"Mothers (both literal and metaphorical) app[ear in the New Tes]tament, both in the form of contemporary in[dividuals and w]hen the New Testament authors interpret biblical texts. Rarely is their status as mothers brought to the fore. When it is, important insights emerge. Bringing all the relevant texts together in one volume, *Under Her Wings* is a unique and valuable resource that no serious student of the New Testament can afford to be without. No matter how long you have been studying the New Testament, you will come away from reading Jennifer Houston McNeel's book with a greater understanding of both the New Testament itself and its cultural background."

—JAMES F. MCGRATH
Clarence L. Goodwin Chair in New Testament
Language and Literature, Butler University

"This engaging and comprehensive study foregrounds an important topic that is too often hidden from view in both biblical scholarship and the church's preaching and teaching ministry: the pervasive presence of mothers and maternal metaphors in the New Testament. Jennifer Houston McNeel illumines the richly nuanced diversity of the New Testament's presentation of both literal and metaphorical motherhood while also drawing attention to underappreciated recurrent themes. Far from being peripheral or merely decorative, maternal language and imagery turn out to be at the heart of the New Testament's theological expression of who God is, how God relates to us, and how we are to relate to each other. This eye-opening volume will be an invaluable resource for the enterprise of theological education and for the life and ministry of the church."

—FRANCES TAYLOR GENCH
Herbert Worth and Annie H. Jackson Professor of
Biblical Interpretation, Union Presbyterian Seminary

"Jennifer Houston McNeel opens our eyes to see mothers and mothering in many places in the New Testament. While the early Roman Empire was a 'man's world,' McNeel's careful analysis of these narrated and named 'mothers' reminds us that these female parents are always there, whether they are recognized or not, appreciated or not. And she demonstrates that attending to the New Testament's 'mother' language and imagery—so often overlooked—

reveals important things about God and the gospel. Carefully researched, full of insight, and designed for group study and reflection, this is a great book to better understand the families in the New Testament, and our own families too."

—NIJAY GUPTA
Julius R. Mantey Professor of New Testament,
Northern Seminary

"In this accessible, elegantly written study of an important but neglected topic, Jennifer Houston McNeel uncovers aspects of motherhood (literal and figurative, human and divine) in the New Testament that will inform—and perhaps also inspire—readers. Laypeople, students, pastors, and scholars alike will benefit from this enlightening and occasionally provocative volume."

—MICHAEL J. GORMAN
Raymond E. Brown Professor of Biblical and Theological Studies,
St. Mary's Seminary & University

UNDER HER WINGS

Mothers and Motherhood in the New Testament

JENNIFER HOUSTON McNEEL

William B. Eerdmans Publishing Company
Grand Rapids, Michigan

Wm. B. Eerdmans Publishing Co.
2006 44th Street SE, Grand Rapids, MI 49508
www.eerdmans.com

© 2025 Jennifer Houston McNeel
All rights reserved
Published 2025
Printed in the United States of America

31 30 29 28 27 26 25   1 2 3 4 5 6 7

ISBN 978-0-8028-8508-1

Library of Congress Cataloging-in-Publication Data

A catalog record for this book is available from the Library of Congress.

For my mother,
Judith Sisson Houston

CONTENTS

	Introduction	1
1.	New Testament Motherhood in Context	7
2.	Unconventional Motherhood	15
3.	Connected Mothers	29
4.	Mothering a Grown-up Messiah	45
5.	Mothers in Crisis	55
6.	Bad Mothers?	70
7.	Mother Jesus	84
8.	A Brief Interlude	93
9.	Motherhood Sidelined	98
10.	Mother Paul	112
11.	Saved Through Childbearing?	133
12.	Foremothers and Spiritual Milk	148
13.	A Dragon in the Delivery Room	163
	Conclusion	177
	Acknowledgments	185
	Notes	187

Contents

Bibliography	201
Index of Authors	207
Index of Subjects	209
Index of Scripture	213

INTRODUCTION

What does the Bible have to say about motherhood? For those doing a surface-level reading, the answer to that question could be "remarkably little." The Bible overall is androcentric (male-centered) and does not spend much time describing the day-to-day lives of mothers or giving mothers practical advice about how to raise their children. But those willing to look deeper will find a different reality—the Bible is, in fact, populated by an intriguing variety of mothers and mother figures who haven't always had the attention they deserve in either the church or biblical scholarship. Sometimes these mothers are hidden in the Bible's side paths, submerged streams, and counternarratives. In other cases, they are in the main story, yet many of the mainstream scholars and preachers of the past have ignored or downplayed their roles in the text. But when we focus on motherhood, we find that the mothers and maternal metaphors of the Bible are centrally important to the biblical narrative and to the theological messages that its authors are seeking to communicate.

Who are the mothers of the Bible? For many readers, iconic mothers such as Eve, Sarah, and Mary may come immediately to mind. But there are many others, such as Hagar, Hannah, Ruth, Rizpah, Gomer, the Syrophoenician woman, Herodias, and the Woman Clothed with the Sun. Some of the Bible's mothers are held up as ideals, some are vilified, and some remain virtually ignored. Some have miraculous pregnancies that are the focus of their stories, while the motherhood of others remains secondary to their main purpose in

Introduction

the narrative. Just as in our world today, motherhood in the biblical world did not look the same for every mother. Nevertheless, some common themes do emerge when we study the mothers of the Bible. This book will explore the stories of mothers and metaphorical uses of motherhood in the New Testament, with an eye to both the diversity of their presentations and the common themes that emerge from a study of these texts.

WHY THIS TOPIC?

There are three primary reasons I chose to write about mothers and motherhood in the New Testament. The first reason is that I am a mother. This is a more significant statement than it might at first seem. To explain why I'll begin with a short personal story. The topic of my doctoral dissertation was an analysis of one of Paul's maternal metaphors (see chapter 10 for more on this topic). In the very early stages of working on that dissertation, I gave birth to my first child. A few years later, at my dissertation defense, I was one week away from delivering my second child. During my defense, my primary advisor asked me, "How did the experience of becoming a mother contribute to your project and your understanding of Paul's maternal metaphors?" This question implied that my own personal experience of motherhood would contribute positively to my interpretation of maternal metaphors in Paul's letters. But about ten minutes later, another professor from the department asked, "How did you keep your own experience of motherhood from interfering with your interpretation of Paul's metaphors?" This question implied the opposite of the other one—that becoming a mother myself had created a bias that would blind me or keep me from faithfully interpreting the text in its own historical context. The fact that I was asked both of these questions within ten minutes illustrates a tension within the biblical studies field around the question of how a scholar's own personal experiences ought to relate to their academic work.

Beginning with the dawn of the European Enlightenment in the late seventeenth century and continuing through much of the twentieth century, academic biblical studies in the West highly valued reason and objectivity. The goal of biblical scholars in this period was to distance their personal lives and feelings from their academic work as much as possible. The idea was that one cannot be objective and therefore arrive at a sense of objective truth if one is overly influenced by one's personal experiences and feelings. Many biblical

Introduction

scholars still feel that way today. But in the second half of the twentieth century, many voices inside and outside of biblical studies began to question the value of objectivity, and indeed, whether true objectivity is even possible. All of us have a perspective. All of us have a worldview that arises from where and when we were born and what has happened to us throughout our lives. And while it is possible to be more objective or less objective, it is never possible to entirely escape the influence of one's own worldview. From this perspective, it would seem rather silly of me to pretend that my interest in the topic of motherhood is unconnected to my own experience of motherhood. Certainly it was becoming a mother that led me to have a particular interest in how motherhood is portrayed in the Bible. However, that does not mean that this book will contain primarily personal or devotional reflections. My interest in the topic of motherhood is both personal and academic. While the former is the catalyst and influences the work I do, it is primarily the latter that you will see explicitly reflected in the pages that follow, as I employ the tools of biblical studies to illuminate the literary, historical, and theological aspects of the stories of mothers in the New Testament. The personal and the academic can exist side-by-side, each informing the other. Ultimately, it is my hope that my own experience of motherhood enriches my academic work, and that my academic work, in turn, affects my understanding of motherhood.

The second reason that I chose to write on this topic is the intriguing paradox that motherhood is both pervasive and ignored in the Bible and in biblical studies. There are many mothers in both the Old Testament and the New Testament, and mothers often play key roles in the biblical narrative, as we'll see in coming chapters. And yet, the mothers of the Bible are often hidden from our view, for two reasons. The first reason has to do with the Bible itself. The androcentric nature of the text means that women's stories are often touched on only briefly in comparison to the long narratives in the Bible that are focused on figures like Abraham, David, and Paul. Women in general and mothers in particular play roles in these stories, but usually only to the extent that their presence serves to move the men's stories forward, for example, by explaining how the man came to have one or more sons. There are, of course, exceptions to this, such as the book of Ruth, but generally speaking, the biblical narrative stays more focused on men than women. The second reason biblical mothers are often hidden from our view has to do with the history of biblical scholarship. Women have always been interpreters of Scripture. But for most of

Introduction

Christian history, academic and ecclesial interpretation has been dominated by men. Most male interpreters throughout the centuries have not considered motherhood a topic worthy of serious investigation and scholarship. So, while the Bible itself somewhat limits our view of biblical mothers, later scholars largely ignored what is there. This pervasive yet hidden nature of motherhood in the Bible makes it ripe for exploration. Sustained attention to the topic of motherhood in the New Testament has the potential to illuminate its importance to the biblical narrative and its relevance for the life of faith today.

The third reason I chose to write on this topic is that motherhood and issues related to it are the focus of debates about all kinds of social issues; this was true in ancient times and still is true today. People associate motherhood with a wide range of family and community issues—the role of women in the home, the role of women in society, who works and who doesn't, who has authority, how children are cared for and disciplined, how the family is structured and how it relates to society, what values are important to us and how we instill them in our children, and so on. Additionally, people often associate motherhood with a variety of emotions, both positive ones, like love and joy, and negative ones, like worry and fear. This is why focusing on motherhood in the Bible can be so interesting: it can be a window into the social and familial values and practices of the ancient world, which can, in turn, cause us to reflect on the social and familial values and practices that characterize our own time and place.

THE CONTENT AND FORMAT OF THE BOOK

Chapter 1 places the mothers of the New Testament in context by exploring two types of background: first a brief exploration of the mothers of the Old Testament, since the Old Testament always serves as the backdrop of the New, and then some historical information about the lives and experiences of mothers at the time that the New Testament was written. The following chapters explore the stories of New Testament mothers and the ways that motherhood is referred to and used metaphorically in the New Testament. My approach is comprehensive: rather than selecting only a few mothers to focus on, I give at least some attention to nearly every mother or mother image that appears in the New Testament. I hope that this will give readers a sense of the significant and diverse ways in which the New Testament canon engages motherhood. The book ends with a conclusion that summarizes the mother-related themes

Introduction

that arose from my analysis throughout the book and offers some closing reflections about why a study of motherhood in the Bible matters.

For those reading this book with a group or class, discussion questions appear at the end of each chapter. If you are not reading with a group, the questions may still help you to reflect more deeply on the passages and issues analyzed in the book. It is by no means necessary to engage the discussion questions or read with a group. It is necessary, though, to be familiar with the stories and passages that I am exploring; therefore, I recommend you read this book with a Bible near at hand, looking up any stories or passages that you are not already familiar with. Except where otherwise indicated, when I quote the Bible I will be using the updated edition of the New Revised Standard Version (NRSVue).

In the chapters that follow we will see that each mother of the New Testament is unique, but we will also see certain common themes begin to emerge, such as the role of motherhood in God's salvation plan, motherhood as symbolic of new life and connection, the caretaking and nurturing role of mothers, and the danger and suffering that ancient people associated with motherhood. It is my hope that the exploration of the stories and passages in this book give readers a greater understanding of the ancient world of the Bible, a deeper appreciation for the roles of mothers in the Bible and in religious life, and an opportunity to reflect on the meaning and influence of motherhood today.

DISCUSSION QUESTIONS

1. When you think of mothers and motherhood, what comes to mind first? What does your culture associate with motherhood?
2. Have you thought much about motherhood in the Bible prior to reading this book? What ideas are you bringing with you about what the Bible says about motherhood?
3. What do you think the relationship should be between a scholar's work and their personal life?
4. The introduction asserted that part of the reason the topic of motherhood in the Bible has been neglected is that, until recently, the majority of biblical scholars were men. In your view, is it important to have people from a variety of backgrounds studying and writing about the Bible? Why or why not?

1

NEW TESTAMENT MOTHERHOOD IN CONTEXT

Mothers in the Old Testament and the Greco-Roman World

This chapter will explore two important contexts for studying the mothers of the New Testament. First, we will look at the mothers of the Old Testament, since the Old Testament forms the backdrop for the New. And second, we will explore what we can know about what motherhood was like and what people thought about it during the time that the New Testament was being written. This cultural context will help us understand what we read about mothers in the biblical text.

MOTHERS IN THE OLD TESTAMENT

Family is central to the Old Testament story. To be more specific, the importance of perpetuating the family of God's chosen people from one generation to the next is central to the Old Testament story. The first commandment given to human beings in the Bible is to "be fruitful and multiply" (Gen. 1:28), which they do, and then they do it again when the same command is given once more after the flood (Gen. 9:1). Abraham is called not to be a king or a priest but to be a father, God promising him as many descendants as the stars he could see above him (Gen. 15:5). The twelve sons of Abraham's grandson Jacob become the fathers of the twelve tribes of Israel. Numerous genealogies populate the Old Testament, showing the importance of kinship and lineage to the people of God.

None of these important descendants would exist if there were no mothers. Therefore, mothers play a central role in the Old Testament narrative. This begins, of course, with Eve, who is given her name because it means she is the "mother of all living" (Gen. 3:20). For Eve, giving birth is something that shows both her own power and her connection to God. When she gives birth to her first child, she says, "I have made a man with Yahweh" (Gen. 4:1, my translation). Here at the outset of the biblical narrative, childbearing is viewed as a collaboration between a woman and God. Though Adam is also involved, since it says he "knew" his wife before she conceived, Eve does not seem to consider his role in the creation of Cain particularly important! After Eve, a series of biblical mothers perpetuate the growth and expansion of God's people, playing a crucial role in the history of God's dealings with humanity. The power of motherhood is somewhat constrained in the Old Testament, however, by the idea that God is the one who controls the womb. Generation after generation the mothers of the Old Testament are barren until God allows them to conceive, and God denies, grants, or promises fertility to many different individuals and groups (Gen. 11:30; 20:18; 25:21; 29:31; 30:2, 22; Exod. 23:26; Deut. 7:14; 28:11; Judg. 13:1–3; 1 Sam. 1:5–6; Ps. 113:9; Isa. 54:1; 66:9; Hosea 9:14). Nevertheless, the central role that motherhood plays in the story of God's people can't be denied.

In addition to this theological role for motherhood in the Old Testament, motherhood's cultural meanings also come through, including the value put on motherhood and the pressure women felt to produce children, especially sons. In ancient Israelite culture women's honor depended on their being wives and the mothers of sons. Since barrenness produced social shame, we see that many of the mothers of Genesis were desperate to produce children, for their own sakes and for the perpetuation of their families and the role that played in God's plan. Leah and Rachel competed with one other in this game of desperation, and it should not be ignored that in the process they exploited and dehumanized the enslaved Zilpah and Bilhah, forcing them to produce children on their behalf (Gen. 29–30). Another example of a woman desperate to be a mother because of the shame of barrenness was Hannah, who mixed her prayers for a son with bitter weeping and promised that if God answered her prayer, she would dedicate the child to the Lord's service (1 Sam. 1:10–11). In response to this prayer, God caused Hannah to conceive Samuel, who lived with his mother only until he was weaned, at which point Hannah left him with the priest Eli so that he could serve God. While Hannah's goodbye to Samuel

Mothers in the Old Testament and the Greco-Roman World

was no doubt heartrending, she was willing to make this sacrifice because the most important thing was that her shame had been removed. She would keep her promise to God.

Ancient Israelite women lived in a patriarchal system, and thus had little if any official authority in government and public religion. However, free women did have some social power that arose from their valued role as mothers, their management of their households, and their influence over the members of their families.[1] A good example of this is the mother described in Proverbs 31, an elite woman who exerts significant influence within her household and beyond. She spins and weaves, provides food for her family, directs the servants, purchases land and plants a vineyard, gives to the poor, keeps her family clothed, sells clothing to the merchants, and teaches wisdom and kindness to her family (Prov. 31:10–31). This passage implies that the mother was the heart of the Israelite home. Proverbs 31 does not give us a picture of a secluded and submissive woman, but one who is active in ensuring the welfare of her family and influences those around her through her example and her teaching. We also see other elite mothers with power in the Old Testament. Some women, like Bathsheba, could even use their role as mother to influence the direction of the nation (1 Kings 1:1–53; 2:13–25). While women were certainly disadvantaged in patriarchal society, financially and in terms of political authority, to say that all women were powerless would be inaccurate. The mothers we meet in the Bible have varying degrees of social power, from queen mothers at one end of the spectrum to enslaved mothers at the other.

Masculine language for God dominates the Old Testament, but God is not portrayed exclusively as masculine. Several passages portray God in feminine terms, usually as a mother. God conceives, gives birth to, carries, clothes, and feeds God's people (Num. 11:12; Deut. 32:13, 18; Neh. 9:21; Isa. 42:14; 45:10–11; 46:3–4; 49:15; Hosea 11:1–4).[2] According to Isaiah 66:13, God's love is like a mother's love: "As a mother comforts her child, so I will comfort you; you shall be comforted in Jerusalem." While God comforts those in Jerusalem as a mother, Jerusalem itself is also portrayed in maternal terms. Mother Zion is in labor (Jer. 4:31; Mic. 4:9–10), gives birth (Isa. 49:19–21; 54:1; 66:7–9), breastfeeds the people (Isa. 66:10–12), and pleads with God on their behalf as their mother (Lam. 2:18–22). When the Bible wants to express ideas of comfort, nurture, carrying, creation, protection, and feeding, it turns to maternal imagery. As Leila Leah Bronner writes, "The mother is a person of influence, and the fact that God poses as a motherly figure demonstrates the power and importance of the mother in the home and beyond."[3]

This brief overview of mothers and motherhood in the Old Testament is just a small sampling of the many stories that one could mention. We will return to some of these and add more examples throughout the book, as they are relevant to the New Testament mothers we will be considering. As we shall see in chapter 2, Old Testament mothers appear in the very first chapter of the New Testament, and they provide an important background for many other parts of the New Testament as well.

MOTHERS IN THE GRECO-ROMAN WORLD

The first-century world in which the New Testament was created was a blending of Greek and Roman cultures. Greek culture had been spread all the way to northwest India by the conquests of Alexander the Great a few centuries before, and the Romans were currently the empire in charge of the entire Mediterranean region. While the lives of a woman in Galilee and a woman in Rome would have been different in many ways, there would also be a lot of similarities because of the pervasiveness of Greco-Roman culture throughout the Mediterranean region in the first century. In most cases, class made more of a difference than ethnic or national origin in terms of what a woman's day-to-day life would have been like. The lives of the elite were far different from the lives of the poor, who made up the majority of the population of the Roman Empire.

What were the lives of mothers like in this context?[4] This varied by culture and class, of course, but some generalizations can be made. First of all, motherhood began earlier for most ancient women than it does for most women today. Women's first marriages typically occurred in the teenage years, with motherhood typically following not too long after marriage. Within a patriarchal system, the procreation of legitimate children was seen as the primary purpose of marriage, and the primary purpose of women, for that matter, and so adolescent girls began fulfilling this purpose shortly after puberty. It seems that upper-class girls were usually married by the time they were sixteen, while for lower-class girls it may have typically been a few years later.[5] Because these teenage girls were often married to older men, widowhood followed by remarriage was common, and one household often included children from multiple marriages.

Mothers in the Old Testament and the Greco-Roman World

It is important for modern readers to understand how dangerous it was to give birth in the ancient world. While precise figures are not possible, historians estimate that the maternal death rate was about 2,500 per 100,000 live births in ancient Rome.[6] For comparison, according to the World Health Organization, the maternal death rate in the wealthiest nations in 2020 was thirteen per 100,000 live births.[7] This means women giving birth in the first-century Roman Empire were about two hundred times more likely to die than women giving birth in a place like the United States today. There are a variety of reasons that maternal mortality was so high in the ancient world. For one thing, there are so many things that can go wrong in pregnancy and childbirth, and medical knowledge in the ancient world wasn't developed enough to deal with many of them (hemorrhages, eclampsia, obstructed labor, etc.). One of the biggest factors would have been infection. Prior to knowledge about germs and especially prior to the creation of antibiotics, maternal mortality was high everywhere. It is important to realize that this was a significant reality for women in the ancient world. It is also important to remember that whenever the Bible uses childbirth as a metaphor, danger and death would have been part of what came to mind for ancient readers.

Women in the ancient world gave birth at home, assisted by midwives and female friends and family members. Men, including fathers and physicians, were not typically present as women gave birth. Midwives were often slaves or former slaves. Some were trained by physicians and others were mentored by other midwives. Midwives guided the birth process, inspected the newborn immediately after birth, and supervised the care of the infant for the first few days. Though practices varied by culture and religion, most cultures in the Mediterranean area had some kind of naming day ceremony about eight to nine days after the infant's birth. This could involve a party and various religious rituals and was considered the day when the infant fully became a member of its family and society. Within Jewish culture, this included the circumcision of baby boys eight days after birth. In both Greek and Jewish cultures, women were considered impure for a period of time after giving birth. A variety of religious and cultural practices in different places regulated and responded to this impurity, including periods of seclusion, refraining from entering sacred spaces, ritual washing, and offering sacrifices. For Torah regulations related to maternal impurity, see Leviticus 12.

Just as the life of the mother was in danger during labor and delivery, so was the life of the infant: infant death during childbirth also occurred at much higher rates than today. And the danger did not end with a safe delivery. In Roman times, about 5 percent of infants born alive would die during their first month, about a third during their first year, and about half by their tenth birthday.[8] The majority of these deaths were the result of disease and infection, though other problems, such as malnourishment, were also common.

In a world without baby formula, the first question upon an infant's birth was not "bottle or breast?" but rather "mother or wet nurse?" Wet nurses were often slaves but could also be poor free women trying to earn a living. Mothers had a variety of reasons to employ a wet nurse rather than breastfeeding their infants themselves: to return more quickly to their work or usual daily activities, to avoid the suppression of fertility that breastfeeding sometimes causes, or to allow time to recover from a difficult labor and delivery. Additionally, if the mother died in childbirth but the infant survived, it would be necessary for another woman to nurse the infant. Wet nursing was particularly common among the Roman elite but could occur at any social level.[9] Some elite male writers in the ancient world expressed opinions about wet nursing and encouraged mothers to breastfeed their own children. These elite writers were concerned about the influence that lower-class and foreign nurses would have on the children of upper-class women, both through the extensive time that the nurse would spend with the young child and because of the belief that morals were directly passed to infants through breast milk. As Lynn Cohick shows, these men were primarily concerned not with the well-being of the women, but with the ability of the husbands to maintain control over their wives and children.[10]

Women giving birth in the first century were doing so in a patriarchal system in which they had few legal rights over their own children. It was the father's right to decide whether the infant was to be accepted as a legitimate member of the family. If a couple divorced, the children usually stayed with the father, not the mother. Nevertheless, mothers had quite a bit of influence over their children, even if they did not have much legal power. Lower-class women were typically the primary caregivers for their children. Upper-class women might employ a variety of caregivers, making them less directly involved in the daily bodily needs of infants and children, but even so, as part of overseeing the household, women of all social levels were intimately involved in the education and moral development of young children.

Not so different from today, in the ancient world love and affection were considered a natural part of the mother–child relationship. Some ancient authors expressed the view that mothers love their children more than fathers do. For example, Aristotle wrote that mothers love their children more than fathers do because parenthood "costs the mother more trouble" (*Nicomachean Ethics*, 8.7.7 [Rackham, LCL]). Other authors, however, felt that maternal and paternal love were equal in strength but expressed differently. Roman statesman and philosopher Seneca wrote about parental love, "Do you not see how fathers show their love in one way, and mothers in another? The father orders his children to be aroused from sleep in order that they may start early on their pursuits, even on holidays he does not permit them to be idle, and he draws from them sweat and sometimes tears. But the mother fondles them in her lap, wishes to keep them out of the sun, wishes them never to be unhappy, never to cry, never to toil" (*De Providentia* 2.5 [Basore, LCL]). This quote reveals one reason why biblical authors might choose paternal imagery in one case and maternal imagery in another: ancient authors had different associations with motherhood and fatherhood.

Finally, it is important to understand that people in the ancient world had a very different understanding of women's bodies, and therefore also mothers' bodies, than we have today.[11] Many people in the ancient world believed that a complete, fully human body was a male body. Women, then, were not really a different sex, but inferior, not fully formed human beings. The silver lining was that this inferiority allowed them to bear children. Therefore, women's bodies were necessary, but always inferior. The ancients thought of women's bodies as softer, colder, wetter, and more porous than men's bodies. Menstrual blood was one of the ways that women's excess moisture escaped the body. Many ancient physicians believed that cold menstrual blood needed to be heated by semen to form the infant in the womb. They also believed that semen-heated menstrual blood turned white and traveled up to women's breasts to become breast milk. Thus, it was believed that breastfeeding infants were nourished by a combination of their mother's blood and their father's semen. When reading the Bible, it is important to know that the people writing it did not have the same understanding that we do today of bodies and how they work.

CONCLUSION

This chapter has laid the groundwork for our study by providing some important background information. The ways that ancient readers of the New Testament would have responded to its mother characters and maternal images would have been influenced both by older biblical literature and by the cultural assumptions, historical practices, and medical realities of their world. There is, of course, much more we could say about the lives of mothers in the ancient world. As we explore motherhood in the New Testament in the following chapters, we will explore other historical and cultural background information relevant to the lives and stories of the mothers of the New Testament.

DISCUSSION QUESTIONS

1. How would you describe the relationship between divine power and maternal power in the Old Testament?
2. Is there a mother or mother figure from the Old Testament that you find particularly interesting? What intrigues you about her or the story she is part of?
3. In what ways was motherhood in Greco-Roman times the same as it is today? How might this help us understand and feel connected to New Testament mothers?
4. In what ways was motherhood in Greco-Roman times different than it is today? What difference might that make for interpreting stories of New Testament mothers well?

2

UNCONVENTIONAL MOTHERHOOD

The Women of Matthew's Birth Narrative

As we saw in chapter 1, mothers played important social and theological roles in Old Testament narratives. Thus, it should not surprise us to find that some Old Testament mothers are mentioned in the New Testament. However, it is surprising that we find four Old Testament mothers listed in the genealogy in Matthew chapter 1. In the Old Testament, genealogies typically only included the names of fathers and sons (see, for example, Ruth 4:18–22). The exception to this general rule was that mothers were sometimes listed to distinguish between sons born to different mothers (see, for example, Gen. 35:22b–26). The genealogy we find in Matthew 1 is for the most part a simple father-son genealogy, tracing a single line of descent from Abraham to Jesus. Therefore, it is unexpected when we find the names of four mothers inserted into the father-son list.

Interpreters have long puzzled over why Matthew[1] chose to include Tamar, Rahab, Ruth, and Bathsheba (called here "the wife of Uriah") in the genealogy. It might be tempting to think that Matthew included them because he was ahead of his time and wanted to be gender inclusive in his genealogy. However, this seems unlikely. If this were the reason, we would expect women like Sarah and Rachel to be included. To simply be inclusive of women, one could easily imagine the genealogy beginning something like this: "Abraham and Sarah were the parents of Isaac, Isaac and Rebecca were the parents of Jacob..." But it is not these well-known matriarchs that Matthew chooses to include. If only four women are included, the question naturally becomes, Why these four in particular? It seems to most readers that Matthew must have had a reason for choosing these specific women.

Unfortunately, there is no definitive answer to this puzzle because Matthew does not provide an explanation. We are left to make educated guesses about the message Matthew might be intending to convey to his readers. Biblical scholars over the years have proposed various answers. Some have suggested that the women were all particularly bad sinners, and Matthew's inclusion of them is meant to show that the gospel story about Jesus offers a path of forgiveness for even the worst sinners among us. This older interpretation is almost universally rejected by modern biblical scholars because, as we will see below, these women are largely portrayed positively in Old Testament narratives. Reformation-era thinkers, Puritans, and those living in the Victorian era may have been scandalized by these women's stories, but the biblical authors themselves don't seem to be. Also, as Beverly Gaventa points out, if Matthew just wanted to give us examples of sinners, many of the men already in the list would have served as more than adequate examples![2]

A more popular suggestion has been that the women were all gentiles, and Matthew's inclusion of them is meant to communicate that this gospel story is for everyone, not just for Jews, and that Jesus himself has some gentile ancestry.[3] Although Matthew's Gospel is often called the most Jewish Gospel because of its focus on the Jewish law and the way it connects Jesus to Moses and David, this Gospel also gives us the gentile magi at the beginning of the story and the "great commission" to all nations at the end of the story, so it makes some sense to think Matthew would begin his story by connecting Jews and gentiles in the family tree that leads to Jesus. Although this suggestion is far more plausible than the idea that the women were egregious sinners, it still fails to be entirely convincing because it is not clear that the women were all regarded as gentiles by the biblical writers. This is especially the case with Bathsheba, who is nowhere identified as a gentile. Her husband was a Hittite, but her own nationality is not given. She has a Hebrew name, however, making it likely that she was an Israelite. Rahab and Ruth were gentiles, but also were accepted into and became part of the people of Israel. Tamar was not an Israelite, but then again, almost no one was at that time. The children of Israel at that time consisted only of Jacob's children and grandchildren, so it is not surprising that Jacob's son Judah would find a non-Israelite wife for his son. It is possible that we are supposed to understand the women as gentiles, but it is by no means clear that this is the best interpretation.

The Women of Matthew's Birth Narrative

We may find an interpretation that is more convincing if we broaden our view from seeing the women as gentiles to seeing their experiences with marriage and motherhood as unconventional. The gentile status of some of the women may be part of what makes their stories unconventional in an Israelite context, but it is not all that makes them so. There is much more that is unconventional in these stories. It may well be that what Matthew intends to convey by including these women in the genealogy is a reminder that God can and often does work through unconventional family situations in order further God's plan of salvation for the world. By beginning his Gospel with that message embedded in the genealogy, Matthew is preparing the reader for the story of Mary and Joseph, which follows—an unconventional marriage and birth story if there ever was one!

Despite their unconventionality, or maybe even in some sense because of it, these women and their stories also demonstrate the Matthean idea of righteousness.[4] The Greek word *dikaiosynē*, usually translated as "righteousness," also means "justice," "fairness," and "uprightness." To define the word, rather than just translating it, we could say that, to Matthew, righteousness is "the character of a life lived as it should be, with a right relationship to God, to other people, and to the world."[5] In Matthew, Jesus's words and actions define what righteousness is.[6] The law is not abolished, but Jesus shows us how to interpret and fulfill it. Three things are needed in Matthew's understanding of righteousness: first, inner faithfulness rather than only an external adherence to the law; second, proper relationships both with God and with other people; and third, compassionate action in the world, as demonstrated by Jesus. Could this kind of righteousness, so important in Matthew's Gospel, have anything to do with what is going on in Matthew 1, both with the genealogy and the story of Mary and Joseph? I believe it does. When we explore these stories in detail, we see how these women's lives were both unconventional and righteous, according to Matthew's definition—and also how they prepare us to hear the story of Mary and Joseph.

TAMAR

When I say that these women's lives were "unconventional," part of what I mean is that the trajectories of their lives, and especially their paths to motherhood, were outside of the norms of patriarchal culture—that is, outside of the expected way that marriage and reproduction were "supposed" to go in their ancient, patriarchal context. This is certainly the case with Tamar, whose

Unconventional Motherhood

story you can read in Genesis 38. Tamar's first marriage was to Judah's oldest son Er. The narrator tells us, however, that Er was wicked and that God killed him before he could produce an heir with Tamar. Therefore, Judah gives Tamar to his second son, Onan, telling him to "perform the duty of a brother-in-law to her" (38:8). This is referring to the practice of levirate marriage, in which the firstborn son of the marriage between the woman and her brother-in-law counts as the offspring and heir of the original, deceased husband (see Deut. 25:5–10). While such a practice might seem strange to us, this is not, in fact, the unconventional part of the story. While levirate marriage is not a part of most modern cultures, it was a part of theirs. This practice provided some protection for childless widows, ensuring that they would be provided for by their deceased husband's family.

Although the marriage between Tamar and Onan was conventional, Onan's behavior in the story was not. Onan does not want to produce offspring for his dead brother, and so uses the withdrawal method to ensure that Tamar would not become pregnant. He probably does this so that he himself could become the primary heir of his father's estate, rather than the son who would count as his brother's child. This selfish behavior displeases God, who puts him to death as well. Once again, Tamar is a childless widow. Judah tells her that his third son, Shelah, is still too young for marriage, and sends Tamar back to live in her father's house until Shelah grows up. Secretly, however, it seems that Judah has no intention of giving Tamar to Shelah. Two of his sons have already died after marrying her—why risk a third?

After some time of continuing to live as a widow in her father's house, Tamar decides to take action. According to the custom of levirate marriage, someone in Judah's family should be giving her offspring. Since Judah is withholding his third son from her, Tamar creates a plan in which Judah himself will end up getting her pregnant. She disguises herself as a prostitute and offers her services to Judah from the roadside. Judah gives her his signet, cord, and staff as a pledge of future payment. Tamar becomes pregnant and returns to live in her father's house. When Judah sends a friend to deliver the promised payment, the supposed prostitute is nowhere to be found.

At this point in the story there is a very interesting parallel to the story of Mary in Matthew 1. Both women have a pregnancy that is legitimate from the point of view of the narrative but considered illegitimate by other characters in the story. When Judah hears that Tamar is pregnant, he is furious, thinking that she has "played the whore," as the gossiping neighbors put it.[7] He demands that she come out from her house and be killed for her crime of adultery. Tamar, however, is able to produce Judah's signet, cord, and staff, proving that she has only "played" the whore in the sense of her disguise, not in the way that the neighbors meant it. Tamar's actions of disguising herself as a prostitute and getting pregnant by her father-in-law are not conventional, by her culture's standards or ours. This is not the "normal" way of becoming pregnant at that time. But Tamar's story reminds us that being unconventional is not the same as being unrighteous. According to the norms of her time and place, Tamar has a right to expect Judah's family to take care of her and provide her with children. Her unconventional actions give her what is rightfully hers, something that Judah acknowledges. When he sees his signet, cord, and staff, he says, "She is more in the right than I, since I did not give her to my son Shelah" (38:26). The Hebrew of this verse could just as accurately be translated as "She is more righteous than I." Tamar is righteous. She cares more about what is right than what the neighbors say about her. This is one part of what it means to be righteous in the Gospel of Matthew, and it is an idea that is relevant to the story of Mary and Joseph, as we will see below. With her unconventional but righteous actions, Tamar secures another branch in the family tree that leads to Jesus.

RAHAB

While Tamar only "plays" at being a prostitute, Rahab actually is one (see Josh. 2:1–24, 6:15–27). She lives in Jericho at the time that the Israelites are coming into the promised land. She is a prostitute and apparently the head of her household, or at least she acts as such. She has a living father and mother as well as brothers and sisters, but she is the one who speaks for them and takes action to protect them. Her profession and her independence both mean that she does not exactly live up the patriarchal ideal for what a woman is "supposed" to be in that time and place. She is an unconventional woman. Nevertheless, like Tamar, she is portrayed as righteous in the narrative. She harbors the Israelite spies who had come to scope out the city, saving their lives by hiding them, lying to the authorities, and helping the men escape by a rope out the window. In return she asks that the Israelites spare her and her family in the attack that follows, a promise that the Israelites keep.

Rahab's motherhood is nowhere mentioned in the Old Testament. According to Matthew, she becomes the mother of Boaz and therefore the great-great-grandmother of David (see Ruth 4:18–22). No one knows what Matthew's source is for this information. It seems unlikely that Rahab was actually David's great-great-grandmother since the entire period of the judges, probably three or four hundred years long, separates their lifetimes from one another. But whether it is historical or not, Matthew chooses to include Rahab as one of the foremothers of the Messiah. This may be because her unconventional life illustrates the kind of righteousness Matthew wants us to think about. Like Tamar, Rahab takes action in ways that run against the grain of her patriarchal culture, but in doing so she proves her faithfulness to God, and, according to Matthew, her motherhood continues the line that leads to the Messiah.

RUTH

Faithfulness, righteousness, and women taking charge of their own lives are themes in the stories of Tamar and Rahab that we again see repeated in the life of Ruth and her mother-in-law Naomi. When the widowed Naomi returns to the land of Israel from her time living in Moab, she brings her Moabite daughter-in-law Ruth with her. The two widows work together to find a way to make ends meet. This includes Ruth "gleaning," a practice in which farmers allow the poor to collect the leftover crops in their fields after the harvest. Ruth happens to glean in a field owned by a kinsman of Naomi's husband, named Boaz. After Boaz is protective of and generous with Ruth, Naomi instructs Ruth to go at night to the threshing floor where Boaz will be sleeping, to uncover his feet, and then do whatever he tells her to. "Feet" is sometimes used as a euphemism for genitals, and that may or may not be the case here. Either way, by uncovering Boaz and asking him to cover her, she is asking him to marry her, and thus serve as the "kinsman redeemer" who provides for the family of his deceased relative. You can read the twists and turns in the book of Ruth, but to fast-forward to the end, Boaz does marry Ruth, and Ruth then gives birth to Obed, David's grandfather.

There are several unconventional aspects to Ruth's life story. First, she is a foreigner, an immigrant to Israel. Her story is one of going to a foreign land and finding a place to belong. This, of course, is the story of countless people through the ages, but it is noteworthy in Ruth's case because elsewhere in the Old Testament her place of origin, Moab, is spoken of quite negatively, as an enemy of Israel. Genesis assigns a very unflattering origin story for the people of Moab, claiming in 19:37 that they are descended from the incestuous relations between Lot and his oldest daughter. Deuteronomy 23:3 says that no Moabite "shall come into the assembly of the LORD" because they did not help the Israelites when they were on their journey from Egypt to the Promised Land. The Books of Ezra and Nehemiah consider foreign wives, including those from Moab, to be dangerous to the nation and a cause of the people's sin (see Ezra 10:6–17 and Neh. 13:23–27). Despite these decrees against foreign wives in general and Moabites in particular, the book of Ruth gives us a beautiful story of an upstanding Israelite man marrying a Moabite woman, and the Moabite woman becoming an accepted and beloved part of an Israelite community. This makes her story unconventional when considered in the context of passages from elsewhere in the Old Testament, but it is also one of the reasons her story has been loved by so many readers for thousands of years.

Another thing that makes Ruth's story unconventional is the circumstances surrounding her path to motherhood. Creeping out to a threshing floor and uncovering a man's body in the middle of the night is not the normal way to get a husband in that day and age or ours! Additionally, there is an unconventionality to the way Ruth and Naomi fend for themselves without male authority or protection for most of the book. This is a story that does not fit neatly into the way that women's lives are supposed to go in patriarchal culture. In addition to subverting xenophobic attitudes, this book can also be seen as subverting patriarchal norms. But as we've already seen, unconventionality is not the same thing as unrighteousness. Far from it. Righteousness and faithfulness abound in this book. Ruth shows faithfulness to her mother-in-law, and Boaz shows faithfulness to his relatives and community. Ruth and Naomi act in ways that secure both their own personal futures and the lineage that leads to David. Like Tamar and Rahab, Ruth doesn't take the most conventional route to motherhood, but along the way she shows righteousness and faithfulness to God and to those around her. This Moabite woman plays a central role in the history of God's saving works.

BATHSHEBA

It may seem at first that Bathsheba does not fit very well in a group with Tamar, Rahab, and Ruth. I have been emphasizing the independent action of the women and their unconventional righteousness, yet what is most known about Bathsheba is her adulterous encounter with David, a story in which Bathsheba is largely passive and David, though he takes action, can hardly be said to be righteous (see 2 Sam. 11:1–12:25). However, when we look closer at Bathsheba's story, some of the same themes we have been seeing begin to emerge. First, one thing we can see quite clearly is that, like the other genealogy women, Bathsheba's path to motherhood is not conventional and includes significant violations of patriarchal norms. This is not Bathsheba's fault. She is innocent and does nothing wrong. But norms are violated nonetheless when King David orders Bathsheba to be brought to him. In the eyes of patriarchy, this was a sin not primarily against Bathsheba, but against her husband.[8] David violates one of patriarchy's most sacred values when he takes another man's wife for himself. But this unconventionality is unrighteous, not righteous, so David's role in the story is not at all like that of Tamar, Rahab, or Ruth.

To find righteousness in the story, we have to look harder. On this point Amy-Jill Levine makes a helpful suggestion. She focuses on the righteousness of Uriah in the story rather than on the righteousness of Bathsheba or David.[9] Readers have often wondered why Matthew refers to Bathsheba as "the wife of Uriah" rather than using her name. It is often suggested that Matthew does so to draw attention to the fact that she was another man's wife when David took her. This could very well be the reason. But it could also be the case that Matthew calls her "the wife of Uriah" because it is actually Uriah, not Bathsheba, that Matthew wants to draw our attention to. Uriah is the one in the story who demonstrates the kind of righteousness that is important to Matthew. When David discovers Bathsheba is pregnant with his child, he tries to cover up his actions by getting Uriah to come home from war and sleep with his wife, so that everyone will assume the baby is Uriah's. This is the part of the story where we see Uriah's faithfulness. Uriah's commander in chief (David) tells him that he has permission to go home and enjoy all the comforts of home. For him to do so would be fine according to the letter of the law. The highest earthly authority in the land has given him permission. But Uriah has a righteousness that exceeds the letter of the law—an internal righteousness that causes him to remain faithful to his fellow soldiers by remaining in solidarity with them in their hardships rather than indulging in comfort only for himself. His faithful behavior could hardly form a sharper contrast with David's unfaithful, selfish, and scandalous behavior. David's unrighteous behavior relates, of course, to the taking of Bathsheba, but also extends to the subsequent killing of Uriah. Uriah's righteousness leads directly to his death, an idea that is relevant to the story of Jesus that Matthew is starting to tell.

Although focusing on the righteousness of Uriah is helpful, and although his name does appear in the genealogy, it is not Uriah but Bathsheba who is the mother Matthew mentions, even if not by name. Is there any more we can say about *her* place in the genealogy, rather than just her husband's? There is, but to see it we need to move beyond the story of David's adultery in 2 Samuel 11. There is another story about Bathsheba in the Old Testament that is much less known but may be helpful to consider in this context. Although Bathsheba seems largely passive in 2 Samuel 11, she is far from it in this later story.

There are many twists and turns in the struggle between David's sons to succeed him as king. Earlier, Absalom had made a play for the throne (see 2 Sam. 15–18). Now, as David is old and weak in 1 Kings 1, Adonijah seeks to establish himself as the next king. This is when Bathsheba acts on behalf of her son Solomon. Upon hearing from the prophet Nathan that Adonijah is making a move for the throne, Bathsheba goes to David and asks him to keep his promise that her son Solomon will be the next king. It is not clear from the story whether David had made this promise in the past or not, but Bathsheba's action in this story prompts the old king to issue orders ensuring that Solomon will be recognized as the next king. If Nathan and Bathsheba had not acted, most likely Adonijah would have become king after David. This was the logical course of events, since he was the oldest of David's living sons (1 Kings 1:6). The preference for a younger son is an ongoing theme throughout the Old Testament, and we see it play out again here as Bathsheba ensures the younger Solomon will sit on the throne, and in the following chapters we also see that both David and God approve of and bless Solomon's kingship. So, although Bathsheba's story is different from the other genealogy women in several ways, we see that all four women (Tamar, Rahab, Ruth, and Bathsheba) take some extraordinary action that leads to an unconventional continuance of the lineage that leads from Abraham to Jesus.

MARY AND JOSEPH IN MATTHEW

We've seen that none of the women in the genealogy had pregnancies that came about through the normal course of events according to patriarchal culture. What was expected would be for a young girl to remain a virgin in her father's house until her teenage years, get married as a teen, and begin having children shortly thereafter. These women did not follow that path. Tamar became pregnant by her father-in-law, Rahab was a prostitute before marriage, Ruth was a widow who got a new husband by uncovering his body on a threshing floor at night, and Bathsheba's marriage to David came about when he forced her into an adulterous relationship. Nevertheless, all these women can be considered righteous in their actions and instrumental to moving God's plan of salvation forward. Does this prepare us to hear Mary and Joseph's story in Matthew chapters 1 and 2? I believe it does. Just like the genealogy women, Mary's pregnancy does not come about through normal or expected means, and both Mary and Joseph can be considered righteous, as they are involved in extraordinary circumstances that move God's plan of salvation forward. As Mary and Joseph's story begins, the genealogy has already reminded us that God is not bound by our cultural norms and expectations, and faithful people can operate outside of them.

After the genealogy, the very next verse of Matthew's Gospel says, "Now the birth of Jesus the Messiah took place in this way. When his mother Mary had been engaged to Joseph, *but before they lived together, she was found to be pregnant* from the Holy Spirit" (1:18, emphasis mine). Once again we find ourselves in a story in which marriage and reproduction are not happening according to the expected norms of patriarchal culture. Young women are not supposed to get pregnant before they are married. Of course, Matthew lets the reader in on a secret, that the child is from the Holy Spirit, but the other characters in the story are not aware of this fact, so Mary's situation would appear scandalous to them. Here it is important to understand that in ancient culture, women who got pregnant outside of marriage were seen not just as immoral, but as threats to the economic and social stability of society. Ancient patriarchal culture as an economic system relied on the stable transfer of property from father to son. Women's main role in this system was to provide *legitimate* sons within marriage who would inherit their fathers' properties. Illegitimate children were a threat to this system. This is something so serious to the book of Deuteronomy that 22:23–24 says that when a man sleeps with an engaged woman, both the man and the woman are to be stoned to death. Such a sentence would not have been carried out in Mary's case, both because Israelite culture had changed since the time Deuteronomy was written and because the Romans, who were in charge, usually reserved the right of capital punishment for themselves. Nevertheless, that law in Deuteronomy still shows how serious patriarchal culture was about young women remaining virgins until their weddings. Like Tamar, Rahab, Ruth, and Bathsheba, Mary's path to motherhood is not following the expected trajectory.

Much like Tamar's story, although Mary's pregnancy is legitimate, others view it as illegitimate. In Tamar's case, Judah is at first outraged by the idea of Tamar's pregnancy, and later acknowledges her righteousness. In Mary's story, Joseph follows a similar trajectory. While Joseph doesn't exhibit the kind of outrage that Judah expresses, it is clear that he at first considers Mary's pregnancy to be illegitimate and later changes his view. Matthew 1:19 says that when Joseph learned of the pregnancy he planned to break the engagement. This is not surprising. From the perspective of patriarchal culture, it appears Mary has shamed Joseph by being unfaithful to him. We would expect Joseph to separate from Mary. However, unlike Judah, Joseph in this moment does not bluster loudly and call for Mary's death. Rather, he resolves to handle the matter as quietly as possible, for Mary's sake. This is where the righteousness of Joseph begins to come through. No doubt feeling hurt and angry, he is also compassionate as he tries to do what is right.

But just as Judah changes his tune upon having his signet, cord, and staff presented to him, so Joseph has an experience that causes him to change his view and change course. An angel appears to him in a dream telling him that the child is from the Holy Spirit, and he should not be afraid to take Mary as his wife (1:20). This may have solved the problem of what is happening between Mary and Joseph themselves, but it does not solve the problem of what the neighbors might think. To them it would still appear that Mary has been unfaithful to Joseph, and now it would appear that Joseph has lost his mind to accept her anyway! Joseph accepts a woman who appears to have committed adultery against him and accepts the baby she is pregnant with that is not his own. This is not how things are supposed to work in patriarchal culture. So, we see in Mary's pregnancy and in Joseph's actions a story in which marriage and pregnancy happen outside of expected norms, like it did with Tamar, Rahab, Ruth, and Bathsheba. But, like Tamar, Joseph cares more about what is right than what is normal or what the neighbors might say.

I proposed above, in agreement with Amy-Jill Levine, that while Bathsheba's story was outside of expected patriarchal norms, it was actually Uriah who demonstrated the Matthean understanding of righteousness, which might be why his name rather than Bathsheba's is mentioned in the genealogy. In parallel fashion, I would propose that, while it is Mary's pregnancy that is outside of patriarchal norms, it is Joseph whom Matthew primarily focuses on to illustrate righteousness in the story. Keep in mind that Joseph's name is also mentioned in the genealogy (see verse 16), and indeed, it is his genealogy, not Mary's, that Matthew records. We'll see a very different portrait of Mary when we get to the Gospel of Luke, but here in Matthew's Gospel Mary is largely passive and silent, like Bathsheba was in 2 Samuel 11. The story focuses on Joseph's actions and his righteousness. He is righteous at first in planning to dismiss Mary with as little public scandal as possible because of his compassionate nature. But later his righteousness is manifest in his willingness to take Mary as his wife in obedience to God, no matter how great the public scandal becomes, because it is the right thing to do. Joseph's righteousness in the story consists both in his willingness to be shamed in the eyes of the world in obedience to God, and his willingness to give up his own rights and aspirations as a man and father to serve God's plan of salvation for the world (something Onan in Tamar's story was unwilling to do!). Mary and Joseph may have lost some respectability in the eyes of their neighbors, but the stories of Tamar, Rahab, Ruth, and Bathsheba and Uriah have already reminded us that we should not confuse righteousness with respectability and conventionality. Sometimes it is within unconventional events and even in "unrespectable" people that we find God at work in the world.

THE MOTHERHOOD OF MARY IN MATTHEW

Just as we felt unsatisfied above, talking only about Uriah, and so dug deeper to find more to say about Bathsheba, so we might also feel unsatisfied giving the whole spotlight to Joseph when analyzing Matthew's birth narrative. It is natural for us to want more from Matthew in relation to Mary herself. Is there any more we can say about Mary and her motherhood in Matthew? As Beverly Gaventa points out, one thing that is clear about Mary's motherhood in Matthew is that it ties her very closely to Jesus. Nearly every time Mary or Jesus is mentioned in the birth narrative the other is also mentioned. Five times in chapter 2 they are referred to as "the child and his mother" or very similar wording (2:11, 13, 14, 20, 21). As Gaventa puts it, "the two belong together."[10] So we see here one important aspect of what motherhood means in the New Testament: connection. Mother and child in Matthew almost form a single unit. Where one goes, there the other goes. Matthew recognizes the importance of the bond between mother and child. This bond is something other New Testament writers recognize as well, and it is one of the reasons motherhood is used metaphorically in the New Testament—to signify connection.

Another thing that is clear about Mary's motherhood in Matthew is that it in no way shields her from the perils of the world. Matthew chapter 2 is a story fraught with danger. Mary and Joseph must survive in a world in which a hostile king is seeking their son's life. It is a story in which they are affected by unusual world events and anxiety over the safety of loved ones, which many of us may be familiar with. And motherhood heightens the anxiety rather than lessening it. The very connection we've seen between Mary and Jesus in the story makes it all the more disquieting when we see that that connection is in danger of being broken by King Herod in the most violent way. Indeed, although the connection between Mary and Jesus remains intact for now, other mothers in this story are not so fortunate. The "slaughter of the innocents" in 2:16–18 brings us the heartrending cries of other mothers who have lost their children to Herod's cruelty and arrogance. These cries are described as the cries of "Rachel weeping for her children," a reference to Jeremiah 31:15 and a poignant picture of maternal grief. In Genesis, Rachel is one of Jacob's wives and the mother of Joseph and Benjamin. In Jeremiah, Rachel becomes a maternal figure for the whole nation, lamenting the sending of her children into exile. Matthew picks up on this image to express the grief of the people over the slaughter of the innocents. Danger, grief, and suffering are connected to motherhood in Matthew's story.

CONCLUSION

In Matthew 1–2 we see motherhood's capacity to bring both connection and suffering. The story provides an intimate portrait of connection between mother and child (Mary and Jesus) and also poetically illustrates the consequences when that bond is severed (Rachel weeping for her children). The inclusion of Tamar, Rahab, Ruth, and Bathsheba in the genealogy sets the stage for Mary and Joseph's actions to illustrate the kind of righteousness that Matthew wants to emphasize and that Jesus's teachings in the rest of the Gospel will more fully explicate. Yet through all this the character of Mary in Matthew is largely passive and silent. For a different portrait of Mary, we will turn in the next chapter to the story of Jesus's birth as Luke tells it.

Unconventional Motherhood

DISCUSSION QUESTIONS

1. How would you define what "conventional" and "unconventional" motherhood look like in your own time and place? Can you think of any examples of unconventional mothers who have impacted their families and the world in positive ways?
2. Why do you think Matthew chooses to include Tamar, Rahab, Ruth, and Bathsheba in his genealogy? Did you find the argument that they were all involved in unconventional paths to marriage and motherhood convincing, or do you think Matthew had some other reason for including them?
3. The chapter talked about the ways in which the genealogy women prepare us for the story of Mary and her motherhood. In what ways does the story of Mary and her motherhood prepare us for the story of Jesus that Matthew tells in the rest of his Gospel?
4. The chapter argues that Mary's motherhood illustrates the themes of connection and suffering. Can you think of other places in the Bible where motherhood signifies connection and/or suffering?

3

CONNECTED MOTHERS

Mary and Elizabeth in Luke's Birth Narrative

As pointed out in chapter 1, motherhood played an important role in the Old Testament because so often God's plans were carried out through the birth of a child. We also saw in chapter 1 that barrenness was a source of shame, and so women cried out to God as the one who had the power to open their wombs. And we saw examples of women who used their roles as mothers to secure their families' futures and to further God's plans of salvation for the world. Readers familiar with these themes from the Old Testament will find themselves right at home in the opening chapters of Luke's Gospel. Luke chapters 1 and 2 evoke a biblical world in which many of the themes and ideas expressed in the narrative ground Luke's gospel story in the Scriptures of Israel. In addition, these chapters also forecast important themes that will play out as Luke's Gospel unfolds. In a sense, then, the opening chapters of Luke look forward and backward at the same time, creating a bridge that connects the story of Jesus to the story of Israel. The stories of two mothers, Mary and Elizabeth, form the central planks of this bridge.

ANGELIC VISITS AND MIRACULOUS PREGNANCIES

Right away we are plunged into a world filled with scriptural themes and connections, as Luke's story opens with a priest in the temple. This is Zechariah, husband of Elizabeth, "serving as a priest before God" in the sanctuary of the temple (1:8). We learn that Zechariah and Elizabeth are righteous before God, that they are an older couple, and that they have no children because Elizabeth is barren (1:6–7). It is worth noting that Zechariah did not divorce Elizabeth for failing to provide him with children, something he had a right to do. Rather, they have grown old together as a couple without children. This doesn't mean, however, that they are unconcerned about their childless state. Later in the story, when she is pregnant, Elizabeth will say that God has taken away the "disgrace" she endured because of her barrenness (1:25). So it is not the case that Elizabeth and Zechariah did not want children, but they stayed together despite their disappointment.[1]

To the reader familiar with the Old Testament, the disgrace Elizabeth felt because she could not have children calls to mind the matriarchs of Genesis who were desperate to have children because of the social shame of barrenness.[2] As an older barren woman, Elizabeth's story especially recalls the story of Sarah, who has a miraculous pregnancy after menopause. There is a similarity in Sarah and Elizabeth both becoming pregnant at an older age, and also a similarity in the narratives involving their husbands. In both stories it is the husband who receives the news that his wife will become pregnant, and in both cases the men express skepticism because of their wives' advanced ages (Gen. 17:17; Luke 1:18).[3] Also, in both stories, the women express joy and gratitude to God once they have become pregnant or given birth (Gen. 21:6–7; Luke 1:25). These literary parallels between Sarah and Elizabeth serve to connect Luke's story to the Old Testament. They show the reader that the story of Jesus about to unfold is directly related to the promises God made to Abraham and Sarah. The promise that the world would be blessed through Abraham's descendants (Gen. 12:3) is about to be fulfilled in the story Luke is telling. With Elizabeth's miraculous pregnancy, John the Baptist comes into the world, preparing the way for Jesus. Just like so many Old Testament stories, this New Testament story of salvation is moved forward by a family that grows because a woman becomes a mother.

Six months after visiting Zechariah in the temple in Jerusalem with the news that Elizabeth would become pregnant, the angel Gabriel pays a visit to their relative Mary in Nazareth in Galilee. In contrast to the older Elizabeth, Mary is identified as a virgin. This word, *parthenos* in Greek, does not mean exactly the same thing as "virgin" in English. The word "virgin" in English means anyone who has not had sexual intercourse. While the word *parthenos* can carry a similar meaning in Greek, the word was usually used with a more specific referent: a female person who is of marriageable age but is not yet married. The identification of Mary as a *parthenos* means that her patriarchal culture considered her no longer a child, but not fully a woman, either, because she was not yet married. While her age is not given in the story, we might reasonably assume that she is a teenager.

The scene in Luke's Gospel in which Gabriel tells Mary about her coming pregnancy, traditionally called the Annunciation, is a well-known and much-studied story. In it we learn that Mary's path to motherhood will be of an unprecedented nature. After Gabriel tells her that she will bear a child, she asks how this could be, since she has not yet had sex with a man. Gabriel replies, "The Holy Spirit will come upon you, and the power of the Most High will overshadow you; therefore the child to be born will be holy; he will be called Son of God" (1:35). Ancient people in the Greco-Roman era had various ideas about how conception occurred. Some ancient physicians and thinkers believed that everything needed for the formation of a child was contained in the man's semen, and the woman's role was only to be the place in which the baby grew—an incubator, so to speak—and to provide nourishment to the growing fetus in the form of menstrual blood. Other ancient physicians and thinkers believed that women's bodies also produced a kind of seed and that the woman's seed mixed with the man's seed to create the fetus. Most people also believed that what made the baby alive—the animating life-force—was contained in semen. This animating force was called the *pneuma*, a Greek word usually translated into English as "spirit" but that can also be translated as "breath."[4] It is unclear from Luke's story whether he thought that Mary's body produced seed or where the male seed would come from, but his story tells us that the *pneuma* would come from God. The life-force animating Jesus would be the Holy Life-Force, the Holy Spirit.[5]

This Holy Life-Force, Gabriel tells Mary, will "overshadow" her, so that the child she conceived would be holy, called the Son of God. As Jaime Clark-Soles points out, this use of the word "overshadow" is significant because the word is only used one other time in Luke's Gospel—in the Transfiguration story.[6] Both stories have to do with Jesus's identity, and both refer to him as the "Son of God." In the Transfiguration story, a cloud "overshadows" Jesus and the disciples, and the voice of God from the cloud identifies Jesus as "my Son"

(Luke 9:35). In Luke's Gospel, both Mary and Jesus are "overshadowed" by God's presence. The description of this presence as a cloud in the Transfiguration story recalls God's presence in clouds in the book of Exodus—in a pillar of cloud (13:21), in a cloud on Mount Sinai (9:9, 16), and in a cloud covering the tent of meeting (40:34). This is the overshadowing presence of God that Mary experiences in Luke 1 and Jesus experiences in Luke 9. As Clark-Soles writes, "*Both* Mary and Jesus and *only* Mary and Jesus are divinely overshadowed. They both have access to the divine and have supernatural experiences reminiscent of Moses. Like Mother, like Son."[7] Mary and Jesus are closely connected to one another by Luke's word choices and the intricacies of his storytelling. Luke does not fully explain the mechanics of Jesus's conception, but Mary is clearly intimately involved in the divine mystery of his origins.

A much-debated question has been how much agency or choice Mary has in the Annunciation story and its aftermath. In most cases of miraculous pregnancy in the Bible, the women in question have been praying to God for some time, asking or even begging for a child. This is not the case with Mary. Mary did not ask for Gabriel's visit or what is happening to her. Being a young *parthenos*, she would have had no reason to ask for such a thing. Additionally, Gabriel does not ask her if she is willing to participate in God's plan. Rather, he simply declares to her, "You *will* conceive in your womb and bear a son" (Luke 1:31, emphasis mine). Also, some readers are uncomfortable with the "overshadowing" language, feeling that it precludes Mary's agency and consent. How much agency can you have when the "Most High" is overshadowing you?[8]

On the other hand, Mary is far from passive in this narrative. From the very beginning of the conversation Mary is characterized as a person who thoughtfully processes what is happening to her. After Gabriel's greeting, we are told that "she was much perplexed by his words and pondered what sort of greeting this might be" (1:29). We see that she is going to be actively engaged in this conversation, both emotionally ("perplexed") and intellectually ("pondered"). Then, after Gabriel tells her she will bear a son, Mary does not acquiesce immediately but seeks more information before she decides on her response. Although Mary's question is similar to Zechariah's (1:18), Mary is not punished for asking it, as Zechariah was (1:20). Why? It is not clear but may have something to do with the fact that Zechariah's question seems to reveal a high degree of skepticism and asks for a sign, whereas Mary's question simply asks for an explanation. At any rate, Gabriel gives Mary what she asks for (more information), and in response Mary gives her famous "Yes" to God's plan: "Here am I, the servant of the Lord; let it be with me according to your word" (1:38). Mary may not have asked for what has happened to her, but she does actively process it and consent to it.

And yet, even in her consent, issues of agency linger because within her statement of consent she calls herself "the slave of the Lord." The Greek word *doulē*, translated by most English translations as "servant" or "handmaid," is more accurately translated as "slave." Mary says yes, but her yes is given because she views herself as God's slave. The slave is bound to do what the master orders. Some readers may feel that this takes away Mary's autonomy in the story. There are several things, however, that can help such readers understand this choice of language. First, there is nothing automatic about Mary's acquiescence; we have already seen how she reacts, ponders, and questions throughout the story.[9] Also, being a "slave of the Lord" puts her in good company. The New Testament elsewhere uses this phrase to describe apostles and believers doing God's work (see, for example, Acts 4:29 and Rom. 1:1).[10] Additionally, as Gaventa points out, if Mary is a "slave of God," then it means she does not belong to anyone else.[11] No human being exercises authority over her in this story; she speaks for herself. Finally, as F. Scott Spencer points out, there is a parallel between Mary's agreement to this difficult task and Jesus's prayer at the end of his life that God's will be done (22:42).[12] In that sense, by identifying her as the "slave of the Lord," Luke's narrative is not so much taking away her autonomy as it is presenting her as a model disciple—the first model disciple in Luke's Gospel.[13] Model disciples do not create God's plans, but they do participate in them willingly. Mary had not asked for motherhood, but after weighing things carefully, she chooses to accept the path of motherhood that God has laid out for her.

MARY AND ELIZABETH

After her encounter with Gabriel, Mary decides to go see Elizabeth. It is these two women who take center stage together in the next part of the story. I explained in chapter 2 that one of things motherhood signifies in the New Testament is connection between mother and child. But here we see that motherhood can also create connections between women. Of course, Mary and Elizabeth were already connected as kin, and women do not need to be mothers to forge deep connections with each other. Nevertheless, any time two people share similar experiences, this can bring them closer together, and for Mary and Elizabeth, this shared experience was becoming mothers at the same time. And not just becoming mothers in general, but experiencing miraculous pregnancies brought about by God for the purpose of the world's salvation! This puts them in a very small club indeed.

The Spirit continues to play a role here, as it does throughout Luke's Gospel. When Mary arrives, we are told that the child in Elizabeth's womb leaps at the sound of Mary's voice and that Elizabeth is filled with the Holy Spirit as she speaks to Mary. Elizabeth proclaims Mary blessed for being Jesus's mother and blessed for believing what Gabriel had told her. Once again the theme of connection is strong in these verses: Mary's connection to Jesus (Elizabeth blesses both of them together in verse 42), Mary's connection to Elizabeth (as the two engage together in a Spirit-filled conversation), Elizabeth's connection to Jesus (she calls him her Lord), Elizabeth's connection to John (the child is currently inside her body), and John's connection to Jesus (leaping at the sound of Jesus's mother's voice).

Engaging the text from a womanist perspective, Stephanie Buckhanon Crowder notes the difference in social status between Mary and Elizabeth.[14] Elizabeth is older and the wife of a priest in Judea. Mary is barely out of girlhood and is from rural Galilee—peasant country. And yet there is a reversal of their statuses in the story when Elizabeth calls Mary blessed and asks, "Why has this happened to me, that the mother of my Lord comes to me?" (1:43). The one with lower social status in the eyes of the world becomes the one elevated by God's action in the story, and Elizabeth can recognize it because she is filled with the Spirit. But class and status don't get in the way of Mary and Elizabeth's relationship. Elizabeth does not look down on Mary for her lower social status. Neither does Mary lord it over Elizabeth because she has been chosen to carry the Messiah. Rather, they are mutually supportive of one another.[15]

MARY AND HANNAH

The theme of social reversals (the lowly being lifted up and those of high status being brought down) continues to be featured prominently in the Magnificat, the words Mary proclaims in response to Elizabeth. Mary's speech (1:46–55) participates in the broader purpose of Luke's opening chapters as discussed at the beginning of this chapter: to connect the story of Jesus to the story of Israel by looking both forward and backward at the same time. The Magnificat looks forward by introducing numerous themes that will be important throughout Luke and Acts, such as worship (1:46–47), honoring God (1:46, 49), salvation (1:47, 50), social reversals (1:48, 51–53), Israel (1:54–55), God's mercy (1:50, 54), and God's faithfulness (1:50, 54–55). Additionally, the Magnificat also points backward, connecting this story to the story of Israel through its similarity to a variety of songs, psalms, and prayers in the Old Testament. As interpreters have long noticed, the most striking similarity is to Hannah's prayer of praise in 1 Samuel 2:1–10. Both speech-prayers begin by exulting and praising God and continue by proclaiming how God has raised up the lowly and brought down the powerful.

Hannah lived near the end of the time of the judges, and like many other Old Testament women, she was initially barren. Her distress over this situation was heightened because her husband Elkanah had another wife, Peninnah, who had already given him children (1 Sam. 1:2). Consistent with the idea that it is God who has control over fertility and birth, we are told that Hannah was barren because "the Lord had closed her womb," though no reason for this is given. But since God was the cause of the problem, God was the one to whom Hannah went, praying through tears and promising God that if he gave her a son, she would dedicate him to the Lord's service (1:9–11). God answered Hannah's prayers, and she bore a son, whom she named Samuel. After his weaning, she took him to live with the priest Eli at the tent sanctuary containing the ark of the covenant, and she gave her prayer of praise, like the one Luke attributes to Mary.

The similarity between their prayers of praise most likely means that Luke is intentionally drawing a comparison between Hannah and Mary. What could he be trying to communicate to the reader by making this comparison? I propose three things. First, as already mentioned, the similarity of Mary's prayer to Old Testament passages connects Luke's story to the story of Israel. Second, the association with Hannah emphasizes Mary's faithfulness. Hannah is an Old Testament figure beloved by many, portrayed positively in her story as a woman who wrestles faithfully with God in prayer and keeps her vow to God after her child is born, despite the difficulty of having to give him up. This connection to Hannah helps us see Mary as a faithful person as well, who also engages boldly with God and is also faithful to the difficult mothering role to which God is calling her. She also will have to let her son go. Third, if Mary and Hannah are being compared, then that implies a comparison also between the sons being born to them. Samuel grew up to be one of the greatest prophets of the Old Testament. The similarity of their mothers' situations implies here at the outset of Jesus's story that he will also grow up to be a great prophet.[16] This comparison is reinforced by a very similar description of each boy growing in years/stature and wisdom/favor in 1 Samuel 2:26 and Luke 2:52. A further connection between Samuel and Jesus is that Samuel is the prophet who anoints David as king (1 Sam. 16:13), and now Jesus will fulfill the Davidic line—in the Annunciation story Gabriel told Mary that God would give to Jesus "the throne of his ancestor David" and that he would reign on that throne forever (Luke 1:32–33).

The connections between Mary/Jesus and Hannah/Samuel clearly imply that Jesus is a prophet. But what about Mary herself? Is she also portrayed by the narrative as a prophet? Luke does not use the word "prophet" to describe her, but several aspects of her story characterize her as a prophetic figure. Barbara Reid points out that three narrative elements in the Annunciation story are also typically found in prophetic call stories in the Old Testament: the call comes to an ordinary person in the midst of daily life, the one called initially resists the call, and their resistance is met with assurances that God will be with the prophet to help them and will make the tasks possible.[17] If the Annunciation is Mary's prophetic call story, then the Magnificat can be viewed as her prophetic speech. As Reid writes, "Mary's prophetic work involves not only giving birth to the one who will claim the throne of his ancestor David and who will rule forever (1:32–33), but also proclaiming what this rule of God will be like (1:46–55)."[18] In the Magnificat Mary declares that God is with the lowly, and God's rule will turn the power structures of the world upside down. This is a message very much in line with Old Testament prophetic traditions. In Luke's opening chapters, "mother" and "prophet" are not mutually exclusive roles.

MARY'S LABOR AND DELIVERY IN LUKE

Luke's Christmas story is a story many people think they know well. Consider the following aspects of Jesus's very familiar birth story:

- Mary riding a donkey to Bethlehem
- Mary and Joseph knocking on the doors of inns all over town

- Everyone turning them away until one innkeeper finally tells them they can stay in his stable
- Mary giving birth in the stable surrounded by sheep and oxen
- A star appearing over the stable

Now consider that none of those elements are found in the story of Jesus's birth in the Gospel of Luke (or any other New Testament Gospel). In Luke there is no mention of a donkey ride, no mention of knocking on doors, no mention of an innkeeper, no mention of a stable, no mention of animals, and no mention of a star.[19] In this section, we will look at the story Luke actually tells.

Mary and Joseph travel to Bethlehem because of a census. With no further information given about where they stay in Bethlehem, it is logical to assume that they stay in the home of extended family members. Most travelers did not stay in inns in the ancient world. Inns were only found in large cities, not villages like Bethlehem, and even where they did exist they would generally have been places of ill repute. If Mary and Joseph are coming to Bethlehem because it is Joseph's ancestral home, then they are most likely staying with his extended kin. While they are staying there (not the night they arrive) the time comes for Mary to give birth. Luke uses momentous language to describe this: "The days were fulfilled for her giving birth" (Luke 2:6, my translation). This is rather majestic language for the experience of being nine months pregnant and going into labor, but it reminds us that this is no ordinary birth—God is at work in these events. To Luke, this is no ordinary time. It is part of salvation history. And like so many stories before, God's plan of salvation is enacted by a woman giving birth.

After Mary gives birth, Luke tells us that she swaddled the newborn Jesus in bands of cloth and laid him in a manger (an animal feedbox) because there was no room for them in the *katalyma*. English Bibles have traditionally translated this Greek word as "inn," but inn is not a good translation for *katalyma*. The word *katalyma* means the place in a house or building where guests are lodged.[20] The 2021 update to the NRSV changed its translation from "there was no place for them in the inn" to "there was no place in the guest room." Luke also uses the word *katalyma* in 22:11. When Jesus and the disciples are preparing for the Passover meal, Jesus sends Peter and John to ask a man, "Where is the *katalyma*, where I may eat the Passover with my disciples?" And the man shows them a large upstairs room in his house. Peter and John are not asking where the inn is that they can use to celebrate Passover, but where the guest space is in the man's house that he is going to allow them to use. In this story *katalyma* clearly means guest room, not inn.

So, in 2:7, when Luke writes that there is no place for Mary and Joseph in the guest room, this most likely means that they are staying in a house but that all the upstairs sleeping rooms are already full, presumably with other census travelers. So why, then, is an animal feedbox the place where Jesus is laid? To understand this it helps to know what village houses were like in that time and place. Archaeology shows us that in ancient Israel/Judea, most village houses consisted of two stories arranged around a central courtyard. Peasant families, who would have only owned a few animals, brought these animals into the first floor of their homes to shelter at night. Upstairs were rooms for sleeping and eating. If there is no guest space available for Mary, it means she has to give birth on the first floor, the family's main living area, near the place where animals were kept. A feedbox for the animals was nearby as a place to lay the baby.

In Luke's story Jesus is not born in some separated, lonely, unusual place; he is born as one of us, surrounded by the hustle and bustle of peasant family life. We also do not need to imagine that Mary gave birth by herself; she was most likely surrounded by female family members and a midwife, as were all women who gave birth in the ancient world. It is true, however, that we can say Jesus was clearly born into a lower-class setting in Luke's story. One aspect of the traditional Christmas story that holds true in Luke's narrative is that you don't expect a future king to be laid in an animal feedbox. And not only is his birth a lower-class birth, but it is in a place that is not his own home. He comes into the world in borrowed space, foreshadowing his statement in 9:58 about the nature of his ministry—that foxes have holes and birds have nests, but the Son of Man has nowhere to lay his head.

MARY'S MINDFULNESS

After Jesus is born, Luke's story shifts scenes to shepherds in a field.[21] Angels appear to the shepherds telling them of the birth of a savior. Though terrified, the shepherds nevertheless decide to go investigate this news and find Mary and Joseph and baby Jesus lying in the manger. When they arrive, they tell the story of what happened to them in the field, and everyone who hears it is amazed. (Notice that this implies there are lots of people around to hear what the shepherds say—again, Mary and Joseph are not off by themselves in a stable!) The general reaction to what the shepherds say is amazement, but Luke tells us something more specific about Mary's reaction to their words: "Mary treasured all these words and pondered them in her heart" (2:19). We already saw in the Annunciation story that Mary thoughtfully processes what is happening to her. Here we see it again. The word translated by the NRSVue as "treasured" can mean "preserve," "keep," "protect," "defend," "hold," or "treasure up." One possible definition of the word is "to store information in one's mind for careful consideration."[22] The word translated as "pondered" can mean "converse," "consider," "ponder," "reflect," or "compare." Interestingly, the word can also be used in the context of battle or an argument—to "engage" with an opponent.[23] I'm not suggesting that Mary was in conflict with what the shepherds said, but merely that this is a very active word. Mary is not passively watching what is happening to her. She is actively engaging with it and trying to figure out what it all means. As Bonnie Miller-McLemore points out, we could call this "theological reflection."[24]

Mary is a person who pays attention. She observes, considers, and reflects on the significance of what is happening in her life. Miller-McLemore focuses particularly on how Mary can be a model for mothers in this regard—especially the mothers of young children who may feel overwhelmed amid busy, chaotic, tiring lives. During her own confusing chaos, Mary "models a certain kind of Christian spirituality of presence" because she "attends to God precisely within the confused messiness of her life."[25] If giving birth in a borrowed living room or courtyard and then having shepherds come in telling wild stories immediately afterward isn't confusing and chaotic, I don't know what is! Mary's intentional engagement with all of it in her mind and heart can be a "vision or sign of hope and guidance" to mothers dealing with everyday challenges.[26] Of course, this does not apply only to mothers but to anyone who ever feels overwhelmed by the chaotic messiness of life. Mary can be a model for everyone, not only mothers, and not only women.

MARY'S SUFFERING IN LUKE

In the previous chapter I wrote about suffering as a theme associated with motherhood in the opening chapters of Matthew's Gospel, particularly in relation to the flight to Egypt and the slaughter of the innocents in chapter 2. The theme of suffering is also present in a couple of ways in the later part of Luke's birth narrative. As in Matthew, Mary's motherhood in Luke does not protect her from suffering but makes the possibility of suffering even more likely and the severity of the potential suffering even more acute. The first scene in which we see this is in the presentation of the infant Jesus in the temple (2:22–38). The second place is in the story of Jesus in the temple as a twelve-year-old boy (2:41–52). The fact that both events are associated with the temple might tell us that Mary's particular suffering as a mother will have something to do with Jesus's religious and vocational calling. Being the mother of the Messiah can't be easy.

After Jesus's birth, Mary and Joseph bring two birds to the temple in Jerusalem for a purification sacrifice. This tells us two things about Mary and Joseph. First, it tells us that they are faithful, observant Jews, following the guidance of the Torah in their family life. Second, it reinforces the idea that they are poor people, which has already been implied by the circumstances of Jesus being born in peasant surroundings. Leviticus 12:1–8 indicates that after childbirth a mother should bring a sheep and a pigeon or turtledove to the temple for a purification offering. But the text indicates that if she cannot afford a sheep, she can bring two birds instead. The fact that Mary brings two birds indicates that she and Joseph cannot afford a sheep. Again, this is not a noble or upper-class beginning for one who will later be hailed as Messiah and king, and it shows us that Jesus is a different kind of king than your typical earthly ruler.

When Mary, Joseph, and the infant Jesus arrive at the temple, they encounter a man named Simeon. Simeon is a man who lived faithfully, with the hope that God would redeem Israel. Guided by the Holy Spirit, Simeon comes to the temple that day and is able to recognize Jesus as the Messiah. He praises God for allowing him to see God's salvation within his lifetime. Then Simeon turns to speak directly to Mary, saying, "This child is destined for the falling and the rising of many in Israel and to be a sign that will be opposed so that the inner thoughts of many will be revealed—and a sword will pierce your own soul, too" (Luke 2:34–35). Simeon makes a direct connection between Jesus's destiny as the Messiah and Mary's future suffering. Interpreters most often understand Simeon's words to be referring to the suffering that Mary will experience when Jesus dies. That suffering is probably included in what Simeon is referring to, but I think we can interpret it a bit more broadly than that as well. Jesus's vocation will cause some hardship for Mary even before the time comes for him to die. For example, it could not have felt good to Mary when she and her other children came to visit Jesus and he responded to the news that they were outside by saying, "Who are my mother and my brothers?"[27] In the Gospels, Jesus's vocation as the Messiah creates some distance between him and his family of origin.

Indeed, when we think about what Simeon's words to Mary mean, we don't have to look further than the next story to see Mary's motherhood of Jesus causing her anguish. This is the story of Jesus in the temple as a twelve-year-old boy. On a trip to Jerusalem for Passover, Jesus becomes separated from his parents and stays behind when the caravan of multiple family groups heads out of Jerusalem. After a day of traveling, Mary and Joseph discover that he is not with their friends and family as they had assumed, and they return to Jerusalem and spend three days searching for him. They finally find him in the temple conversing with the teachers there. Mary says to Jesus, "Child, why have you treated us like this? Your father and I have been anxiously looking for you" (Luke 2:48). As Gaventa points out, this translation is rather "bland"—the underlying Greek word indicates that Mary and Joseph have not just been "anxiously" looking for Jesus, but that they have been doing so "in anguish." They are not just worried but experiencing "the real and present terror of parents who do not know where their child is."[28] Jesus's response to Mary, that he is in his "Father's house," indicates again that Jesus's calling will put some distance between him and his family of origin.

MARY AS JESUS'S TEACHER

In the ancient world, parents were the primary teachers of their children. This is still true today but was even more true in ancient times because only a small minority of children went to school (primarily boys from elite families). For most children, education occurred in the home. Both mothers and fathers played a role in children's religious education and moral development. This was true in both Roman and Jewish culture.[29] At the end of the story of Jesus as a twelve-year-old in the temple, Luke writes that Jesus goes home with his parents to Nazareth and is obedient to them. In the same verse we also learn that Mary is continuing to remember and consider carefully all that is occurring (2:51). As for Jesus, all we find out about his life between age twelve and age thirty is, "Jesus increased in wisdom and in years and in divine and human favor" (2:52). Jesus did not already know everything he needed to know as a twelve-year-old boy. He grew in wisdom as he grew into an adult. Who was teaching him what he needed to learn during these growing years? Like other children of his time, place, and social status, it would have been primarily his parents, to whom the story tells us he was obedient. And perhaps it might be safe to venture that, of his parents, Mary was his primary teacher, since Luke tells us almost nothing about Joseph, but continually focuses on Mary's role in Jesus's life, including her memory and deep reflections on what is occurring in her life and Jesus's life. She is the one who is paying attention. She must have had a key role to play in Jesus's increase in wisdom through his childhood, teenage, and early adult years.

Jaime Clark-Soles makes this case, drawing especially on the content of Mary's Magnificat in 1:46–55. Clark-Soles shows many connections between Mary's words in the Magnificat and the later themes of Jesus's teachings, arguing that Jesus got his ideas primarily from his mother.[30] For example, there are strong parallels between the social reversals expressed in the Magnificat and Jesus's choice of the Isaiah passage for his inaugural sermon in Luke 4:18, a passage that speaks of bringing good news to the poor and letting the oppressed go free. A similar parallel exists between the Magnificat and the Beatitudes in Luke 6:20–26. Clark-Soles also draws a comparison between Mary's words in the Annunciation ("Let it be with me according to your word") and Jesus's words in the Garden of Gethsemane ("Not my will but yours be done"). If the themes of the Annunciation story and the Magnificat are any indication, much of what Jesus later taught may have originally been taught to him by Mary.[31]

But even this theme of Mary as Jesus's teacher participates in the theme of Mary's suffering. For the more she leads him toward his ministry, the more he will grow away from her. Not because there is something wrong with Mary that he needs to get away from but because this is something all children must do as they gradually move from childhood to adulthood. We've seen some of the ways that Mary's suffering is distinctive, in that there are particular hardships associated with being the mother of the Messiah. But this aspect of Mary's hardship is something that all parents can relate to. Just like all other parents, Mary experienced what Miller-McLemore calls the "infinitesimal leave-takings that occur daily and at each life stage."[32] Children do not simply leave their parents suddenly and all at once when they reach eighteen or twenty-one or some other set age. Rather, childhood in its entirety is a long, slow process of children gradually leaving their parents, becoming just a bit more independent with every milestone and stage of development. For Jesus to grow into his vocation he had to grow away from Mary. This was bound to cause Mary some sorrow, as it does for all who care for children. But parents and other caregivers can take some comfort in the fact that these leave-takings are also a sign that they are doing their jobs well. We may nostalgically wish we could hold on to the time when our children are small, but we know that to do parenting well is to guide children along the path that will lead them away from us. This was a truth that Mary seems to have deeply understood, as she protected and nurtured Jesus while he was small, and then guided him into an adulthood that would change the world.

CONCLUSION

No other New Testament Gospel gives as much attention to women and motherhood at the beginning of the story as Luke does. The opening chapters of Luke's Gospel are remarkable for their focus on Mary instead of Joseph, the character of Elizabeth and her interactions with Mary, and just how much women speak and are filled with the Holy Spirit. Mary engages and ponders, Elizabeth exclaims, Mary proclaims. As I stated at the beginning of the chapter, these women connect Jesus's story to Israel's story and lay the theological groundwork on which the rest of Luke's Gospel is built. And yet we also cannot fail to notice their near absence from the rest of Luke's story. After chapter 2, Mary appears only in one brief episode in 8:19–21 and is mentioned indirectly in 11:27–28.[33] Her name is not used in either passage.[34] Elizabeth is never seen or mentioned again after chapter 1.

In this Gospel, Mary's and Elizabeth's motherhoods are first emphasized and then eclipsed. This is partly because Luke is primarily telling Jesus's story, not Mary's or Elizabeth's, and it is partly because of the androcentric nature of most of the Bible. What's unusual here is not that we don't hear more about Mary and Elizabeth later, but that we do hear about them so much at the beginning of the story. Their absence from the rest of the story should not make us think that they had no ongoing role in the lives of their adult sons. Rather, it should make us think about what kind of lives historians have typically paid attention to and recorded: Whose stories get remembered and told? In the ancient world these were primarily men's stories. We can be glad for what Luke has given us in chapters 1 and 2 while still wishing that he and other biblical authors had told us more about women, children, and other groups of people whose lives are mostly lost to history.

Connected Mothers

DISCUSSION QUESTIONS

1. What stood out to you in the chapter's analysis of the Annunciation story? Does it make a difference for our understanding of the story to know something about how ancient people understood conception? Which is more important to Luke and to you: Mary's virginity (i.e., the lack of male seed), or the fact that her child's *pneuma* (animating life-force) came from God? Why?
2. In your view, how much agency does Mary have in the Annunciation story? Does she consent to motherhood?
3. In what ways does motherhood bring women together, as it did for Mary and Elizabeth? Are there times or circumstances when motherhood drives women apart?
4. What difference does it make to picture Jesus's birth in a home rather than a stable? What difference does it make to imagine Mary surrounded by supportive women as she gives birth, rather than doing so alone or only with Joseph?
5. Is it troubling to you to think of Jesus as needing to be taught by Mary? Why or why not?

4

MOTHERING A GROWN-UP MESSIAH

The Mother of Jesus in the Gospel of John

I ended the previous chapter by acknowledging that Luke tells us almost nothing about Mary after the birth story is over in chapter 2. In Matthew, Mark, and Luke, we get very little indication that Mary had any significant ongoing role in Jesus's life after he was grown up. But most mothers (in both the ancient and modern worlds) do not stop having relationships with their children when those children reach maturity. In the Roman era, mothers did not have much in the way of legal rights over their children, but it was common for them to have a lot of influence over their children, and this continued for as long as both mother and child were alive.[1] So it is natural for us to wonder what Mary's relationship with Jesus was like after he was grown and his ministry had begun. The Gospel of John is the only New Testament Gospel to give us more than the briefest glimpse of this relationship. Jesus's mother appears in two significant stories in John when Jesus is an adult—the wedding at Cana (2:1–12) and the crucifixion (19:25–27). Interestingly, his mother is never named in this Gospel. For convenience I will continue to refer to her as Mary, but John does not name her. It seems that for John, Mary is significant not so much for her individual identity as for her role in relation to Jesus. In this chapter we will consider that role, beginning with her significance for one of the most important theological themes in the Gospel of John—Jesus as the Word made flesh. Following that, we will explore the role Mary's motherhood plays at Cana and at the cross.

THE WORD MADE FLESH IN MARY'S BODY

In the Gospel of John, Mary is not mentioned at all in connection with Jesus's birth. In fact, there is no birth story in John. Instead of taking us back to the beginning of Jesus's earthly life, John takes us back to the beginning of creation, identifying Jesus as the incarnation of the *logos*. The word *logos* in Greek most often refers simply to the content of spoken language and thus is almost universally translated into English as "word." But in addition to this dictionary definition of *logos*, the word also had a deeper meaning in Greek philosophy, where it was used to refer to the divine principle of reason and order that structures the universe. The ancient Jewish philosopher Philo identified the *logos* of Greek philosophy with the personification of Wisdom as a female figure in the Jewish Scriptures. The author of John seems to be making the same connection, since he uses the term *logos* to describe the divine reality that was incarnate in Jesus, but he describes that *logos* in ways that are very reminiscent of the Old Testament figure of Wisdom (see especially Prov. 8:22–31).

In John 1:14 the *logos* becomes flesh, but no mention is made of Mary. For John, the important thing is not to establish the circumstances of Jesus's birth but to establish the idea that God was the one at work in Jesus. In this Gospel, this is simply the truth about Jesus's identity, and it is not dependent on how Jesus was conceived or born. On the one hand, the lack of focus in John on Jesus's conception marginalizes Mary in the narrative, since she does not play a starring role in John's opening chapters as she had in Matthew and especially in Luke. On the other hand, reading between the lines, this theme of incarnation makes Mary's role even more significant. When the *logos* becomes flesh, it is Mary's maternal body that plays the central role in bringing this about, even if John does not say so explicitly.

Sometimes we pay more attention to the idea of Jesus as the *logos* than we do to the idea that the *logos* became flesh. The fact that the *logos* became flesh in Mary's body means that Jesus was a real human being. He didn't just appear to be human but was as human as you and me. He was flesh. According to Beverly Gaventa, this is the primary role that Mary plays in John's Gospel: her presence as his mother reveals his humanity and connects him to the world.[2] This may be why John does not use her name. What is significant about her is not her identity as an individual but her role as Jesus's flesh-and-blood mother, revealing his humanity. Therefore, it is significant that of the two places Mary appears in this Gospel, one is at the very beginning of Jesus's public ministry and one is at the very end. Mary's motherhood, as a reminder of Jesus's humanity, frames his ministry in the Gospel of John, essentially marking off the time period in which the *logos* walked as flesh among us.

THE WEDDING AT CANA

Each New Testament Gospel writer chooses to narrate the beginning of Jesus's public ministry with a different story. In each case, the story tells us something important about the portrait of Jesus that the Gospel writer wants to emphasize.[3] In Mark, the first major event after Jesus's baptism is an exorcism story (1:21–28), an event that demonstrates Jesus's power and sets up the central conflict of the story—Jesus versus the forces of evil. In Matthew, the first public thing Jesus does is to give the Sermon on the Mount (5:1–7:27), which shows us Jesus as a Jewish teacher, interpreting Torah and laying out the contours of a life of righteousness for his followers. In Luke, Jesus's first ministry event is his sermon in Nazareth (4:16–30), in which he draws on Isaiah to proclaim that his ministry will be one that brings good news to the poor and release to those in captivity. In John, Jesus's first public act is to transform water into wine at a wedding (2:1–12). We should expect, then, that this story will tell us something about how John views what is most important about Jesus's ministry. Indeed, as we walk through this story we will see all kinds of connections to Jesus's identity and where the story of his ministry is heading. Mary's motherhood plays a central role in revealing these connections.

After Jesus calls his first few disciples to follow him in John 1, he attends a wedding with his disciples and his mother at the beginning of chapter 2. The story begins, "On the third day there was a wedding in Cana of Galilee" (2:1). Presumably, this means that the wedding took place on the third day after Jesus had called Philip and Nathanael to follow him. However, the Gospel of John is filled with symbolism, and many elements in the narrative have both a literal and a figurative meaning. While at one level these words simply inform us about the timeline of this part of the story, at the same time they will also ring a bell for many of John's readers who are already familiar with something else that occurred "on the third day," namely, Jesus's resurrection from the dead. Here at the outset of the story John is establishing a link between the beginning and end of Jesus's ministry. We will see several more of these links as we keep reading.

During the wedding celebration the wine runs out. This is not just a minor inconvenience but a moment of crisis for the family hosting the wedding. Weddings were multi-day events, community celebrations enjoyed by the family, friends, and neighbors of those getting married. Hosting such an event took a significant number of resources. Not many families in the ancient world had the resources to pull off such a celebration on their own. For this reason, according to Bruce Malina and Richard Rohrbaugh, it was common for friends and relatives to send the hosting family gifts of food and wine in advance of the celebration to help with the great number of provisions needed for a wedding feast. The fact that the wine ran out at this wedding threatens the honor of the hosting family: not only were they unable to provide adequately for their guests, but the "lack of wine" suggests a "lack of friends."[4] Their connections were not sufficiently generous in helping them prepare for this event.

When Jesus's mother learns that the wine has run out, she goes to Jesus and says, "They have no wine" (2:3). It is a simple statement but seems to imply that she expects him to do something about it. At least, that is how Jesus seems to interpret her statement, since he replies, "Woman, what concern is that to me and to you? My hour has not yet come" (2:4). The first half of this statement is notoriously difficult to translate into English because the language of the original text is ambiguous. Gaventa translates the text very literally as, "What is to me and to you, woman?"[5] It is up to the translator to determine what that is supposed to mean. Here is a sampling of how different translations render the text in English:

- "O woman, what have you to do with me?" (Revised Standard Version)
- "Woman, how does your concern affect me?" (New American Bible)
- "Woman, why do you involve me?" (New International Version)
- "Woman, what concern is that to me and to you?" (NRSVue)

How much Jesus is distancing himself from his mother with this statement depends greatly on which of these interpretations we choose.

The RSV puts the greatest distance between Jesus and Mary, interpreting his statement to mean that they don't have anything to do with each other at all. They may as well be strangers! The NAB softens this, implying that it is not Mary herself who has nothing to do with Jesus, but that her concern about the wine has nothing to do with him. The NIV is similar in that Jesus rejects Mary's concern about the wine, but this translation also seems to imply more of a criticism of Mary for sharing her concern with him at all. In other words, Jesus is essentially saying to her, "why are you bothering me about this?" The NRSVue is the translation that allows us to retain the closest possible relationship between Jesus and his mother. In this interpretation, Jesus's words imply that he and his mother are (or at least ought to be) unified in their lack of concern about the wine. They can stay on the same side, so to speak, if she will see it his way. It is also important to realize that we have no access to tone of voice when we read Bible stories. While most commentators interpret Jesus's words as dismissive of Mary and her concerns, Clark-Soles suggests that we should hear his words as "familial, playful banter."[6] I think this may be wishful thinking, but it is important to recognize that tone of voice and body language would play a crucial role in a scene like this, and we don't have access to that in the written narrative.

Unfortunately, it is not possible to say which of the above interpretations is "right" because of the ambiguity of the original text. But no matter Jesus's tone, and whether he is distancing himself from his mother or only from her concern about the wine, it is at least fairly clear that Jesus initially does not want to take any action in response to his mother's information about the wine, because he follows his first statement with the words, "My hour has not yet come." Like the use of the words "on the third day" at the beginning of the story, these words seem to have an immediate meaning and a deeper meaning. First, they imply that Jesus does not want to take action because he feels the time has not yet come for him to begin revealing himself in this way. But elsewhere in the Gospel of John, Jesus's "hour" refers to the time of his crucifixion (see 7:30; 8:20; 12:23, 27; 13:1; 17:1; and 19:27). So, like the words "on the third day," these words about Jesus's hour also create a link between this story and the climax of Jesus's ministry at the end of the Gospel.

When considering the relationship between Jesus and his mother in this story, another important factor to consider is his use of the word "woman" to address her. Jesus calling her "woman" sounds rude to our English-speaking ears, but this was a common rather than a rude way to address women in that culture. However, even though it is not rude, it is surprising, because it was not a common way to address one's own mother.[7] Jesus uses the same word to address the Samaritan woman in 4:21, the woman caught in adultery in 8:10, and Mary Magdalene in 20:15. The fact that Jesus addresses his mother in the same way as these other women implies that Jesus is creating some distance between himself and his mother. This might remind us of stories in other Gospels in which Jesus distances himself from his mother and siblings, proclaiming faith relationships more important than biological ones.[8] In this story, Jesus's identity as Son of God takes precedence over his identity as son of Mary.

Mary, however, seems undeterred by Jesus's manner of addressing her. Though Jesus has just indicated at least a reluctance if not an unwillingness to act, his mother turns to the servants and says to them, "Do whatever he tells you" (2:5). Mary's confidence that Jesus will act is then vindicated by Jesus, in fact, telling them what to do. Jesus's words have just distanced him from his mother, yet she is still his mother. And as such she knows him well and has spent roughly thirty years watching the development of his character and the unfolding of his calling. She seems to be able to see more clearly than even he does that the "hour" has come for him to act and that it is in his nature to show compassion in this situation. Jesus does not say she is right, but his subsequent actions show an acknowledgment that she is right in her reading of him and her reading of the situation. Jesus may be grown up, but Mary is still mothering him.

Jesus points to six large stone jars used for ritual washing and tells the servants to fill them with water. They do so, and then follow his further instructions in drawing some out and taking it to the chief steward—the highest-ranking servant, who was in charge of running the banquet. At some point along the way, the story doesn't tell us exactly when, the water had become wine. And not just any wine—a fine wine that inspires words of praise from the steward when he calls the bridegroom over. In addition to being of fine quality, the wine is also generous in its abundance. Six jars of twenty or thirty gallons each were filled with water, creating somewhere between 120 and 180 gallons of wine. That's a lot of wine! In this part of the story there are also more links to the story of Jesus's crucifixion. The Cana story features water and wine. Water and wine both appear in the story of Jesus's crucifixion as well. In John 19:29 Jesus is offered sour wine while on the cross, and in 19:34, when Jesus's side is pierced after his death, blood and water flow out.

Near the end of the Cana story, the narrator tells us that this miracle was the first of Jesus's "signs" (2:11). John is the only Gospel to use the language of "signs" to describe Jesus's miracles. The thing to remember about signs is that they are meant to point us to something else. If we get fixated on the sign itself, we've missed the point. So, what is this miracle of water into wine supposed to point us to? It could be that the abundant quantity of wine is meant to point us to the abundant nature of God's grace that will be manifest though Jesus's ministry—after all, he will tell his followers later that he came that "they may have life and have it *abundantly*" (John 10:10, my emphasis). It could be that it is meant to show Jesus's compassionate nature as he assists a family in crisis. It could be that it is meant to point us to the fact that the beginning of Jesus's ministry signals a new stage in the unfolding of God's salvation plan, since Old Testament prophets like Isaiah and Amos reference abundant wine in their descriptions of what life will be like in the glorious future that would come when God's new age dawns (See Isa. 25:6 and Amos 9:13).[9] It probably signifies all these things and more.

The wedding at Cana is the beginning of Jesus's ministry in the Gospel of John, but as we've already seen, here at the beginning of the story the reader is already being pointed toward the end of the story through numerous narrative links between this story and the story of Jesus's death and resurrection. Jesus's hour hasn't come yet, but with these words about abundant wine we are already being pointed toward that hour. We are supposed to realize that this story of water turned into an abundance of wine is just a foretaste of the up-to-the-brim and over-the-top abundance of grace and love that will be expressed by Jesus when he lays down his life for his friends at the end of the story. And it is Jesus's mother who is the catalyst for bringing this about. She is the one to bring Jesus's attention to the lack of wine and the one who seemingly won't take no for an answer when Jesus tries to rebuff her. As his mother, Mary knows Jesus well and can see that the time has come for him to begin his ministry. The miracle at Cana provides a preview of the abundant life and grace available through Christ and occurs at the instigation of Jesus's mother.

At the end of the story the narrator tells us that when the wedding was over, Jesus's mother and her other children traveled with Jesus from Cana to Capernaum. This would seem to indicate an ongoing closeness between Jesus and Mary, as she travels with him to the next stop of his ministry. But we also saw the ways that Jesus distanced himself from his mother through his language toward her in the Cana story. And we hear nothing of her presence in his life or ministry between 2:12 and 19:25, which is quite a gap. This tension between closeness and distance in their relationship illustrates the tensions and dualities at play in Jesus's identity in the Gospel of John: that Jesus is both Son of God and son of Mary—the *logos* made flesh.

JESUS AND HIS MOTHER AT THE CROSS

In the previous section I noted several narrative links between the Cana story and the story of Jesus's death and resurrection: the words "on the third day," the words about Jesus's hour, and the presence of water and wine. To these links we can add another: the presence of Jesus's mother. These two stories are the only two in John where she appears, so her presence creates yet another link between the beginning and ending of Jesus's ministry. When Jesus is on the cross, a small group of followers is standing nearby, including his mother, the Beloved Disciple, and a few other women.

The narrator does not give us any direct access to Mary's thoughts and feelings as she stands at the foot of the cross. But it does not take a great deal of imagination to think that Mary suffers deeply as she stands there, watching her son die. In previous chapters I wrote about suffering as an aspect of Mary's motherhood that is expressed in the stories about her in Matthew and Luke. This theme is also present here, at least in the minds of most readers, and as represented over and over through the years in various movies, stories, and works of art that portray Mary's grief as she watches Jesus being crucified.

The author of John, however, focuses not on Mary's grief, but on what Jesus does from the cross. Jesus addresses his mother and the Beloved Disciple, saying to his mother, "Here is your son," and to the Beloved Disciple, "Here is your mother" (19:26–27). The narrator then tells us that Mary lived with the Beloved Disciple from that time onward. In addition to being the mother of Jesus, Mary can now also be understood as an adoptive mother, becoming at the cross the mother of the Beloved Disciple. They are now family to one another, a biblical illustration of what we already know—that not all families are related to one another by blood. Some are related by adoption and by the choice to love and be in relationship with the chosen.

Although the Bible does not tell us this, most readers presume that Mary was a widow by the time Jesus died, since Joseph makes no appearances in the Gospels after the birth stories. Related to this, I think most readers also assume that the reason Jesus "gives" his mother to the Beloved Disciple is so that her needs will be provided for, since most widows in ancient patriarchal culture could not support themselves on their own. However, there are two factors that I believe argue against the idea that provision for Mary's needs is the primary motivating factor of Jesus's words from the cross. First, Jesus does not tell the Beloved Disciple to care for his mother, but rather redefines the very nature of their relationship. They are both given new family roles in relation to each other. They are both addressed in a parallel fashion, rather than one being told to care for the other. Second, the Gospels tell us that Mary had other children (Matt. 12:46; 13:55; Mark 3:31; 6:3; Luke 8:19; John 2:12).[10] This means that she would probably not have been left destitute after Jesus's death. She would have been able to go to one of the homes of her other children. Since Jesus was living an itinerant lifestyle, if Mary was a widow, she was probably already living with one of her other children even before Jesus died. It is not as though Jesus had been providing a stable home for her up to this point, such that now he would need to make sure someone else does that.

If Jesus was not primarily ensuring that Mary would be provided for, what was he doing when he says, "Here is your son.... Here is your mother"? One popular interpretation that remains compelling is that, in saying these words, Jesus gives birth to the church from the cross.[11] As we have already begun to see, and we will explore even further in chapter 6, relationships within the faith community that Jesus builds are more important to him than biological ones. By giving his mother and the Beloved Disciple to one another as a new mother-son pair, Jesus is establishing his followers as a new kind of family. This interpretation is even more compelling when we consider that neither Jesus's mother nor the Beloved Disciple are named characters in the Gospel of John, raising the possibility that their roles can be understood symbolically. The Beloved Disciple is a mysterious, unnamed character who appears only from chapter 13 onward. He has often been assumed to be the disciple John (son of Zebedee), but the Gospel itself leaves his identity a mystery. The Mother and the Beloved Disciple given to one another in this scene can be understood to represent all who share faith in Jesus.

Mary's relationship of adoption with the Beloved Disciple forms the foundation of the community that will become the church. In the prologue of John's Gospel, the narrator says of Jesus, "To all who received him, who believed in his name, he gave power to become children of God" (1:12). In the Gospel of John, believers become children of God—that is, they become the family of faith. As Gail O'Day writes, even those without supportive biological families of their own can now have "the possibility of a future marked by acceptance, not rejection. The new family that is born at the foot of the cross is marked by love and faith."[12] And as Clark-Soles points out, if those who believe in Jesus are the children of God, then "Jesus's mother is the matriarch of the family."[13]

CONCLUSION

Mary only appears in two stories in John, but it is at two of the most crucial moments in the narrative—the beginning of Jesus's public ministry and the end of his earthly life at the cross. There are a lot of different aspects of Mary's motherhood that we see illustrated by her appearance in the Gospel of John, and all of them are theologically significant. Her biological motherhood plays a role in the incarnation and affirms Jesus's humanity. At the cross she becomes also an adoptive mother and the matriarch of the family of faith. Mary is a catalyst for Jesus's ministry beginning at Cana, and her presence in the narrative ties together the beginning and end of Jesus's ministry.

In Matthew and Luke, Mary is a model mother primarily in her actions related to her pregnancy and in relation to Jesus as an infant and child. In John, Mary and Jesus relate to one another as mother and son, but also as two adults. We see her in this Gospel as a woman supporting her grown son. She continues to mother him by prompting him to begin living out his calling at the right moment, and then by staying with him through the bitter end. In the end she remains his mother but also becomes one of the foundations of the family of faith. Therefore, her presence in John's narrative represents the believer's connection to Jesus and to all who become his family through faith.

DISCUSSION QUESTIONS

1. In what ways is Mary's relationship with Jesus different in John than it is in Matthew and Luke? What do you think are the reasons for these differences?
2. What tone of voice do you imagine Jesus using when he addresses his mother in the Cana story? What do you think his words to her are meant to communicate?
3. Do you think that Jesus gives his mother and the Beloved Disciple to each other so that his mother will be provided for, or to "birth" the church community from the cross? Or both? What difference does this make for our interpretation of the passage?
4. Why do you think the author of John creates so many narrative links between the Cana story and the crucifixion story? What are we supposed to learn by reading these two stories together?
5. What might it mean for Mary to be the "matriarch" of the Christian family, as Clark-Soles puts it? How might different Christian traditions view the meaning of this differently?

5

MOTHERS IN CRISIS

Motherhood in the Miracle Stories of the Synoptic Gospels

If you were to ask people to list the mothers of the New Testament, Mary would probably be the first to come to mind for almost everyone. For many people, Mary would be the only New Testament mother they could think of. But, in fact, there are more mothers in the New Testament. One of the primary places that mothers other than Mary show up in the New Testament is in the miracle stories of the Gospels. Here we have several stories of mothers in crisis. In one case it is the mother herself who needs healing, but in the rest of the stories featured in this chapter we see mothers desperate for the healing of one of their children. In some cases, their desperation emboldens them to seek help from Jesus. In other cases, they have not sought Jesus out at all, but Jesus is the one who initiates the healing. Often in these stories we are given a little window into the challenge of being a mother with an unwell child, especially in an era when medical knowledge was more limited than today. In some cases, we are also given a window into the love ancient mothers had for their children and the way that mothers sought to protect and advocate for their children.

THE HEALING OF SIMON'S MOTHER-IN-LAW

In the Synoptic Gospels (Matthew, Mark, and Luke) there is a healing story that comes near the very beginning of Jesus's ministry. In this very short story,

Mothers in Crisis

Jesus heals the mother-in-law of Simon, who is later called Peter. Each Gospel writer tells the story in a similar way, but also with some differences. Read the story carefully in its three versions:

> As soon as they left the synagogue, they entered the house of Simon and Andrew, with James and John. Now Simon's mother-in-law was in bed with a fever, and they told him about her at once. He came and took her by the hand and lifted her up. Then the fever left her, and she began to serve them. (Mark 1:29–31)

> When Jesus entered Peter's house, he saw his mother-in-law lying in bed with a fever; he touched her hand, and the fever left her, and she got up and began to serve him. (Matt. 8:14–15)

> After leaving the synagogue he entered Simon's house. Now Simon's mother-in-law was suffering from a high fever, and they asked him about her. Then he stood over her and rebuked the fever, and it left her. Immediately she got up and began to serve them. (Luke 4:38–39)

In all three versions Jesus goes to Simon's house and heals Simon's mother-in-law from a fever. The fact that Simon has a mother-in-law also means that Simon has a wife, but his wife is not directly mentioned in this or any other Gospel story.[1]

Before we get into the details of the story, it is worth noting the presence of Simon's mother-in-law in the house. Does she live with them, or was she visiting when she came down with the fever? If she is living with them, this probably means she is a widow. Widows who were not financially independent were often taken in and cared for by male relatives (sons, brothers, or others), but we should not assume it was only men who took on this role.[2] Whether she was living with them or just visiting, in this story we have an example of a daughter and her family making sure that a mother was being cared for. We often think of mothers as the ones providing care, but of course we all know that the time comes eventually when parents need to be cared for. Both Jewish and Greco-Roman writings express the expectation that adult children will care for their elderly parents.[3] This brief story provides a glimpse of one family fulfilling that expectation.

Motherhood in the Miracle Stories of the Synoptic Gospels

Turning now to the story itself, we'll begin with Mark's version, since most scholars agree that Mark was written first and that Matthew and Luke copied from Mark and other sources in creating their Gospels. In Mark's version Jesus enters the house with some of his newly called disciples. An unspecified "they" tell Jesus that Simon's mother-in-law is sick with a fever. It could be the disciples that tell Jesus, or other members of Simon's household. Jesus takes her by the hand, lifts her from the bed, and her fever is gone. Then, the story says she began to serve "them." Again, the "them" is not specified but presumably includes all those present in the house, including Jesus and his disciples. This miracle is only the second miracle that Jesus has performed in Mark's Gospel, coming right after the exorcism story in 1:21–28. Word apparently gets around about the mother-in-law's healing, because after that Jesus is kept busy performing healings and exorcisms for many people, as "the whole city" gathers around the door of Simon's house (1:33–34).

Matthew and Luke tell the story similarly but with some alterations. Matthew focuses in on Jesus and the mother-in-law, with no other characters appearing in the story. He does not mention disciples entering the house with Jesus. No one tells Jesus about the sick woman; he seems to see her all on his own. And at the end of the story, she serves "him" rather than "them." It seems that Matthew does not want us to get distracted by the presence of others, but to focus only on Jesus's actions and presence in the story. Luke also eliminates the mention of disciples entering the house but does indicate that some people in the house told Jesus about the sick woman. Luke also makes the moment of the healing a bit more dramatic, indicating that Jesus "rebuked" the fever. This is in keeping with one of the major themes of Luke's Gospel—that Jesus came primarily for the sake of the poor, unwell, and downtrodden. Jesus's presence here banishes the evil forces that were oppressing this woman, making her well and enabling her to serve.

The fact that she begins to serve as soon as she is healed is one of the most discussed aspects of the story. This can be interpreted in different ways. Some view this as a return to her culturally prescribed gender role. As soon as she is healed, she is expected to serve the men a meal. No rest for the recovering! Other interpreters, however, note the significance of the verb used to describe her action in the story. The verb translated as "served" in the NRSVue is *diakoneō* in Greek. This verb means to serve as an intermediary, to perform duties, to wait on someone at table, to help, to take care of, or to minister to. "Serve" is a good translation, and within the logic of the story it likely means that she served them a meal. This would be in keeping with her role as a woman in the house, and there is little reason to doubt that the members of Simon's household followed this kind of pervasive cultural gender norm.

However, this service that she rendered can be viewed as having a deeper meaning as well, especially considering how the verb *diakoneō* is used elsewhere in the Gospels. This verb appears four times in Mark. The first time it is used is in Mark 1:13, in which angels serve Jesus while he is in the wilderness being tempted by Satan (translated as "waited on" in the NRSVue). From the start of this Gospel we know that service is not only done by lowly figures. The second time it is used is in this story about Simon's mother-in-law. The third time is in Mark 10:45, in which Jesus says, "For the Son of Man came not to be served but to serve and to give his life a ransom for many." Here Jesus defines his own mission as service, using the same verb used to describe the actions of Simon's mother-in-law after her healing. In the same passage Jesus also indicates that service is also to characterize his followers, using the noun form of the same root (*diakonos*), translated as "servant": "You know that among the gentiles those whom they recognize as their rulers lord it over them, and their great ones are tyrants over them. But it is not so among you; instead, whoever wishes to become great among you must be your servant, and whoever wishes to be first among you must be slave of all" (Mark 10:42–44). The fourth time the verb *diakoneō* is used in Mark is to describe the actions of Jesus's female followers in Mark 15:41 (translated as "provided for" in the NRSV and "ministered to" in the NRSVue). These women are living out the service that Jesus said his followers should do.

Simon's mother-in-law serves, which is a traditional woman's role, but in the Synoptic Gospels that is what angels, Jesus, and disciples do, not only women.[4] This mother's service illustrates what life in the community of Jesus's followers is supposed to look like. She is freed from her ailment so that she can serve the community gathered in her house. Mothers have been serving meals and taking care of others for as long as humanity has existed. Mothers have been doing this kind of work in the church for as long as the church has existed. The church, however, has not always valued this work as equally important as the work of those who preach. The Gospels of Matthew, Mark, and Luke teach us, however, that when Simon's mother-in-law serves a meal, she is doing the work of a disciple. She is doing the work of the gospel. For it is truly "good news" when people are healed and when people are cared for and when everyone has something to eat.

THE MOTHER OF JAIRUS'S DAUGHTER

One of the most striking and memorable stories in the Synoptic Gospels is that of the healing of the woman with a flow of blood and the raising of Jairus's daughter. The three versions of the story are in Mark 5:21–43, Matthew 9:18–26, and Luke 8:40–56. The stories of the bleeding woman and Jairus's daughter are intertwined with one another. The story begins with Jairus's request for Jesus to come heal his sick daughter. They are interrupted on the way by the bleeding woman reaching out to touch Jesus, and Jesus's subsequent conversation with her. In the intervening time Jairus's daughter dies, but Jesus continues his walk to Jairus's house and raises her up. I'm not going to analyze the story in detail, because the character I want to focus on is almost completely absent from the story. The mother of Jairus's daughter is mentioned in the story, but because the role she plays is so small we will have to use our imaginations to think about how she might have experienced this event and what role she might have played in it.

What can we know about this woman, who was wife to Jairus and mother to an unnamed daughter? Not a lot. We don't know her name. We don't know what town she lives in.[5] We don't know how old she is. We don't know if she had other children. We do know that she is married, and that she is probably a person of significant social standing in the community, since she is married to one of the leaders of the local synagogue. And we know she has a twelve-year-old daughter. This mother makes a brief appearance in the biblical story: When Jesus arrives at her house, he only allows four of his disciples and the girl's father and mother to enter with him into the room where the girl is lying (Mark 5:40 and Luke 8:51). There, those six individuals witness Jesus raising the girl from the dead. When this occurs, those present, including her mother, are "overcome with amazement" (Mark 5:42) and "astounded" (Luke 8:56).

Beyond those bare-bones details, what else can we imagine about this mother and her role in the story? Can we imagine her sitting by her daughter's sickbed day after day, bringing her something to drink and a cool cloth for her forehead? Can we imagine her lifting up prayers to God for her daughter's healing morning, noon, and night? Can we imagine her mild worry turning to anxiety as her daughter got worse instead of better? Can we imagine her conversations with Jairus about what else could be done? When they heard Jesus had arrived on the shore of their town, were they in immediate agreement that one of them should go to him, or did one of them have to convince the other that this was what they should do? Did she stay at home to stay with her daughter, or because it was more socially appropriate for her husband to approach this male miracle worker? Was it hard to be the one waiting at home? How slowly did the minutes pass? Can we imagine how time seemed to go from a slow march to a complete stop at the moment her daughter died? Can we imagine the feeling of all hope being lost and her husband still out of the house? Then, how does she feel when Jesus arrives? Can we imagine why she and Jairus reacted negatively when Jesus told them the girl was just sleeping (Luke 8:53)? Words of hope can seem cruel when one believes all hope is lost. And what about when her daughter got up? The Gospels tell us she was "amazed" and "astounded," but what would that have looked like? What would that have sounded like? What would that have felt like? Did she praise God aloud? Did she thank Jesus over and over? Did she collapse to the floor with the weight of the relief?

There is little we can know and much we can imagine about the mother of Jairus's daughter. To focus on her in our interpretation of the story is an exercise in trying to bring to light the overlooked and underdeveloped characters of the Gospels. And that, in turn, is practice for starting to pay attention to the overlooked and unnoticed people in our communities and world today.

THE SYROPHOENICIAN/CANAANITE WOMAN

While the mother of Jairus's daughter was largely hidden in the Gospel stories about her daughter's resurrection, a different mother boldly takes center stage in the next story we are going to consider. This woman's story appears in Mark 7:24–30 and Matthew 15:21–28. She is nameless in both. In Mark she is called a Syrophoenician woman, and in Matthew she is called a Canaanite woman. Let's look at each version in turn.

In Mark 7:24 Jesus goes to the gentile region of Tyre, northwest of Galilee, and enters a house seeking seclusion. But a woman whose daughter had an unclean spirit heard about him and came into the house, bowing down at Jesus's feet. The narrator identifies her as a gentile of Syrophoenician origin. Phoenicia was the region in which the cities of Tyre and Sidon were located, and this was part of the Roman province of Syria, hence the term "Syrophoenician." This woman begs Jesus to cast the demon out of her daughter, and Jesus replies, "Let the children be fed first, for it is not fair to take the children's food and throw it to the dogs" (7:27). In this mental picture Jesus is presenting her with, the children at the table represent the people of Israel, who are the primary recipients of Jesus's ministry. Jesus indicates that what is primarily intended for Israel should not be thrown to the gentiles, at least not until all Israel has been filled. The woman replies, "Sir, even the dogs under the table eat the children's crumbs" (7:28). In this reply, the woman seems to accept Jesus's "feed Israel first" stance, but subtly shifts the image from one of scarcity to abundance. The way Jesus puts it, one might worry that there is not enough food to go around; therefore, we need to make sure the children are fed first. But in the woman's reply we see a world in which there is enough for everyone, even the dogs under the table. God's grace and provision are not limited to the children only but encompass all in the house. Jesus seems to accept the woman's revision of his image, because he then replies, "For saying that, you may go—the demon has left your daughter" (7:29). The woman goes home and finds her daughter free of the demon.

Matthew contains the same basic story, but with several significant differences. In Matthew 15:21, Jesus goes to the district of Tyre and Sidon, but no mention is made of him entering a house. Rather, as soon as he arrives in the border area we are told that a Canaanite woman "came out" and started shouting at him. In this version it seems that Jesus is outside, likely walking down a road with his disciples, when a woman comes out and begins shouting at him. She is identified as a "Canaanite." This is rather surprising because there were no people called Canaanites in Jesus's day. Canaanites were the ancient enemies of Israel from more than one thousand years prior to Jesus's lifetime. So why would Matthew choose this word to describe her? More than any other word, this would immediately and clearly mark her as an outsider to Jesus and the disciples. And not just any outsider, but someone who comes from a group viewed as completely hostile to God's people—one of the peoples that, according to Deuteronomy 20:16–18, the ancient Israelites were supposed to utterly destroy. So now we wonder, what will Jesus's reaction to this outsider be?

This outsider does not come out meekly but comes out shouting. Women shouting at men in public was not socially acceptable behavior in either Jewish or Greco-Roman culture, so we might not be surprised that the woman is not well received by Jesus and his disciples. What is surprising, though, as Frances Taylor Gench notes, is the fact that this outsider addresses Jesus with insider language: "Have mercy on me, Lord, Son of David; my daughter is tormented by a demon" (15:22).[6] She is using thoroughly faith-filled language in addressing Jesus as "Lord" and "Son of David" and asking for mercy. But Jesus seems to respond more to her outsider identity or her manner of behaving than to her use of insider language, because Jesus's response according to the story is this: "He did not answer her at all" (15:23). Drawing on the work of John Meier, Gench notes that Jesus makes four kinds of responses in Matthew's version of the story, and silence is his first response.[7] She is calling for his help. He ignores her and continues on his way. Why? That is a good question to ask, since Jesus does not usually ignore people who are asking him for help. Something unusual is happening here, and it's natural to wonder why Jesus does not respond.

The disciples, however, do have a response to this woman's persistence. They say to Jesus, "Send her away, for she keeps shouting after us" (15:23). The disciples are annoyed with the woman for continually shouting after them. Could this annoyance have anything to do with the perceived inappropriateness of her behavior as a woman? It could, though that is not certain. At any rate, it is important to note that their request of Jesus is a little ambiguous in the original language. In the English translation I just shared, the words "send her away" seem to imply that the disciples want Jesus to make her leave immediately. But the original Greek implies that they might really be saying, "Send her away satisfied." In other words, what the disciples really want is for Jesus to give her what she wants so that she will stop bothering them. (Anyone who has ever cared for small children knows this kind of temptation!) This interpretation of the disciples' words makes Jesus's words in response make more sense, since he seems to be refusing to give the disciples what they want when he replies, "I was sent only to the lost sheep of the house of Israel" (15:24). This is Jesus's second response in the story: a refusal to help based on theological grounds.[8] Jesus says that he was only sent to the lost sheep of the house of Israel, implying that he will not help the woman because she is a gentile. Not even to get her to be quiet.

But the woman persists. She comes and kneels before Jesus, saying, "Lord, help me." Remember that in Matthew's version Jesus is not sitting in a house but is outside on the road. The woman has been trailing after them, shouting. But at this point she comes and kneels before him. This time she physically impedes Jesus's progress, forcing him to respond to her. And at this point he speaks directly to her for the first time. He says, "It is not fair to take the children's food and throw it to the dogs" (15:26). This is Jesus's third response: theological insult.[9] This statement is even harsher than in Mark's version because it does not even leave open the possibility of the dogs being fed later—there is no mention of the children being fed *first*. Rather, the food belongs only to the children. Over the years people have tried to find ways to soften this statement, but it is hard to get around the fact that Jesus calls her and her people dogs and that it has always been insulting to be called a dog. In ancient times this was a "standard insult."[10] Jesus's words here imply again that he will not help her because she is a gentile.

But this woman is not done. Faced with this insulting picture, she has a comeback: "Yes, Lord, yet even the dogs eat the crumbs that fall from their masters' table" (15:27). Two things are particularly noteworthy about her response. The first is obscured by the NRSVue translation I just quoted. You cannot tell by reading the NRSVue that the word translated as "Lord" and the word translated as "masters'" are the same in Greek (one in the singular and the other plural). So the woman addresses Jesus as Lord and speaks of the lords' table. Or, if you prefer, she addresses Jesus as Master and speaks of the masters' table. It is as though she is saying, "It is your table, Jesus." The second noteworthy aspect of her response is the way it reframes Jesus's picture from scarcity to abundance in the same way as it does in Mark's version of the story, as I described above. What the woman is really saying to Jesus with her words is, "It's your table, Jesus, and I know there's enough to go around." Her words challenge Jesus to move from scarcity to abundance, from exclusion to inclusion. And it works. Jesus's fourth response in the story is very different from his first three: "Woman, great is your faith! Let it be done for you as you wish" (15:28). Jesus's response in Matthew seems much more animated and excited than it is in Mark. He seems somewhat astounded to find this kind of faith in a gentile woman and is pleased enough with it to heal her daughter.

In considering both Mark's and Matthew's versions of the story, the motherhood of the Syrophoenician/Canaanite woman is an important aspect of the story. If she had only come for herself, she might have walked away when Jesus called her a dog. She might have thought to herself, "I don't need this. I'll find some other way to cope." But she wasn't there for herself. She was there for her daughter. Mark tells us that she "begged" Jesus to help her. Matthew records that she shouted to Jesus about how her daughter was being "tormented" by a demon. Both versions give us a window into the woman's desperation. The daughter is being tormented. The mother is desperate to help her. She will do what it takes to get help for her daughter. She will risk her reputation by shouting in the street. She will absorb the insulting language of a foreign miracle worker whom she believes can help her. She will keep going even when rebuffed multiple times. We can find examples of this kind of motherly behavior in every era, including in women today who are the mothers of sick children and in some cases may be facing a medical bureaucracy no more inviting than Jesus initially was in this story. Mothers take care of sick children, of course, but they also advocate for them and fight for them. They do this out of love and out of a deep sense of solidarity with their children. Notice how the Canaanite woman in Matthew 15:22 asks Jesus to have mercy on *her* rather than on her daughter. She has completely identified with her daughter's suffering, as have many parents before and since. For Jesus to have mercy on her daughter is for Jesus to have mercy on her.

We should also consider the power of this mother's words to bring about change. In Matthew's version of the story, it seems as though the woman's bold words cause Jesus to change his mind and heal her daughter. And her words seem to create a lasting change in Jesus as well. Up to this point in the story Jesus has been ministering almost exclusively to Jews, but afterward he also begins teaching and performing healing and feeding miracles among gentiles.[11] Jesus seems to have learned something about God's inclusiveness and the potential extent of his own ministry from his encounter with this gentile mother. Jesus's encounter with the Canaanite woman is a turning point in the Gospel, setting Jesus on a path that will culminate in the Great Commission at the end of the story—Jesus sending his disciples out to make disciples of "all nations" (28:19).

In Mark's version, this mother's words may be powerful in a completely different way. It may be that her words had not only the power to persuade Jesus to change his mind, but also the power to cast the demon out of her daughter. In the NRSVue, Jesus says, "For saying that, you may go—the demon has left your daughter" (7:29). Translated more literally, Jesus says, "Because of this word [*logos*], go; the demon has gone out of your daughter." Jesus's words could imply that it was the woman's speech, not his own action, that cast the demon out. She has cast the demon out with her bold, faith-filled speech. This is the interpretation of the story given by Mitzi Smith. Smith interprets the text from a womanist perspective and in light of the ways that "sass" or "talk-back" is used by Black women and other marginalized persons as a way of resisting oppressive authorities and reclaiming power.[12] In Smith's interpretation, when Jesus refuses to help the Syrophoenician woman, she talks back to him, and in the end, "Jesus simply affirms the power of this Greek Syrophoenician woman's sass."[13] The narrator never says that Jesus cast the demon out; rather, Jesus tells her that if she goes home she will find her daughter well, because of the words she has spoken. This may or may not be how the author of Mark originally intended the story to be understood, but the ambiguity of the language leaves it open as a possibility.

The story of the Syrophoenician/Canaanite woman is difficult to interpret. People react differently to what Jesus says to the woman and what happens in the story. Many readers feel that Jesus does not behave in the manner they usually expect from him. Sometimes people attempt to soften the story by suggesting that Jesus secretly intended to heal the woman's daughter all along but was either just testing her or was seeking to provide a lesson for the disciples. Such attempts are ultimately unsatisfying. I don't find the idea that Jesus would toy with this desperate woman, stringing her along, any more palatable than the idea that he is initially unwilling to help her and calls her a dog. The only satisfying interpretation of the story for Jesus's character is the one in which Jesus changes his mind—the one in which an encounter with a sassy, faith-filled, foreign mother opens Jesus's mind and heart to new possibilities. Jesus was fully human. Human beings naturally form in-groups and have to learn not to be prejudiced against outsiders. The reason Jesus is worthy of admiration is because he was open to learning that lesson. As Surekha Nelavala writes, "The evangelizer ultimately was evangelized."[14] When his attitude and path were shown to be inadequate, he was willing to change course. What a valuable lesson for us to learn in these polarized times we live in! The woman in this story provides an example of a mother capable of changing the world, and Jesus provides an example of learning to be open to seeing the full humanity of those on the other side of the boundary lines we draw between ourselves and others.

THE WIDOW OF NAIN

In Luke 7:11 Jesus goes with his disciples to a town in Galilee called Nain. Upon arriving there they see a funeral procession coming out of the town's gate. The narrator fills us in on the fact that the dead man was his mother's only son, and that this mother is also a widow. Jesus is filled with compassion when he sees the funeral procession. He tells the mother not to cry, stops the procession by touching the bier, and tells the dead man to rise. Then "the dead man sat up and began to speak, and Jesus gave him to his mother" (7:15). As interpreters frequently note, the story of Jesus raising a widow's son recalls the story of Elijah and the widow of Zarephath in 1 Kings 17:8–24 and is part of Luke's portrayal of Jesus as a great prophet. Indeed, after the man is raised, the people who witness the miracle praise God and say, "A great prophet has risen among us!" (Luke 7:16).

When Luke tells us that the woman is a widow and has just lost her only son, he most likely assumes his readers will understand what a precarious position this puts her in. Most women in the ancient world did not earn an independent living but relied on being part of a family headed by a male relative.[15] This woman is now without that support system. It was possible for women to inherit property in the ancient world, but more commonly resources passed down the male line. Also, even if the woman was able to inherit, it's important to remember that most people in the ancient world had a subsistence-level existence. Most families did not have a lot to pass down to the next generation. Rather, family members who were older relied on younger family members to work and keep the family afloat. The woman in this story is quickly running out of family members to rely on. We don't know if the men of this family farmed a piece of land, practiced a trade, or earned a small income as day laborers. But whatever they did, they are not around to do it anymore.

That said, we also want to be cautious about assuming that this woman would have ended up destitute or living on the streets. This is the assumption many readers make, that no one in her extended family or community will do anything to help her—that no one cares about what happens to her. This is a very dim view to take of members of a culture for whom a core ethical value is the care of the orphan and widow (see, for example, Exod. 22:22–24; Deut. 14:28–29; 24:17–22; Pss. 68:5; 146:9; Isa. 1:17; 10:1–2; Zech. 7:8–10; and Mal. 3:5). Of course, it would be foolish to assume that orphans and widows were always cared for just because these texts say they ought to be. But it would be equally foolish to assume that these ethical commands were always ignored. We've already seen an example in this chapter of someone who was likely a widow being provided for by someone other than a husband or son (Peter's mother-in-law living with her daughter and son-in-law). Additionally, we might want to notice how in the story of the widow of Nain, the text says that "a large crowd" is walking with the woman in the funeral procession. The community has gathered around her in the midst of her tragedy. Should we really assume that no one from that crowd will help her in any way when the funeral is over? We should not assume that no one will help her, but as I said earlier, with the death of her son, her situation becomes much more precarious than it was before. Rather than being embedded in the social and economic system of a typical household structure, she will now most likely be dependent on the kindness of others. When Jesus raises her son, he also restores the woman's security.

Regardless of what this woman's financial future would have been had Jesus not raised her son, one thing we know for sure is that when Jesus enters the scene, she is grieving. To lose a husband and then one's only son is a devastating experience, regardless of all other factors. When Jesus approaches the funeral procession, he says to the woman, "Do not cry" (Luke 7:13). Very few English translations express the nuance of the Greek here, which more accurately means "do not continue to cry" or "stop crying." In other words, the language implies that the woman was already crying, and Jesus tells her to stop. Even if we weren't told that she was crying, we could easily imagine that she would be based on her situation. But the text makes it explicit. The woman is weeping as she walks behind the body of her son. The text also makes explicit that when Jesus sees her, he is moved with compassion for her. He interrupts the procession and interrupts this woman's expression of grief to reach out and raise the young man back to life.

That Jesus is doing this primarily for the woman's sake can be seen after the miracle, when the story says that as soon has the man sits up and begins to speak, Jesus gives him to his mother (7:15). At this point we have to use our imaginations to picture the woman's reaction to the miracle. While Luke had told us the woman had been weeping, he does not describe her reaction to the miracle at all. We are told that the reactions of those who witnessed the event were to feel fear, to praise God, and to identify Jesus as a great prophet. Perhaps the woman also joins in some of these reactions, but presumably she is also feeling a great deal of joy and gratitude.

CONCLUSION

The four stories we explored in this chapter all contain a mother in crisis. Simon's mother-in-law is seriously ill. Jairus's wife and the widow of Nain have children who have died. The Syrophoenician/Canaanite woman's daughter is being tormented by a demon. Though they are all mothers and have all experienced some kind of crisis, their stories also have significant differences. For example, who requests or initiates the healing and how old the child is vary from story to story. There are differences in whether and how faith is expressed in each story as well. The Syrophoenician/Canaanite woman shows faith before her daughter is healed. Simon's mother-in-law does not directly express faith, but her service as soon as she is healed is a good sign that she has been listening to Jesus's teachings. We don't know anything for sure about the faith of Jairus's wife or the widow of Nain either before or after their children are raised.

Despite these differences, there is something all these mothers have in common: None of them is given a name. Of course, there are some unnamed men in these stories as well (such as the widow of Nain's son), but far more of the women remain unnamed. The story of the healing of the bleeding woman and Jairus's daughter is particularly striking in this regard. There are eight individual characters in Mark's version of the story (Mark 5:21–43): Jesus, Jairus, Peter, James, John, the bleeding woman, Jairus's wife, and Jairus's daughter. All the men are named and none of the women are named. Similarly, the characters in Mark's version of the healing of Simon's mother-in-law are Jesus, Simon, Andrew, James, John, and Simon's mother-in-law. There is not a single named woman in any of the four stories we explored in this chapter. This doesn't mean that their stories are not remarkable. But it does call attention to the androcentric nature of our biblical narratives.

The motherhood of these women plays into their stories in various ways. It defines Simon's mother-in-law's place in the household. It gives the Syrophoenician/Canaanite woman her boldness. It causes the despair of Jairus's wife and the widow of Nain. We see in their stories the lengths mothers will go to get help for their children, typified by the Syrophoenician/Canaanite woman. But we also see in the silence of Jairus's wife, Simon's mother-in-law, and the widow of Nain the social norms that circumscribed their roles. As with any number of other ancient writings, we are grateful for the places where women appear, but we are always left wishing the ancient authors would have told us more about them, beginning with their names. Their names were forgotten but their stories are not, and their strength and determination shine through the patriarchal narrative.

Motherhood in the Miracle Stories of the Synoptic Gospels

DISCUSSION QUESTIONS

1. Do you see the service of Simon's mother-in-law as returning her to her proper domestic/female role or as modeling what followers of Jesus are supposed to do? Why do you view the story this way?
2. The chapter gives an imaginative account of how the mother of Jairus's daughter might have experienced various parts of the story. If you were writing that part of the chapter, what would you imagine her thinking and feeling?
3. Jesus praises the Canaanite woman for having great faith. How does she show faith in this story?
4. What do you think about Mitzi Smith's idea that it was the Syrophoenician woman's word, not Jesus's, that cast the demon out of her daughter?
5. What does the story of the widow of Nain reveal about the way Jesus is characterized in the Gospel of Luke?
6. Does it matter to you that none of the women in this chapter are named? Why or why not?

6

BAD MOTHERS?

Ambivalent and Negative Portraits of Motherhood in the Gospels

So far in this book we've looked at New Testament passages that portray women's motherhood in largely positive ways. In Matthew, Mary's motherhood in relation to Jesus revealed her and Joseph's faithfulness to God amid unconventional circumstances. In Luke, Mary's motherhood was wrapped up in the way she served as a model disciple and prophet of the good news. In John, Mary's motherhood played a central role in the incarnation, the beginning of Jesus's ministry, the ending of Jesus's ministry, and the founding of the community of the church. In chapter 5 we saw examples of mothers serving and protecting their families. There may have been a few moments along the way, however, when we began to see that the picture of motherhood in the New Testament might not be entirely positive. For one thing, we noted how Mary is almost entirely absent from the Synoptic Gospels after the birth stories are over. We also saw the way that Jesus seemed to distance himself from his mother in the Gospel of John. Finally, we saw in chapter 5 how many mothers go unnamed in the Gospels and how little we are told about them. These more negative aspects were worth noting but did not seem worth dwelling on at length since these mothers are, for the most part, portrayed very positively by the Gospel writers. However, there are other stories in the New Testament in which mothers are portrayed negatively, and even cases where motherhood itself does not seem to be valued very much. First, we will look at what the

Ambivalent and Negative Portraits of Motherhood in the Gospels

Synoptic Gospels have to say about family relationships in general. Then we will consider three stories of specific mothers in the Gospels who are portrayed in ambivalent or negative ways: the mother of the man born blind in John, the mother of James and John in Matthew, and finally, Herodias, the most vilified "bad mother" in the Gospels.

AMBIVALENT WORDS ABOUT FAMILY IN THE SYNOPTIC GOSPELS

Family was centrally important in the ancient world—both close family and extended kinship networks. Both Greco-Roman and Jewish cultures were group-oriented rather than individual-oriented, and kinship groups were the most important groups that people belonged to. Loyalty, cooperation, affection, and the sharing of resources were some of the values and behaviors expected of people within family groups. But the Gospel writers recognized that the loyalty that kinship requires and the constraints that families place on people can sometimes interfere with the path of following Jesus. For this reason, the Gospel writers had some countercultural things to say about families. We'll begin our exploration with a look at Jesus's relationship to his own family and then consider a few passages that address the topic of families and discipleship in general.

As we've already seen in previous chapters, Matthew and Luke portray Jesus's parents in a positive light in their birth narratives, and John provides a vitally important, albeit limited, role for Jesus's mother in his Gospel. But what we see elsewhere in the Gospels about Jesus's relationship to his family is more ambiguous. This is especially the case in the story of Jesus's mother and brothers trying to visit him, found in all three Synoptic Gospels. Here's how the story appears in Mark:

> Then he went home, and the crowd came together again, so that they could not even eat. When his family heard it, they went out to restrain him, for people were saying, "He has gone out of his mind." . . . Then his mother and his brothers came, and standing outside they sent to him and called him. A crowd was sitting around him, and they said to him, "Your mother and your brothers are outside asking for you." And he replied, "Who are my mother and my brothers?" And looking at those who sat around him, he said, "Here are my mother and my brothers! Whoever does the will of God is my brother and sister and mother." (Mark 3:20–21, 31–35)

Bad Mothers?

One thing to appreciate in this story is that Jesus calls those who do the will of God his "brother and sister and mother" (3:35). There are not only brothers in the family of faith, but also sisters and mothers. Women in the early church and in today's church, whether they have children of their own or not, can be viewed as sisters and mothers in the family of faith—indeed, even as sisters and mothers of Jesus!

But other aspects of the story can trouble readers, especially because of what it seems to imply about Jesus's relationship with his mother and siblings. Keep in mind that Mark has no birth narrative, so when Jesus's family comes out to restrain him in 3:21, this is the first thing we learn about Jesus's family in Mark's Gospel. If we had only Mark's Gospel, we would probably conclude that Jesus had an adversarial relationship with his family. They try to restrain him from continuing with this ministry. He, in turn, seems to reject any connection to his mother and brothers when they try to see him. When looking only at Mark's Gospel, even Mary seems to have a negative relationship with Jesus.

The picture is more complicated in Matthew and Luke, since they include positive portrayals of Mary and other members of Jesus's family in their birth narratives. They also soften some of the harshest aspects of the story of Jesus's family coming to visit him (see Matt. 12:46–50 and Luke 8:19–21). Both remove the part of the story in which Jesus's family is said to try to restrain him in response to reports that he is out of his mind. Additionally, Luke removes Jesus's question, "Who are my mother and my brothers?" In this way, Jesus in Luke's version merely identifies those who do God's will as his family without explicitly implying a rejection of his family of origin. Taking the evidence of all the Gospels together, it is probably not right to conclude that Jesus had an entirely positive or negative relationship with his mother and the rest of his family.[1] Jesus lived an unconventional life and acted in countercultural ways. Therefore, it is not surprising that some of his family members would have been unhappy with what he was doing. But Jesus believed that the most important thing was not his family, but his mission to proclaim the Kingdom of God to those who needed to hear about it the most. His mission took precedence over his family. And this was a standard that he set not only for himself but also for his followers. We see that in other passages in the Synoptics in which Jesus talks about strife within families.

One such passage is Matthew 10:34–39, in which Jesus says he has not come to bring peace, talks about the division he will cause in families and elaborates on the high cost of discipleship:

Ambivalent and Negative Portraits of Motherhood in the Gospels

Do not think that I have come to bring peace to the earth; I have not come to bring peace but a sword.

> For I have come to set a man against his father,
> and a daughter against her mother,
> and a daughter-in-law against her mother-in-law,
> and one's foes will be members of one's own household.

Whoever loves father or mother more than me is not worthy of me, and whoever loves son or daughter more than me is not worthy of me, and whoever does not take up the cross and follow me is not worthy of me. Those who find their life will lose it, and those who lose their life for my sake will find it. (Matt. 10:34–39)

Taking verse 34 out of context, it might seem that Jesus is advocating violence. But when we read it in the context of Matthew's larger story we realize that Jesus must be speaking symbolically, because we know that Jesus is not an advocate of violence. Luke's parallel version of this teaching provides an interpretation for what Jesus means: "Do you think that I have come to bring peace to the earth? No, I tell you, but rather division!" (Luke 12:51). In addition to killing, swords can also divide one thing from another. What Matthew presents symbolically with the image of the sword, Luke presents in a more literal fashion: Jesus brings division. Both Matthew and Luke follow their statements about the sword and division with a description about how family members will be divided against one another because of Jesus's teaching. Jesus's message will be so divisive that it will divide households, even setting mothers and daughters against each other. Jesus felt such division was inevitable because of the countercultural nature of his teachings.

First and foremost, these words from Jesus show us how vitally important his mission was to him—proclaiming the kingdom of God was more important to him than family relationships, and he expected his followers to think this way, too. If their proclamation of the gospel put them at odds with their family members, then they were to prioritize the gospel mission over their family relationships. This would have been a hard message for ancient people to accept. For ancient Mediterranean peoples, the extended family was almost everything—it was the source of one's stability; one's income, food, and cloth-

Bad Mothers?

ing; one's social connections; one's religion; one's security. To be cut off from family was to be cut off from all those things. And if that's not enough, Jesus is speaking to a Jewish audience, for whom one of the greatest commandments is, "Honor your father and your mother" (Exod. 20:12). When Jesus talks about leaving family or about conflict in the family his words were even more radical in that time and place than they are today. But this is the urgency of the Kingdom message. God's reign takes precedence over anything that would keep you from living the Kingdom's values, even family relationships.

If this teaching seems challenging, consider the even harder teaching in Luke 14:26: "Whoever comes to me and does not hate father and mother, wife and children, brothers and sisters, yes, and even life itself, cannot be my disciple." The verb translated here as "hate" can mean "hate," "detest," "disfavor," or "disregard."[2] While it may be tempting to choose the translation "disregard" because it is less shocking than "hate," I think Jesus is trying to be shocking with this statement. Even the idea that one should disregard family would be highly shocking to Jesus's hearers. It shows just how serious he is about loyalty to God coming first. On the other hand, it is reasonable to assume that Jesus is using hyperbole here to get the hearer's attention, and that he does not literally mean that people should hate their parents, spouses, children, and siblings. Matthew gives a softer interpretation of Jesus's meaning in the parallel passage found in his Gospel: "Whoever loves father or mother more than me is not worthy of me, and whoever loves son or daughter more than me is not worthy of me, and whoever does not take up the cross and follow me is not worthy of me" (Matt. 10:37–38). This is still a challenging teaching, but it at least allows for some love of family members.

The idea that loyalty to God and the Kingdom mission comes before loyalty to family is also reinforced in Luke 11:27–28, when a woman in the crowd shouts to Jesus, "Blessed is the womb that bore you and the breasts that nursed you!" and Jesus responds, "Blessed rather are those who hear the word of God and obey it!" Even Mary gets no preferential treatment in Jesus's view. She is not blessed simply for having given birth to him and nursed him. She is blessed only if she hears the word of God and obeys it. This, of course, is how Luke portrays her in chapters 1–2, as hearing the word of God and obeying it. Therefore, she is blessed, but, according to Jesus, it is not because she is his mother.

Motherhood has the potential to either weaken or strengthen discipleship. To be a mother is to constantly negotiate competing priorities and loyalties,

Ambivalent and Negative Portraits of Motherhood in the Gospels

and Jesus sets a high bar for prioritizing the Kingdom over everything else. Real life is messy, though, and no one gets it right all the time. We'll turn now to the stories of three New Testament mothers who are caught in that messiness and are evaluated by the Gospel writers in ambivalent or negative ways for their discipleship (or lack thereof).

THE MOTHER OF THE MAN BORN BLIND

The story of the man born blind is an extended story that takes up all of chapter 9 of the Gospel of John. After Jesus heals a blind man, much controversy ensues with some of the religious leaders, particularly because the healing had taken place on the Sabbath. The man is questioned, his parents are questioned, and much discussion occurs. In typical Johannine fashion, the story becomes about much more than a literal healing—it becomes an occasion to meditate on the nature of true sight. Who is really blind—the blind man, or the religious leaders who cannot accept that God is at work in Jesus? We will not trace every twist and turn of this story here, but simply note that the mother of the man born blind does play a role in the story, albeit a small one and undifferentiated from the man's father—they operate together in the story as a parental unit.

Before the man's parents make an appearance in the story, they are first mentioned by the disciples near the very beginning of the chapter. When Jesus and his disciples first see the blind man, the disciples ask Jesus, "Rabbi, who sinned, this man or his parents, that he was born blind?" (John 9:2). One understanding of disorders and disabilities in the ancient world was that they were punishments for sin. The disciples seem to be taking this view because they are wondering whose fault it is that the man is blind. Jesus replies that neither he nor his parents had sinned, but that the man had been "born blind so that God's works might be revealed in him" (9:3). Some readers may find the idea that God caused a baby to be born blind so that he could be healed by Jesus decades later to be only marginally more comforting than the idea that God caused the baby to be born blind as a punishment for sin. Nevertheless, at least we can take some comfort from the fact that Jesus indicates that it is not the parents' fault that their son was born blind. Parents take the blame for a lot of things that go wrong with children. Sometimes the blame is truly deserved, such as if children have problems that result from abuse or neglect. But in so many other cases, parents have the best of intentions and do the best they can with the resources they have, and yet things can still go wrong, like illness, accidents, or poor choices made by the children themselves.

After Jesus heals the blind man, some of the Pharisees begin questioning the man because the healing had taken place on the Sabbath. Then some begin to question the man's parents about whether he had in fact been born blind, and if so, how it was that he could now see. The man's father and mother reply, out of fear, that he was indeed born blind, but they don't know anything about how he came to see (9:20–23). They indicate that anyone who wants to know should ask the man himself, since "he is of age." They are no longer obligated to speak for him. Although they speak out of fear, this still raises interesting questions about when parents stop being responsible for their children. To some extent, of course, this never stops, as parents continue to care about their children throughout their lifetimes and can be a source of wisdom for their children even after they become adults. Yet there does come a time when children are of age and speak for themselves. If the man's parents could not be blamed for his condition at birth, they certainly cannot be answerable for events that have occurred when he is an adult. And clearly the man does not need his parents to speak for him. Throughout the story, he repeatedly speaks for himself competently and even eloquently to his neighbors, to the Pharisees, and to Jesus.

Nevertheless, even if this mother cannot be blamed for her son's blindness and is justified in letting him speak for himself as an adult, there still does seem to be a coldness in the way this man's parents refuse to get involved in the situation. They seem to be more concerned for their own well-being in this case than for their son's. Readers also sometimes wonder if the man's parents had abandoned him, since he is said to be a beggar in verse 8. This is impossible to say. It could be that his parents were not taking care of him, and that is why he has to beg. But it could also be that the whole family is poor, and in poor families, all members must try to do something to contribute to the family income. Begging may have been this man's way to try to contribute to the family income, since few other options would have been available to a blind man in the ancient world. But whether his parents had abandoned him or not, we can still see their refusal to get involved as an illustration of the idea that parents do not always advocate for their children well. Sometimes, they look out for their own interests rather than the interests of their children. Also, in distancing herself from her son's healing, this mother is also distancing herself from Jesus the healer. She is not interested in having anything to do with Jesus. Unlike Mary, this woman's motherhood does not lead her to discipleship.

THE MOTHER OF JAMES AND JOHN

The mother of the man born blind plays such a small role in that story that it is hard to come to any firm conclusions about how negatively she is portrayed. The story of the mother of James and John (the sons of Zebedee), found in Matthew 20:20–28, gives us a little more to go on, since this mother plays more of an active role in the beginning of the story. In some ways, she is the opposite of the mother of the man born blind. While the mother of the blind man only appears in the story when summoned and then only very reluctantly, the mother of James and John is the one to take the initiative to approach Jesus about her sons. While the mother of the blind man refuses to speak for her son, the mother of James and John actively advocates on her sons' behalf.

Although this mother's story appears only in the Gospel of Matthew, we need to begin our study in the Gospel of Mark. As explained in the previous chapter, biblical scholars are nearly unanimous in thinking that Mark was written first and the author of Matthew adapted Mark's material to fit the narrative he was constructing. If this is indeed the case, it is interesting to consider the rather significant difference between how the older form of the story begins in Mark and how Matthew's revised version begins:

> James and John, the sons of Zebedee, came forward to him and said to him, "Teacher, we want you to do for us whatever we ask of you." And he said to them, "What is it you want me to do for you?" And they said to him, "Appoint us to sit, one at your right hand and one at your left, in your glory." (Mark 10:35–37)

> Then the mother of the sons of Zebedee came to him with her sons, and kneeling before him, she asked a favor of him. And he said to her, "What do you want?" She said to him, "Declare that these two sons of mine will sit, one at your right hand and one at your left, in your kingdom." (Matt. 20:20–21)

In Mark, it is the brothers themselves who come to Jesus and ask for places of honor. Matthew received this story from Mark but made a big change: rather than the brothers asking for themselves, it is now their mother who comes to Jesus with the request.

Determining why Gospel writers wrote their stories the way they did is always speculative, because they do not provide us with explanations. One common suggestion, however, for why Matthew inserts James and John's mother into this story is that Matthew is trying to protect James and John, who do not come off well in Mark's version. The story in Mark comes immediately after Jesus predicts his passion for the third time. Jesus has just said that he will have to suffer, be rejected, and die—this is his calling and destiny as the Messiah—this is the kind of Messiah he is. But the disciples, including James and John, are not listening. If James and John had been paying attention, they would have understood that Jesus came to teach the way of service and suffering, and therefore it is wildly inappropriate to ask for places of honor. The disciples generally seem clueless throughout Mark's Gospel, and James and John here are no exception. Jesus rebukes them, telling them what they should have already known as his disciples: "Whoever wishes to become great among you must be your servant, and whoever wishes to be first among you must be slave of all" (Mark 10:43–44).

Matthew and Luke copy a lot of their material straight from Mark, but one thing that they regularly change about Mark's Gospel is how negatively the disciples are portrayed. It seems a good guess that when Matthew went to incorporate this story into his narrative, he was uncomfortable with how poorly James and John are portrayed. He softened the blow by making it their mother who comes to Jesus with this misguided request.[3] Now she is the one who seems not to have been listening to Jesus's teachings about humility, service, and suffering. At the same time, maybe she doesn't come off quite as badly in Matthew's version as James and John do in Mark's version. After all, we expect mothers to advocate for their children. In Mark, the brothers are asking for something for themselves; this clearly goes against Jesus's teachings. In Matthew, their mother is asking for something for her sons, not herself. She seems to be proud of and protective of her sons, ready to be involved for their well-being. She seems to have missed the boat on fully understanding Jesus's teachings, but this does not automatically make her a "bad mother." Perhaps she is a "good mother" but a "bad disciple."

But just how bad a disciple is she? First, she is there, and that counts for something. The fact that she is present in this story shows that she is traveling with Jesus. She is one of the disciples. When Jesus called her sons, they left their father in the boat (Matt. 4:22), but apparently their mother went with them. She also responded to Jesus's call. Additionally, Stephanie Buckhanon Crowder, analyzing the story from the perspective of African American motherhood, makes the intriguing suggestion that perhaps Mrs. Zebedee (as Crowder calls her) understood more about Jesus's teachings than she is usually given credit for. After all, Jesus didn't only say that he would soon be rejected, suffer, and die. He also added that, on the third day, he would be raised from the dead (20:19).[4] The disciples never seem to hear this part. Perhaps Mrs. Zebedee was the only one to pay attention to the end of Jesus's statement. This promise of resurrection may have been something she wanted her sons to participate in.

Nevertheless, even if she was responding to the promise of resurrection, she was not listening fully to the way of life Jesus was teaching. There is hope that comes to believers through the promise of resurrection, but one does not seek the Kingdom of God by seeking places of honor, for oneself or for one's family members. This is why Jesus must teach his disciples, in response this mother's request, that his followers are not to seek power over others or seek places of honor, but rather to be servants and even slaves to one other, following his example (20:25–28). This mother was thinking of the Kingdom of God in terms closer to the Kingdom of Rome than the kind of Kingdom Jesus taught about.[5] I think the mother of James and John understood Jesus's teachings partially, but her maternal desire for her sons to have the best of everything kept her from entering fully in the way of life Jesus was teaching. It was her motherhood that got in the way of her discipleship. In this way she is an excellent illustration of why the Synoptic Gospels have ambivalent attitudes toward family relationships.

HERODIAS AND HER DAUGHTER

The Gospel writers knew that families sometimes have a corrupting influence, that family loyalty can sometimes lead people astray, and that not all parents are good parents. If there is any story in the Gospels that shows the dire consequences of family corruption and bad parenting, it is the story of Herodias and her daughter.[6] This story appears in Mark 6:14–29 and Matthew 14:1–12. It is gruesome and disturbing, and also one of the only stories in the Gospels

Bad Mothers?

that does not focus on Jesus. The story involves John the Baptist, the ruler Herod Antipas, Herod's wife Herodias, and Herodias's daughter. Mark has the longer and more detailed version of the story, so I will primarily analyze Mark's version.

Herod the Great was a client king ruling Judea, Samaria, Galilee, and surrounding regions under Roman authority. He was known for overseeing a major renovation of the Jerusalem Temple as well as other building projects. According to the Gospel of Matthew, he was also responsible for the slaughter of the innocents recorded in Matthew 2:16–18. Upon Herod's death, his kingdom was divided among his sons. His son Herod Antipas ruled over Galilee and Perea. Herod Antipas is the Herod referred to in the story of Herodias and her daughter. According to the story, Herod had arrested John the Baptist because John had criticized him for marrying Herodias, who had been his brother's wife. Herodias also hates John for the same reason and wants to have John put to death. Herod, however, denies her wish because he is afraid of killing a "righteous and holy man" (Mark 6:20). But Herodias's opportunity to get her revenge on John comes during Herod's birthday party, when Herodias's daughter comes in to dance for the guests.

Here we have some name confusion because the story in Mark says that "his daughter Herodias" comes in and dances. This would mean that both Herod's wife and their daughter are named Herodias. This is possible, of course, but does not fit with other historical sources we have. The ancient Jewish historian Josephus indicates that Herodias had a daughter from a previous marriage whose name was Salome. The Gospel of Matthew solves the problem by calling her not "Herodias" but "the daughter of Herodias" (Matt. 14:6). Matthew does not give the girl a name and seems to imply that she was only Herodias's daughter, not Herod's. This is probably a more accurate depiction of the Herodian family tree and a case of Matthew making a correction to Mark's story as he incorporated it into his Gospel. In any case, whatever her name and whatever her relation to Herod (whether daughter or stepdaughter), the story tells of a girl who dances for a group of people at a party, pleasing Herod so much that he offers her whatever she wants.

How old is the daughter, and what is the nature of this dance? These things are uncertain. Mark calls her a "girl" in verses 22 and 28, so she is not full grown, but whether she is five, ten, or twelve years old we cannot say. In interpretations and depictions of this story she is often portrayed as a teenager or older, and her dance is depicted as sexual and seductive. Herod, therefore, in this interpretation, is not only careless in his oath-making but also lecherous toward his daughter or stepdaughter. This could be the way Mark intends us to understand the story, but it is important to acknowledge that this is an assumption we make as readers—the text does not describe what the dance was like, nor does it indicate in what manner it pleased Herod. F. Scott Spencer points out that imagining a little girl who delights her father as he watches her do her ballet routine would fit Mark's details and language just as well as the usual sexual interpretation.[7] At any rate, what is clear, no matter her age or the nature of the dance, is the foolishness of Herod's pledge to give her whatever she asks for. Herod's pledge echoes some Old Testament stories. The statement that he will give her up to half his kingdom echoes the line that king Ahasuerus says to Esther (Esther 5:3, 6; 7:2). Herod's promise also recalls Jephthah's foolish pledge to sacrifice whoever comes first out of his front door after his victory in battle, leading to the death of his daughter (Judg. 11:1–40). In Herod's case the vow does not lead to the death of the daughter in the story, but it does lead to the death of John the Baptist.

This is where Herodias's motherhood enters the story. She uses the opportunity of Herod's vow to get her revenge on John. When the daughter asks her mother for advice about what to ask for, Herodias instructs her to ask for the head of John the Baptist on a platter. The girl is obedient to her mother's wishes, and John is executed and his head brought to the girl, who in turn gives it to her mother. This is a rather shocking bit of parenting. Herodias not only uses her daughter to achieve her own ends, but also subjects her to the gruesome experience of carrying a freshly severed human head on a platter. All this is done seemingly without a thought for what is best for the girl, or what effect the experience will have on her. This is certainly an illustration of maternal power, as the girl does as she is told, but it is certainly not an illustration of maternal love, care, or protection.

Why do the Gospel writers choose to include this story? "Because it happened" is not a good enough answer. Regardless of what you believe about the historicity of this event,[8] Luke and John do not include the story, so it is certainly possible to construct a Gospel without it. So why do Mark and Matthew include it? This is not an easy question to answer, but it is the case that this story contains numerous thematic connections to the rest of the Gospel story. Regina Janes explores these connections, which include death by execution, food imagery, and blood imagery.[9] John's execution in this story foreshadows Jesus's later execution. Food imagery is another connection, with the head being served on a platter and meals being prominently featured throughout the Gospels. Interpreters have long noted, for example, that it is probably not a coincidence that the gruesome feast imagery of John's head on a platter comes right before the feeding of the five thousand by Jesus, a very different kind of feast. Janes also draws an important comparison between this story and the story of the bleeding woman and Jairus's daughter in Mark 5.[10] The woman in Mark 5 and Herodias are both "bloody" women, Herodias causing a bloody death and the woman bleeding for twelve years. Yet one is healed of her infirmity while the other remains unrepentant of her bloody deeds. Perhaps even more significantly, there is a connection between the two daughters in these stories. The Greek word *korasion*, translated as "girl," is used to describe both Herodias's daughter and Jairus's daughter, and these two stories are the only times in the New Testament that Greek word *korasion* is used. These two girls form quite a contrast, the dance of one representing death, and the resuscitation of the other representing life. In Mark and Matthew, John the Baptist's death foreshadows Jesus's death, and the raising of Jairus's daughter foreshadows Jesus's resurrection.[11]

CONCLUSION

The mothers in this chapter have ranged from ambiguous to practically evil in their portrayals by the Gospel writers. Compared to the mothers advocating for their children in chapter 5, the mothers in this chapter either look out for their own interests rather than the interests of their children (the mother of the blind man), or they seek to promote the welfare of their children but do so in a way that is contrary to the teachings of Jesus (the mother of James and John). These are specific illustrations of the general principle that the Synoptic Gospels emphasize in various passages, that motherhood and other family relationships have the capacity to interfere with discipleship because they cause us to prioritize human matters over the divine calling of discipleship. But in terms of bad mothers in the Gospels, no one can compare to Herodias, who uses her motherhood as a tool for bloody revenge, showing no concern for the effects this might have on her daughter. If Mary and the mothers in chapter 5 serve as examples of how to be devoted disciples as mothers, Herodias and the

Ambivalent and Negative Portraits of Motherhood in the Gospels

other mothers in this chapter serve as examples of how *not* to be—cautionary tales, so to speak, of the ways that family loyalty can lead people astray.

DISCUSSION QUESTIONS

1. How would you describe Jesus's relationship to his own family?
2. Are you uncomfortable with the Synoptic Gospels' words about prioritizing discipleship over family relationships? Why or why not? Have you experienced households being divided because of Jesus's teachings?
3. What do you think of the mother of the man born blind? Does the story give us enough information to decide whether she is a good mother or not?
4. Do you think the mother of James and John was justified in asking Jesus for places of honor for her sons? How well do you think she understood Jesus's teachings?
5. In what ways can motherhood make discipleship harder? In what ways can it deepen discipleship?
6. Why do you think Mark and Matthew tell the story of Herodias and her daughter? What are readers supposed to learn from this story?
7. Do you think that Herodias's daughter deserves any blame for the death of John the Baptist, or is she entirely manipulated by an abusive mother? What share of blame do you place on Herod?

7

MOTHER JESUS

Metaphorical Motherhood in the Gospels

In addition to the mothers who appear as characters in Gospel stories, there are also passages in the Gospels that present us with metaphorical mothers. Motherhood is employed in parables, images, and figures of speech to evoke meanings like connection, suffering, and new life. As we will see, these images are not superficial or incidental to the text but go to the heart of the theology expressed in the Gospels. In this chapter we will consider the image of Jesus as mother hen, the connections the Gospels make between Jesus and Woman Wisdom, and birth imagery in the Gospel of John.

JESUS AS MOTHER HEN

The story of Jesus lamenting over Jerusalem appears in both Matthew and Luke, though the two authors place it in different parts of their narratives. In Matthew it occurs when Jesus is in Jerusalem teaching in the temple during the last week of his life. After an extended denunciation of the scribes and Pharisees for hypocrisy, Jesus laments, "Jerusalem, Jerusalem, the city that kills the prophets and stones those who are sent to it! How often have I desired to gather your children together as a hen gathers her brood under her wings, and you were not willing! See, your house is left to you, desolate. For I tell you, you will not see me again until you say, 'Blessed is the one who comes in the

Metaphorical Motherhood in the Gospels

name of the Lord'" (Matt. 23:37–39). The passage appears with very similar wording in Luke 13:34–35, but in Luke it is in the context of Jesus's journey to Jerusalem and in response to some Pharisees warning him that Herod is seeking to kill him.

In both Matthew and Luke, the passage evokes numerous associations and allusions. One might think of prophetic oracles in the Old Testament that warn disobedient cities and nations (e.g., Isa. 1, Amos 1–2). Additionally, the line "Blessed is the one who comes in the name of the Lord" quotes Psalm 118:25 and also creates a connection between this story and the story of Jesus's entry into Jerusalem, where the same line is quoted (Matt. 21:9 and Luke 19:38). The passage also recalls places in the Old Testament where God is described as a bird, such as Deuteronomy 32:11–12: "As an eagle stirs up its nest and hovers over its young, as it spreads its wings, takes them up, and bears them aloft on its pinions, the LORD alone guided him." In most passages that describe God as a bird, the wings are described as a place of protection and refuge (see Ruth 2:12; Pss. 17:8; 57:1; 61:4; 91:3–4). This is the focus of the passage in Matthew and Luke as well, in which Jesus, perhaps speaking on God's behalf, laments that he has longed to provide such a place of protection and refuge under his wings for the inhabitants of Jerusalem, but they have rejected this offer. While this is described as a desire he had in the past and into the present, it also foreshadows his own future rejection and death in the city of Jerusalem, in which the leadership of the city will be unwilling to accept the vision of peace and justice he brings.

There are two mothers in this passage. The first is Jesus, portrayed as a mother hen. The other is Jerusalem, mother of the people of the city, who refuses the offer of protection for her children. Jerusalem was sometimes portrayed as a mother in Israel's prophetic tradition (see Isa. 49:19–21; 66:7–12; Jer. 4:31; Mic. 4:9–10). The portrayal of Mother Jerusalem in Matthew and Luke forms an interesting contrast with the portrayal of Mother Jerusalem in Lamentations 2:18–22. In Lamentations, following the devastation of the Babylonian invasion of the city, Mother Jerusalem pleads with God on behalf of her children. Whereas in Lamentations Jerusalem is a devastated mother who weeps and cries out to God for her children, in Matthew and Luke Jerusalem seems to be either an uncaring or an unwise mother, refusing to accept what is in the best interest of her children. In a sense, Jesus longs to be the mother that Jerusalem is failing to be, and he warns that this lack of mothering is going to have devastating consequences for the people.

Mother Jesus

Though this book has focused mostly on the power of mothers, this image reveals the power of children in the mother-child relationship. Jesus longs to mother the children of Jerusalem, but they refuse to be mothered. Mothers can be consistent in offering care and guidance, but children have the power to reject that care and guidance, especially as they grow older. And when they do reject it, it sometimes has devastating consequences. Nevertheless, the image of Jesus as mother hen retains a note of hopefulness. Jesus continues to offer the city protection and care, and his words include the promise that one day in the future he will come to the city and, instead of being rejected, he will be greeted with joy as "the one who comes in the name of the Lord." Then he will be the city's true mother.

JESUS AS SOPHIA, SOPHIA AS MOTHER

As I explained in chapter 4, John 1 presents Jesus as the incarnation of the *logos* (the Word) and describes the *logos* in a way that identifies it with the female personification of Wisdom in Proverbs and other Israelite wisdom literature. The Gospels draw on Woman Wisdom imagery in their portrayal of Jesus elsewhere as well. For example, Jesus's invitation to come to him in Matthew 11:28–30 echoes Wisdom's call to the people in Proverbs 9:4–6 and the description of Wisdom and her yoke in Sirach 6:24–28 and 51:23–26. The image of Jesus as mother hen discussed above is reminiscent of Proverbs 1, in which Wisdom's call goes unheeded, and the people are left to the consequences of their folly. Understanding Jesus as the incarnation of Wisdom is called Wisdom Christology or Sophia Christology, because *sophia* is the Greek word for wisdom.[1]

While strongly hinted at elsewhere, the association between Jesus and Woman Wisdom is made explicit in Matthew 11:19 and Luke 7:35. In Matthew 11 messengers come to Jesus from John the Baptist, and afterward Jesus speaks to the crowd about John. Then he says:

> But to what will I compare this generation? It is like children sitting in the marketplaces and calling to one another,
>
> > "We played the flute for you, and you did not dance;
> > we wailed, and you did not mourn."

> For John came neither eating nor drinking, and they say, "He has a demon"; the Son of Man came eating and drinking, and they say, "Look, a glutton and a drunkard, a friend of tax collectors and sinners!" Yet wisdom is vindicated by her deeds. (Matt. 11:16–19)

Jesus compares those who hear and criticize him and John to children who refuse to play with other children no matter what the game is—whether they play a joyful wedding game or a sad funeral game. Like those children, the people who criticized both John *and* Jesus just could not be made happy no matter what. John was serious and lived an ascetic lifestyle and they accused him of demon possession; Jesus engaged in the joyful pleasures of life and they accused him of being a glutton and a drunkard. But here's the punchline—Jesus doesn't have to defend his choices because his deeds of healing and compassion speak for themselves, revealing that his life is guided by Wisdom. In fact, his deeds don't just reveal that he is guided by Wisdom but that he *is* Wisdom at work in the world. His deeds are her deeds and vice versa.

In Luke the setup for the story is the same (visitors from John the Baptist and discourse about John), and the parable of the children in the marketplace is very similar. But the last line of the passage is quite different. Rather than saying, "Wisdom is vindicated by her deeds," Luke's version reads, "Wisdom is vindicated by all her children" (7:35). Rather than being Woman Wisdom, in Luke Jesus is her child. She is his mother in the sense that he heeds her call and teaches her ways to others. And since Wisdom is vindicated by *all* her children, Luke's version is emphasizing that John the Baptist was also a child of Wisdom. Though John and Jesus lived very different lives and made very different choices, both were walking in the ways of their mother Wisdom.

Luke portrays Wisdom as a mother to Jesus, and Matthew portrays Jesus as Mother Wisdom. If this seems like it is getting rather complicated, perhaps that is the point. As Barbara Reid writes, "As Sophia incarnate, the Christ integrates divine femaleness with human maleness, overcoming gender dualism. Wisdom Christology enables both women and men to see themselves as children of Wisdom, made in her image, redeemed in her love, and continuing her mission."[2] The androcentric nature of the Gospel narratives means that this Sophia Christology is somewhat buried, but for those who take the time to excavate it, it is clearly there, and its presence in the text reminds us that within the Bible there are counternarratives to the gender dualisms and hierarchies that seem to dominate the Bible when we read it only at a surface level. Mother Wisdom can help us see that. Let's heed her call.

BIRTH IMAGERY IN THE GOSPEL OF JOHN

The Gospel of John contains a lot of birth imagery.[3] Some of this imagery is well known (such as the image of being born again or from above in John 3:3) and some of it is often overlooked (like the parable of birth in 16:20–22). All of it goes to the heart of the gospel message as expressed in this book. The birth imagery begins in the first chapter, which says that those who believed in Jesus were given the "power to become children of God, who were born, not of blood or of the will of the flesh or of the will of man, but of God" (1:12–13). Throughout the Gospel of John, some will accept the message of Jesus and others will not. Chapter 1 sets up this dichotomy with the metaphor of birth— those who do not accept the message are those born the usual way (through blood, flesh, or will of a man) and those who do accept it are those who are born of God. It might seem at a surface reading that women are missing from this metaphor despite it being one of birth. Yet, in the idea of physical birth, women are probably referenced in the mention of blood. Some ancient people believed that menstrual blood was the material that became a fetus when heated by male semen. The mention of blood represents the woman's contribution to conception. The man's contribution is represented by the words "will of a man" (my translation). The word "will" here can also be translated as "desire." Both the blood and the "desire of a man" are components of conception according to "the will of the flesh." By contrast, believers are "born of God," meaning that God is the one who gave birth to them; God is their mother. So female imagery is present in both types of conception described in 1:12–13.

Birth imagery returns in chapter 3, playing a central role in the story of Nicodemus's visit to Jesus. In this well-known passage, Jesus tells Nicodemus that to see the kingdom of God he has to be born *anōthen*. That Greek word can mean either "again" or "from above," which leads to Nicodemus's misunderstanding. He thinks Jesus means "born again," which is why he begins to talk about how a person cannot reenter their mother's womb to be born a second time. Jesus, however, may somewhat intend both meanings of the word but leans more toward the "from above" meaning, since he goes on to talk about what it means to be "born of the Spirit." The Spirit of God is the mother of those who believe. This birth imagery can be connected to the famous expression of the gospel message a few verses later: Those who have the Spirit as their mother are those who have believed in the Son sent from God, and so are saved, according to God's loving action of sending the Son into the world. Their life and their identity come from the one who gave birth to them. It is quite striking that most readers and interpreters through Christian history seem to have trained themselves and others to read John's birth imagery without the obvious implication of God's maternity.[4]

Another possible instance of birth imagery occurs in John 7:37–39. In this passage Jesus is teaching in the temple and cries out, "If someone is thirsty let him/her come to me and let the one who believes in me drink. Just as the Scripture said, 'Rivers of living water will flow from his *koilia*'" (my translation). The word *koilia* can mean either stomach or womb. There are numerous examples of both meanings in the Septuagint and in the New Testament, so either reading is possible here. Unfortunately, the meaning is not clarified by going to the Scripture passage being quoted, because this quote does not appear in the Old Testament. We do not know where the quote comes from. We will have to use the context of John to decide whether stomach or womb would be a better translation here. We will return to that question in a moment.

The other important interpretive question in this passage is who the *koilia* belongs to. The NRSVue interprets it as belonging to the one who believes. However, since Jesus has just invited people to satisfy their thirst by coming to him, it makes more sense to read the *koilia* as belonging to Jesus. The NRSVue adds the words "the believer" into the text where the Greek just says "his." With a more literal reading, it seems most straightforward to understand the *koilia* as belonging to Jesus. Alternatively, you could understand it as belonging to the Spirit, since the next verse says that Jesus was speaking about the Spirit. This would create a strong connection between this passage and the reference to those who are "born of the Spirit" in 3:5–8, especially if *koilia* is translated as womb rather than stomach.

How should *koilia* be translated? The NRSVue translates it as heart, but this is not the meaning of the word, only the reading that the translators feel will be more palatable to English readers. As I said above, stomach and womb are the main options. While I acknowledge that either meaning of *koilia* can work in this passage, there are a few reasons to lean toward translating it as womb rather than stomach. For one thing, the only other time the word is used in

John it clearly has the meaning womb (Nicodemus asks how someone can reenter their mother's *koilia* in 3:4), so this may be the meaning of the word most prominent in this author's mind. Also, the idea that water flows from the *koilia* strengthens the association with birth and the womb rather than with the stomach, since water flows from the womb during the birth process. It would be strange to have water flowing from the stomach. Also, water and the Spirit are connected with birth in chapter 3, and so it would be natural to see birth imagery associated with water and the Spirit in this passage as well. Additionally, birth represents the idea of new life, and life and eternal life are associated with "living water" in John 4:10–14. If "living water" represents life in John's Gospel, then these living waters that flow out of the *koilia* in John 7 would be more logically associated with womb imagery than stomach imagery. This connection with life is also made in chapter 3—the believer receives eternal life through birth by water and the Spirit (3:5, 16). We see that the image of living water flowing from the womb of Jesus or the Spirit connects deeply with John's broader theology of new life for those who believe.

Birth imagery occurs again in a short parable-like illustration that Jesus tells his disciples during the "farewell discourse" prior to his arrest. Jesus, trying to prepare them for what is coming, tells them that soon they will not see him, then later they will see him again. When the disciples do not understand what he means, he says to them, "Very truly, I tell you, you will weep and mourn, but the world will rejoice; you will have pain, but your pain will turn into joy. When a woman is in labor, she has pain because her hour has come. But when her child is born, she no longer remembers the anguish because of the joy of having brought a human being into the world. So you have pain now, but I will see you again, and your hearts will rejoice, and no one will take your joy from you" (16:20–22). Once again birth is used to illustrate new life, in this case new life and joy that will follow a time of pain. Jesus warns the disciples that they will face a time of pain and mourning when he is crucified. But this pain will not be hopeless; like the pain of birth it will be temporary and part of the process of new life coming into being. And the pain and joy are not just related temporally (one after the other), but the joy will swallow up the pain, as a woman's joy in her new infant causes her to stop thinking about the pain of labor. The joy that the disciples will feel at the resurrection will be a joy that overcomes.

The culmination of all the birth imagery in John occurs when blood and water flow from Jesus's side after he dies.[5] I already talked in chapter 4 about

Jesus birthing the church from the cross when he gives his mother and the Beloved Disciple to one another to form a new community. Moments later, after he dies, one of the soldiers pierces his side, and blood and water come out (19:34). These are the two fluids most associated with the birth process. Mention of water flowing from Jesus's body also reminds us of the water flowing from his *koilia* in 7:38. Mentions of water (19:34) and spirit (19:30) in this passage also take us back to the images of birth and life in chapters 3 and 4. All the promises of new life from earlier in the Gospel have been fulfilled in Jesus's act of giving his life on the cross.[6] In that sense, Jesus gives birth from the cross and becomes the mother of all who believe.

CONCLUSION

It is important to highlight lesser-known female imagery in the Bible. The greater the variety of images we employ for God, the easier it will be for us to remember that nearly all the ways we have of describing God are metaphorical—whether we describe God as a Mother, a Fortress, a Shepherd, or a Father. Highlighting female imagery in particular can also help us overcome the narratives of gender dualism and hierarchy that have dominated society and the church through much of history. Images such as those described in this chapter can open our minds to new ways of thinking and allow women to see themselves as part of the biblical narrative. Seeing Jesus as a mother hen or as the incarnation of Woman Wisdom or as giving birth can help men to break out of rigid and unhelpful ways of thinking about their own gender identities as well. Insisting on only male imagery for God has had destructive consequences in the home, the church, and society.[7] There are plenty of resources in the Bible itself for helping us move beyond male-only language and imagery for God, if only we will take the time to notice them.

When the Bible employs female imagery, motherhood plays a prominent role. God, Jesus, Jerusalem, Woman Wisdom, and the Spirit are all portrayed as mothers in the Gospels. This imagery helps readers explore themes of connection, longing, suffering, protection, wisdom, and especially the new life that is given to believers through Christ. In this way, a focus on the maternal images of the Gospels doesn't just help us overcome the problems of using male-only language for God; it also takes us into the very heart of the theology about Christ that is expressed in these New Testament books.

Mother Jesus

DISCUSSION QUESTIONS

1. In what ways is the passage about Jesus as a mother hen illuminated by its connections to Old Testament imagery for God as a mother and as a bird? What does the passage tell us about Jesus's character and identity?
2. What is the significance of viewing Jesus as the incarnation of Woman Wisdom? What implications might this theology have for people's lives and for the church if we focused on it more?
3. Were you persuaded by the argument that *koilia* should be translated as womb in John 7:38? Why does this translation choice matter?
4. How would you describe the role that birth imagery plays in the Gospel of John?
5. Why do you think female imagery for God in the Bible has often been ignored or downplayed? What have people found threatening about this imagery?

8

A BRIEF INTERLUDE

Mothers in the Acts of the Apostles

As we've seen in previous chapters, literal and metaphorical mothers populate the pages of the Gospels with regularity. However, when we move from the Gospels to the book of Acts and the letters of the New Testament, the situation changes. The later parts of the New Testament continue to employ motherhood metaphorically on occasion, but literal mothers are few and far between. In part, this is because most of these books are letters rather than stories, so we might not expect as many mothers to make an appearance. And yet, a good number of women are mentioned in Acts and in the letters of the New Testament—we just don't know which, if any, are mothers. It seems that authors of this part of the canon just don't focus on literal motherhood. In this chapter, we will look for and explore the stories of the few mothers that we do find in the Acts of the Apostles, and subsequent chapters will explore the complex place of motherhood in the letters of the New Testament.

MOTHERS IN THE ACTS OF THE APOSTLES

The Acts of the Apostles tells the story of the growth of the church in its earliest period. It is the sequel to the Gospel of Luke, written by the same author. Acts contains several interesting stories about women, including Sapphira (5:1–11), Tabitha (9:36–43), Lydia (16:11–15, 40), a slave woman with a spirit of divination (16:16–18), Priscilla (18:1–4, 18–21, 24–28), and Philip's daughters (21:7–9). We don't know whether any of the women I just listed are mothers or not—it is simply not mentioned one way or the other. What is important about them to the author of Acts is their relationship to the gospel and its spread, not their status as mothers. In some ways it is refreshing that we get to hear about Tabitha's good works, Lydia's hospitality, and Priscilla's gospel ministry, instead of only seeing these women as wives and mothers. In the narrative they are not reduced to their primary value to a patriarchal society. On the other hand, as with so many other people in the Bible, we wish we knew more about them, including their family life and whether they had children. Motherhood might not be central to their stories, but it would be nice to know if we had some examples of "working moms" in the New Testament: women who raised children and engaged in business endeavors or the work of spreading the gospel. None of the women said to be engaged in work or evangelism in the Acts of the Apostles is identified as a mother. The same is also true for the rest of the New Testament. Although little is known about the maternal status of most of the women in Acts, there are three women in Acts who are explicitly identified as mothers: Mary the mother of Jesus, Mary the mother of John Mark, and the mother of Timothy.

MARY IN THE ACTS OF THE APOSTLES

Jesus's mother Mary appears very briefly near the beginning of the story. After the story of Jesus's ascension, Acts tells us that Jesus's followers are staying in Jerusalem. This includes the eleven remaining apostles, Mary the mother of Jesus and some other women, and Jesus's siblings (Acts 1:12–14). This group, along with some other followers of Jesus, makes up the earliest church, and according to Acts, their main activity at this stage is prayer. That is all we hear about Mary in Acts, so it is not a lot to go on, but at least we know she was there. When we looked at Mary in the Gospels in chapters 2, 3, and 4 of this book, we saw that Mary was a faith-filled disciple who spoke prophetic words, taught her son as a child, stayed with him to the end of his life, and became the matriarch of the church at the cross. Her presence here at the start of Acts creates a connection between this story and those Gospel stories, even if we don't hear much about her. She may be in the background, but she is still there, a faithful part of the community.

Although Mary isn't mentioned in the Pentecost story in Acts 2, we can easily imagine that she is there. In Acts 1, the church is identified as the eleven disciples, Mary, Jesus's siblings, and other followers, totaling about 120 persons. In Acts 2, the story of Pentecost begins by telling us that "they" are "all together" in one place. This would seem to imply that all 120 of the earliest church's members are present when the Holy Spirit descends on them at Pentecost, which would include Mary. She had given a Spirit-filled speech at the beginning of the Gospel of Luke; now she is present as the Spirit fills the church at the beginning of Acts. Although the story does not explicitly mention her, artwork has often depicted Mary as present at Pentecost. We might wish Luke had said more about her, but the church has claimed her as its mother in the subsequent tradition.

MARY, THE MOTHER OF JOHN MARK

The second woman identified as a mother in Acts is also named Mary. This Mary is the mother of a church member named John Mark. In Acts 12 an angel springs Peter from prison. Once Peter is free, he goes straight to Mary's house, where the community is gathered to pray. The slave Rhoda is so excited to hear Peter's voice at the door that she runs to tell the rest of the community, forgetting to first unlock the gate and allow Peter inside.[1] Peter, who has just escaped from prison and may be worried about being pursued, is left in the street continuing to knock. He is eventually let inside.

Nothing more is said of Mary, so this story does not have a lot to contribute to our ideas about motherhood in the New Testament. It is interesting, however, that the house is said to belong to Mary, and no mention is made of her husband. It could be that she is married, but her husband isn't mentioned because he is not a believer or not as prominent a church leader as she is. Or it could be that she is unmarried—perhaps one of the lucky widows who was able to inherit property from her husband rather than becoming dependent on other relatives. Either way, she is portrayed in the story as the owner of the house with at least one slave, so she is probably a woman of some means. She is one of many examples of women in the New Testament who use their wealth or their homes to support the Christian movement (see also Luke 8:1–3; Acts 16:13–15; Rom. 16:3–5; and Col. 4:15). In providing hospitality, Mary acts as a mother not just to John Mark but to the whole community of Jesus's followers.

A Brief Interlude

THE MOTHER OF TIMOTHY

The final mother mentioned in Acts also only gets a brief mention. Acts 16:1–5 tells the story of how Paul met his coworker Timothy. Verse 1 says that Timothy has a Jewish mother, who is a believer, and a Greek father. That's all we learn here about Timothy's mother—she is a believer in Jesus and she is in a mixed marriage, her husband being a gentile and presumably not a believer in Jesus. In that sense, although the text tells us very little, we might imagine a woman who is strong in her convictions, since she stands firm in them despite potential pressures from her unbelieving husband. In this faithfulness she is also able to raise a son to be a faithful believer, so faithful that Paul invites him to become his traveling companion. Timothy's mother is unnamed here, but 2 Timothy 1:5 says her name is Eunice. I will say a bit more about Eunice in chapter 11.

CONCLUSION

It is important to keep in mind that although only these three briefly mentioned women are explicitly called mothers in Acts, they are probably not the only mothers in Acts. Nearly all women in the ancient world got married, and the majority of these would also have become mothers. Therefore, it is reasonable to assume that many of the women mentioned in Acts are also mothers. Sometimes motherhood is what women are most remembered for; other times they are remembered for other accomplishments even if they had children. I entitled this chapter "A Brief Interlude." This is partly because Acts does not have much to say about motherhood, and therefore this chapter is quite short. But it is also because Acts holds a transitional position in the canon. It is connected back to the Gospels because it is a narrative and the sequel to the Gospel of Luke. But Acts also pushes us forward because it is the story of the early church and introduces to us some of the people we will encounter in the letters of the New Testament. Some of the letters, especially those written by Paul, give us the earliest direct evidence we have for what the earliest church was like.[2] It is to those letters that we now turn, to see what they reveal about the place of motherhood in that earliest church.

Mothers in the Acts of the Apostles

DISCUSSION QUESTIONS

1. Why do you think so few of the women of Acts are identified as mothers? What does this tell us about Acts and/or about the early church community?
2. What else do you wish Luke had told us about Mary (Jesus's mother) in the book of Acts?
3. What strikes you as most significant about the brief mentions of Mary (mother of John Mark) and the mother of Timothy in Acts?

9

MOTHERHOOD SIDELINED

Mothers in the Earlier Letters of Paul

The first eight chapters of this book focused on the Gospels and Acts, which present us with vibrant story worlds with characters, conflicts, and plot twists. In terms of the subject of this book, we found that the Gospels in particular were populated with a variety of mothers who were significant to the plotline and showed strength of character in various ways. When we move from there into Paul's letters, it may seem at first as though there is not much to observe about motherhood. We are no longer in a story world full of dramatic action in which mothers play a part, but have entered the realm of the mind and ideas—specifically, the mind of Paul and his ideas about the gospel and how to live it out. Of course, to many people this world of Paul is just as vibrant and relevant as the world of the Gospels. But others remain less comfortable with Paul, uncertain about whether his words are still meaningful for life today, or if they are simply a relic of a patriarchal and authoritarian past. While it is beyond the scope of this book to comment on Paul's relevance in general, in this chapter and the next we will find that his letters are indeed relevant to this book. We just have to look for motherhood in less expected places—especially the realms of allegory and metaphor. It is the case, however, that Paul mostly overlooks literal motherhood. In this chapter we will explore the places where Paul mentions Old Testament mothers and the little we can know about particular mothers in Pauline communities. But first, we will briefly consider authorship issues and why we are not considering evidence from the entire Pauline corpus in this chapter.

AUTHORSHIP QUESTIONS

One of the most significant issues in the study of Paul's letters is the question of authorship. Although there are thirteen letters in the New Testament attributed to Paul, many biblical scholars do not think Paul himself wrote all of them. There is broad scholarly consensus that Paul did write seven of the letters (Romans, 1 and 2 Corinthians, Galatians, Philippians, 1 Thessalonians, and Philemon). Scholars debate and disagree about whether Paul wrote the remaining six letters (Ephesians, Colossians, 2 Thessalonians, 1 and 2 Timothy, and Titus). Since there is debate and disagreement, these letters are called the "disputed" letters, while the letters most scholars agree Paul himself wrote are called the "undisputed" letters.

The idea that Paul did not write all thirteen letters that bear his name is not as surprising as it might at first seem, because we know that pseudonymity (writing in the name of another person) was commonly practiced in the ancient world. Therefore, when scholars see clues in a text that may indicate the document was written later than the lifetime of the person listed as the author, they consider the possibility that the text may be pseudonymous. Scholars consider a variety of criteria when trying to determine whether a text is pseudonymous. I'll explain these criteria further in chapter 11, when we turn to studying the disputed letters. For now, I will just note that, in my own view, there are enough grammatical and theological differences between the undisputed letters and the disputed letters that it makes sense for us to consider them separately. For that reason, we will limit our analysis in this chapter and the next to the undisputed letters, and in chapter 11 we will turn to the disputed letters and the unique issues that they present to readers.

OLD TESTAMENT MOTHERS IN PAUL'S UNDISPUTED LETTERS

Paul makes frequent reference to the Old Testament in his writings. He often quotes the Jewish Scriptures, and, even when he is not directly quoting, his thought world is grounded in the story of Israel. However, though Old Testament references permeate the letters, the mothers of the Old Testament are only rarely mentioned. In this section we will explore the places they do come up in Paul's writings.

Eve

Eve is a figure that is for the most part overlooked in Paul's undisputed letters. Paul makes much theological use of the figure of Adam, but with hardly any reference to Eve. In Romans 5 and 1 Corinthians 15 Adam alone represents humanity, an example of androcentrism. Eve is mentioned once, briefly, in 2 Corinthians 11:3, there the focus is not at all on her status as "the mother of all living" (Gen. 3:20), but only on how she was deceived by the serpent, something that Paul uses as a lesson for the Corinthians at a time when he is particularly concerned about them being led astray.

Sarah and Abraham

Similarly, Paul talks extensively about Abraham but only minimally about Sarah. For example, in Romans 4, even though the focus is on God's promise to give Abraham many descendants, Sarah, as the mother of those descendants, is barely mentioned. She is mentioned in 4:19, but not as a subject in her own right—only that the barrenness of her womb was not an impediment to Abraham's own faith. The focus remains firmly on Abraham, his faith, and the timing of his circumcision. In Paul's letters, believers in Christ are identified as the descendants of Abraham, not the descendants of Abraham and Sarah. In ancient patriarchal thinking, it is the father who matters for heritage and inheritance, not the mother. This situation is similar in Galatians 3, where Paul also talks extensively about the faith of Abraham and the fulfillment of God's promise to give Abraham offspring. In this chapter, no mention is made of Sarah, promises to her, or the fact that she was the mother of the offspring that was promised to Abraham.

Sarah and Hagar

In Galatians 4:21–31 Paul gives an allegorical interpretation of the story of Sarah and Hagar. As I said in the introduction to this chapter, motherhood gets more attention from Paul when he considers it in an allegorical or metaphorical sense than when he is talking about literal mothers. So this allegorical treatment of Sarah and Hagar is more extensive than the other passages we are considering in this chapter, where Paul mentions Old Testament mothers only very briefly.

Genesis tells the story of the barren Sarah giving her slave Hagar to Abraham as a way for Abraham to father an heir (Gen. 16:1–16). Once Hagar becomes pregnant, she begins to look down on Sarah. Sarah is furious at this role reversal and begins to treat Hagar so harshly that Hagar flees into the wilderness. There she encounters the angel of the Lord, who instructs her to return and submit to Sarah, but also promises her that she will bear a son through whom she will receive multitudes of descendants. Hagar names the angel "El-roi" ("The God who sees"), identifying the angel as a manifestation of God.[1] Hagar returns to Abraham's household and gives birth to Ishmael. Later in the story, after Isaac has been miraculously born to Sarah and Abraham, Sarah views Ishmael as a threat to her son Isaac's inheritance and instructs Abraham to send Hagar and Ishmael away (Gen. 21:8–21). Once again, Hagar finds herself in the wilderness, this time with her young son. She fears they will both die when they run out of water. God hears Ishmael's cries and shows Hagar the location of a well. Then they make it through the wilderness. The story of Hagar and her divine encounters is remarkable. Although most Jews and Christians have focused more on Sarah's story than on Hagar's, Hagar has become an important figure for African American women and others reading from the margins who identify with Hagar's situation and her resiliency.[2]

In Galatians Paul is trying to convince gentile church members that they do not need to keep Jewish laws to be followers of Jesus—especially that the men don't need to be circumcised. According to Paul, the faithfulness of Christ on the cross has made it possible for all to be reconciled to God through faith without a need for gentiles to convert to Judaism. Sharing in the faith of Jesus makes them part of the family of Abraham. As part of his case, Paul refers to the story of Sarah and Hagar, interpreting it allegorically. Paul says in 4:21–31 that the two women represent two covenants. Hagar, as a slave, represents the covenant of law given at Mount Sinai, since Paul talks about being bound by the law as a form of slavery. Sarah, as a free woman, represents the covenant of faith that Paul is inviting the Galatians to enter into. Paul's point is that it is not enough to be physically descended from Abraham. One has to be a descendant of Abraham who is also an inheritor of the promise. To Paul, those who have come to share the faith of Abraham are Abraham's true heirs, even if they are not his literal descendants (i.e., Jews). And since those who share Abraham's faith are considered inheritors of the promise, they are also described as being Sarah's children, since it was Sarah's son who inherited the promise. By contrast, Paul considers those who do not share in the faith of Christ to be in bondage, and therefore children of the enslaved Hagar, even if they themselves are Jews who would claim descent through Sarah and Isaac. In this allegorical interpretation, Paul intentionally ignores Hagar and Sarah's literal motherhood in favor of presenting them as spiritual mothers for two different perspectives on faith and life in relation to God.

Using images that share much with other Jewish and Christian writings of the era, especially those of an apocalyptic nature, Paul also speaks in this passage of "the present Jerusalem" and "the Jerusalem above," connecting the former to Hagar and the latter to Sarah. The "present" city of Jerusalem Paul identifies as being in slavery, due to its bondage to Torah observance. It is, of course, important to keep in mind that this is Paul's perspective, not the way the residents of first-century Jerusalem would have viewed themselves! Some of the residents of first-century Jerusalem may have viewed themselves as being in bondage, but only in bondage to the Roman Empire, not to the Torah, which Jews considered (and still consider) to be a gift from God, not a burden that they need to be liberated from. Nevertheless, it serves Paul's rhetorical goals in the letter to connect the literal Jerusalem with bondage and with Hagar. Paul contrasts this with what he calls "the Jerusalem above." This is the idea that a perfect version of Jerusalem exists in the heavenly realm, and that believers can have access to that city. Currently they have access to it in a spiritual sense, and in the future they will have access to it in a more physical sense.[3] Paul connects this version of Jerusalem to freedom and to Sarah, and he urges the gentile believers to align themselves with her.

Central to this allegorical interpretation is the fact that Hagar and Sarah are not only women, but also mothers. In Roman times, children would inherit the status of their mother—that is, children born to a free woman would be free, and children born to an enslaved woman would be slaves themselves. This is how Paul interprets the story of Sarah and Hagar, but in terms of spiritual descendants, not physical ones. If we are bound by the law then we are children of Hagar, in bondage as she was. But if we claim Sarah as our mother, then we will be free as she was. This also fits well with the way these women represent two different versions of Jerusalem, since cities in the ancient world were often personified as female figures, and indeed, Jerusalem/Zion is portrayed as a mother in several passages in the Old Testament prophets (Isa. 49:19–21; 54:1; 66:7–12; Jer. 4:31; Lam. 2:18–22; Mic. 4:9–10). Cities were portrayed as women, and to claim a city as mother was to claim citizenship in that city.[4] In that way, Paul urges the Galatians to choose citizenship in a heavenly city, not a physical one.

Looking to a heavenly city rather than an earthly one opens up many inspiring possibilities. As David deSilva puts it, "Christian hope is no longer bound up with the future of an earthly city . . . Christ-followers . . . do not set their sights on any disputed stretch of land in the Middle East. . . . While the earthly Jerusalem is bound up with the history of a particular ethnic people (the Jewish people), Paul looks to a heavenly city as an appropriate future dwelling place for the multinational, multi-ethnic people of God formed in Christ."[5] Within Paul's allegory is the potential for a beautiful, inclusive vision—a city where all are welcome no matter their race, gender, or social class. There are no particular identity markers required for entry. The residents of the city exhibit a glorious diversity but are united by their faith. It's a beautiful picture. But something is being overlooked if we leave it there. Because, according to Paul, it's not actually the case that all are welcome in this city. In fact, for the children of Sarah to enjoy the city, Hagar must be cast out, along with her children (Gal. 4:30). The freedom of some comes at the expense of others.

To claim Sarah as our mother, must we reject Hagar? Must these two women stand forever opposed to each other? We could remind Paul, as he rejects again the already rejected Hagar, that God did not, in fact, reject her. Rather, God saved her, spoke to her, and promised her a multitude of offspring, that is, a future. As Carolyn Osiek writes, "There is no denying that for Genesis and Paul, Hagar is rejected. But precisely because of this interpretation, she becomes the symbol and heroine for all those women who feel rejected or less desired because of personal, economic, ethnic, or racist practices. While Paul's allegory, for his own purposes, ends with Hagar still rejected, the reader of the Bible cannot forget Jesus' outreach to just such oppressed and forgotten ones."[6] Osiek notes that Paul constructs the allegory this way "for his own purposes." This is key. To interpret Paul's allegory well, we must keep Paul's context, purpose, and perspective in mind. Paul has a very specific purpose in constructing this allegorical interpretation—to get the Galatians to remain faithful to the message of faith he had preached to them, and not be led astray to thinking that they must take on the marks of Jewish identity and law observance in order to become acceptable to God. This is what leads Paul to create such a stark contrast between Sarah and Hagar, between the idea of slavery and the idea of freedom. That particular interpretation of Hagar's story in Galatians doesn't prevent us from imagining her story differently in different contexts.

We should also keep in mind that Paul was frustrated by the activities of particular Jewish missionaries in his communities, whom he felt were leading the congregation members astray from the truth of the gospel, and that, from Paul's perspective, the Galatians' salvation was at stake. This caused him to portray certain aspects of Jewish practice negatively in the allegory. Our context and perspective are different from Paul's, however, and so our interpretation of Sarah and Hagar's stories can be different as well. We can seek out reconciliation rather than rejection. We can reject the idea that others must be enslaved for us to have freedom. With Jesus we can seek out the lost and rejected. And more than that, we can ask ourselves hard questions. Those of us who would consider ourselves free should ask, who has been trampled on our march to freedom? Who has been harmed so that we can have what we have? How can we build a city in which there is a place for both Sarah's children and Hagar's? Paul leaves Hagar rejected and enslaved at the end of his allegorical interpretation, but we don't need to do the same. For while Hagar is enslaved, are any of us truly free?

Sarah and Rebecca

Sarah and her daughter-in-law Rebecca get a little attention from Paul in Romans 9. In this part of the letter, Paul is embarking on an extensive reflection on the salvation of the Jewish people. He is distressed that so many of his fellow Jews have not accepted the gospel message about Jesus. This causes him to reflect on the mystery of election—that God seems to choose some people for salvation and hardens the hearts of others. This may seem unfair to us, but Paul insists that it is beyond our knowledge and ability to fully understand the ways of God. To illustrate this, Paul refers to the stories of Sarah and Rebecca. First, he references the fact that not all of Abraham's children carry the promise. Abraham already had a son, Ishmael, but only Sarah's son Isaac would receive the promise that his descendants would become God's chosen nation and inherit the promised land (Rom. 9:6–9). So, as we saw in the Galatians passage about Sarah and Hagar above, just being a literal son of Abraham is not enough—you have to be the son who inherits the promise. Similarly, Isaac's wife Rebecca was pregnant with twins when God said that one would be chosen to serve the other, one would be beloved and the other hated (Rom. 9:10–13). Paul notes that this is before they were even born, so it is dependent on God's election, not on anything the children did right or wrong. It is beyond our ability to understand why one would be chosen and the other not.

Again, this may seem unfair to us, that the destinies of two boys are set before they even exit the womb, but to Paul this seemed relevant as he wrestled with understanding the unbelief of his people and why some seemed to be on the path of salvation while others rejected it. Perhaps we can relate to this wrestling. Parents may wonder why one of their children follows a successful path in life while another takes wrong turn after wrong turn. Why does life work out for some but not for others? Why do some believe but others don't? Like Paul wrestling with the salvation of Israel, it is beyond our comprehension to understand why some people in our own lives seem to be "chosen" for any number of things, while others are not. It is a mystery. Nevertheless, we can take some comfort from where Paul's wrestling led him. Paul believed that some were presently chosen for belief and others were not, but Paul also believed deeply in God's goodness and God's faithfulness to promises, which is why he came to this conclusion: Although he presently saw unbelief in Israel, he also believed that, in the end, "all Israel will be saved" (Rom. 11:26) because "the gifts and calling of God are irrevocable" (Rom. 11:29).

MOTHERS IN PAULINE COMMUNITIES

We will turn now from Paul's commentary on Old Testament mother characters to searching for mothers in Pauline communities. The first thing to note is that we will not find very many. Paul mentions quite a few women whom he calls his coworkers in the work of spreading the gospel, such as Euodia and Syntyche (Phil. 4:2–3), Chloe (1 Cor. 1:11), Phoebe (Rom. 16:1–2), Prisca (Rom. 16:3–5), Mary (Rom. 16:6), Junia (Rom. 16:7), Tryphaena and Tryphosa (Rom. 16:12), and Persis (Rom. 16:12). However, we don't know if any of these women were mothers. As we noted in the previous chapter about the women of Acts, it is likely that many of them were (because most adult women in the ancient world would have been married and given birth to children), but Paul does not mention it one way or the other. There are only three women in Paul's undisputed letters, all mentioned very briefly, that we can identify for sure as mothers.

Rufus's Mother

One of the few specific mothers mentioned in Paul's letters is the mother of Rufus, greeted in Romans 16:13. In Romans 16, Paul sends greetings to a large number of people in the Roman house churches. While many readers skip this, as it appears to be a boring list of names, it gives us an important window into the rich diversity of the early church community. In this list we see names that are Jewish and Greco-Roman, male and female, slave and free. All these people were breaking down the well-established religious, cultural, social, and economic barriers that had previously separated them, brought together by the new kind of community that was being formed around Jesus. Two of these people were Rufus and his mother.

Paul greets Rufus and calls him "chosen in the Lord," and then greets his mother and calls her "a mother to me also" (Rom. 16:13). This unnamed woman was a literal mother to Rufus and a metaphorical mother to Paul. What was this woman like, and what was her relationship with Paul like, that he would say she was like a mother to him? We can only speculate, of course, because Paul says nothing further about her. But we can make some educated guesses based on what most ancient people in the Greco-Roman era would have associated with motherhood. Most likely, this woman had fed and provided for Paul in his life and ministry, and she may also have been a wise, experienced older presence in his life, giving him counsel and comfort. These are the kinds of things that would have made him likely to think of her as a mother.

An Unnamed Stepmother

The Bible does not make much mention of stepparents, partly due to differences between the way families were structured in the ancient world versus the modern world, and partly because the Bible is not interested in giving us intimate details about what family life was like in the ancient world. But there is one brief mention of a stepmother in 1 Corinthians 5:1. The NRSVue translates the verse this way: "It is actually reported that there is sexual immorality among you and the sort of sexual immorality that is not found even among gentiles, for a man is living with his father's wife." More literally translated, Paul writes that "a certain man has his father's woman." This is usually interpreted to mean that a man in the Corinthian community is sleeping or living with his stepmother. No further details are given, so we don't know if the man's father is still alive (and presumably has divorced the woman in question) or if the father has died. At any rate, influenced by his Jewish ethics, Paul considers the relationship to be incestuous and abhorrent, even though the man and woman in question are not biologically related. The practice is forbidden in the Torah (see Lev. 20:11 and Deut. 22:30, 27:20) and was also prohibited by Roman law.[7] Paul views such sexual immorality as corrupting the community and urges them to cast the man out ("hand him over to Satan") in hopes that "the spirit might be saved in the day of the Lord" (5:5). It's not entirely clear what this means, but it may be that Paul hopes that if the man is forced out, this will not only protect the community but will also ultimately lead to the man's repentance, and therefore his salvation.

This passage is primarily about sexual taboos, immorality, and church discipline. Does it have anything to say about motherhood? Perhaps not much, other than the fact that we might surmise that Paul would say that the woman in question should think of herself as a mother to the man, not as a potential lover. She is not his biological mother, but when she married his father, a maternal relationship was created. In that sense, Paul's outrage at what has occurred can be viewed as a sign of the sacredness of relationships that are not biological but are nevertheless family relationships. Being a stepmother, a foster mother, a guardian, or a mother-in-law is a responsibility and a gift. These relationships are not always easy but provide opportunities for nurture and care that can be crucial and life-giving for all involved if they are engaged in with patience, persistence, humility, and love. In this case the man and woman act in ways that are taboo in their society and that Paul feels are harming the community. Nevertheless, this example can cause us to think about how such nonbiological relationships can provide support and be filled with love when entered into with good intentions.

Paul's Own Mother

There is one more literal mother mentioned in Paul's letters, and that is Paul's own mother. He makes a passing reference to her, or at least to her womb as his place of origin, in Galatians 1:15. Paul reminds the Galatians that he used to persecute Christians before his conversion experience. Then he says,

> But when the one who had set me apart before I was born and called me through his grace was pleased to reveal his Son to me, so that I might proclaim him among the gentiles, I did not confer with any human, nor did I go up to Jerusalem to those who were already apostles before me, but I went away at once into Arabia, and afterward I returned to Damascus.

What the NRSVue translates as "set me apart before I was born" is more literally translated as "set me apart from my mother's womb."[8] So we have here a brief reference to Paul's own mother. Unfortunately, he does not tell us anything about her, and we do not have any other sources to give us more information. Who was this woman? What was she like? Before his conversion her son was very traditional, closed-minded, and motivated to persecute those who believed and behaved outside of the boundaries he thought proper. Did Paul get these ideas from his mother? Or did the apple fall far from the tree? Did he have a bad relationship with her and that is why he seems to speak more warmly of Rufus's mother than his own? Did he never know her because she died in childbirth? We can speculate, but we will never know.

With this language of being set apart from the womb, Paul claims that God's plans for him were in place even before he was born. This echoes prophetic call stories from the Old Testament (see Isa. 49:1 and Jer. 1:5). We might also be reminded again of what Paul said about Rebecca's children in Romans 9—how from the time they were in her womb one was chosen and the other wasn't. Parents like to think they have control over their children and their children's futures, but the reality is that so much is out of our hands. Parents may do their best, but ultimately their children's lives may be influenced by any number of factors, whether they are called by God to a particular purpose or not. Sometimes it can seem as though their direction in life is set "from the womb." Paul seems to have viewed his own life that way.

THE SIDELINING OF MOTHERHOOD IN THE LETTERS OF PAUL

The preceding tour of mothers mentioned briefly in Paul's letters shows that Paul did not spend a lot of time thinking about the women of his communities as mothers. When Paul focused on women he tended to focus on them as women, not as mothers. We might be surprised that Paul was not more inclined to think of the women of his communities as mothers, since motherhood in the ancient Greco-Roman and Jewish worlds was generally thought to be the ideal state for women—indeed, the very reason for women's existence. So why, contrary to his culture, was motherhood sidelined in the mind of Paul? One reason is that Paul seems to have shared with many other early Christians the general idea that believers formed a new family of faith, which became more important than their families of origin or their marital families (see also my discussion of family in the Synoptic Gospels in chapter 6). Therefore, women's roles as mothers or their potential to be mothers were subordinated to their role as members of God's family and their participation in the work of spreading the gospel. I am speaking here of the earliest decades of the church. As church history progressed into the end of the first century and beyond, traditional Greco-Roman family values would return to dominance within the church. But in these earliest days the church as family took precedence over biological family.

There is more we can say, however, about Paul's reasons for overlooking motherhood, beyond the family identity issues we have already seen. We see this when we look at 1 Corinthians 7, in which Paul talks about marriage and family issues. Paul tells us something about his thought process in 1 Corinthians 7 that is very important for our interpretation of his words. He has one major guiding principle in this chapter that gets applied to issues like marriage, slavery, and circumcision. That guiding principle is, "Remain in the condition in which you were called" (7:20). Don't try to make major changes to your circumstances—whatever your circumstances may be, seek to serve God and spread the gospel where you are.

Why does Paul take this perspective? Why not seek freedom if you are a slave? Why not get married if you are engaged? Why not get divorced if you are in a bad situation? In the chapter, Paul tells us explicitly why this is his advice: "I mean, brothers and sisters, *the appointed time has grown short*; from now on, let even those who have wives be as though they had none, and those who mourn as though they were not mourning, and those who rejoice as though they were not rejoicing, and those who buy as though they had no possessions, and those who deal with the world as though they had no dealings with it. *For the present form of this world is passing away*" (7:29–31, emphasis mine).

Motherhood Sidelined

This is one of several places in Paul's undisputed letters that clue us in to the fact that Paul believed that the world as they knew it was going to be ending soon. Paul believed that Jesus would return soon to fully inaugurate a new age in which the world will be reborn, the dead raised, and all enemies defeated, and in which God will reign with peace and justice (1 Cor. 15:12–28; 1 Thess. 4:13–5:11). Paul seems to expect this to happen within his own lifetime (1 Thess. 4:15, 17). In other words, Paul does not think that there will be future generations; history is about to come to an end. The end of history means the end of our human-made social structures, including marriage and slavery. If the world as we know it has no long-term future, there is not much point to getting married, having children, or making changes to society such as better treatment of women or the ending of slavery. This is why Paul is not always as interested as twenty-first century readers want him to be in social justice issues. It is also one of the reasons that Paul doesn't focus on women as mothers—because he doesn't focus on the importance of children for the continuance of the Christian community, or indeed, even for the continuance of humanity.

Paul's belief in Jesus's imminent return eliminates the need for him to think about the next generation, and therefore sidelines the importance of motherhood for women. In 1 Corinthians 7 we see that Paul wants the same thing for both the men and the women of his communities: to have lives as unencumbered by worldly concerns as possible, so that they can concern themselves with "the affairs of the Lord" rather than "the affairs of the world" and live in "unhindered devotion" to God (1 Cor. 7:32–35). For Paul, in the short time he believes is left, it is more important for women to dedicate themselves to the work of the gospel than to get married and have children.

CONCLUSION

Like other male authors in the ancient world, Paul was androcentric in his writings. It did not always occur to him to consider women's lives and women's perspectives. But, as we've seen in this chapter, when Paul did focus on women in his writings, he tended to focus on them as women and as coworkers in his gospel mission, not as mothers. This is because, for Paul, the church community had surpassed the family in importance, and because he believed that the world as he knew it was going to end soon. Androcentrism, church social dynamics, and Paul's eschatology all conspired to sideline in Paul's mind the importance of literal motherhood for the women in his communities. This does not mean, however, that Paul did not focus at all on the idea of motherhood. In fact, when we leave behind the idea of the literal motherhood of women in Pauline communities and move into the realm of metaphor, we will find in Paul's undisputed letters rich maternal images to inspire theological and social reflection. That is what we will turn to in the next chapter.

DISCUSSION QUESTIONS

1. What do you find challenging or troubling about Paul's Hagar/Sarah allegory? What do you find interesting or inspiring about it? What are the potential promises and pitfalls of reading and interpreting Paul's allegory today?
2. What might it look like to create a community in which both Hagar's and Sarah's children are welcome?
3. Why do you think Paul felt the relationship between a man and his stepmother was so harmful to the community? How do we determine when a matter is a private matter within one family and when it should be a concern to the whole community?
4. The attitude of Paul and other early Christians toward family was countercultural. Do you think these ideas are still countercultural today? What are the variety of ways that modern readers might react to the sidelining of motherhood (and other family relationships) in Paul's undisputed letters?

10

MOTHER PAUL

Metaphorical Motherhood in the Earlier Letters of Paul

We saw in the previous chapter that Paul did not focus much on motherhood in relation to the women of his communities. But that does not mean that Paul did not think about motherhood at all. On the contrary, Paul's undisputed letters contain a surprising number of metaphors that draw on the concept of motherhood. Although Paul does not seem to have thought of the women of his community as mothers, he did sometimes think of himself as a mother to his communities! In addition, he used the idea of childbirth to think about the state of creation and what was going on in the world. These metaphors are not simply "fancy" ways of writing that Paul engages in to make his writing more colorful. They are images used to express concepts that are deeply embedded in his understanding of the world and his understanding of gospel ministry.[1] In this chapter we will first consider the places in which Paul uses birth metaphors (1 Thess. 5:3; Rom. 8:22; Gal. 4:19; and 1 Cor. 15:8) and then turn to the passages in which Paul uses breastfeeding metaphors (1 Thess. 2:7 and 1 Cor. 3:2). Finally, I will conclude with some general reflections on the implications of Paul portraying himself as a mother.

Metaphorical Motherhood in the Earlier Letters of Paul

THE END TIMES AND BIRTH PANG IMAGERY (1 THESS. 5:2–3)

As discussed in the previous chapter, Paul seems to have believed that the world as he knew it was going to end soon. A radical change would be brought about with the return of Jesus, the defeat of God's enemies, and the inauguration of a new age of peace and justice. Paul talks about this in 1 Thessalonians. In the letter, Paul is seeking to comfort the community because some of its members have died. He reminds them that all believers, those alive and those who have died, will one day soon be together with Christ in this new age. This is a message of comfort for the Thessalonians. For those who are not already followers of Jesus, however, Paul indicates that this dramatic change to the world will come as something of a shock: "For you yourselves know very well that the day of the Lord will come like a thief in the night. When they say, 'There is peace and security,' then sudden destruction will come upon them, as labor pains come upon a pregnant woman, and there will be no escape!" (1 Thess. 5:2–3). Although Paul believed that the end was coming soon, he never claims to know precisely when it was going to come. In this passage Paul compares the unknown timing of the end to the experience a woman has at the beginning of labor. Even if you know labor is coming soon, there is no way to predict the exact moment it will begin, and so it can still come as a surprise. And just as the onset of labor can produce feelings of fear, so the onset of these world-ending changes would be experienced as fearful events by unbelievers.

In creating this metaphor Paul is drawing on the scriptural and literary tradition of his people. Similar metaphors are used in oracles of judgment against the nations in the Old Testament prophets. For example, in the context of describing the future judgment of Babylon, in Isaiah 13:6–8 we read,

> Wail, for the day of the Lord is near;
>   it will come like destruction from the Almighty!
> Therefore all hands will be feeble,
>   and every human heart will melt,
>   and they will be terrified.
> Pangs and agony will seize them;
>   they will be in anguish like a woman in labor.
> They will look aghast at one another;
>   their faces will be aflame.

This passage is very similar to 1 Thessalonians 5:2–3, with mention of the day of the Lord, destruction, and the birth pangs metaphor. But one thing that is different between Isaiah and Paul is that the Isaiah passage, written centuries earlier, applied the metaphor to a particular nation—the Babylonians—and indicated that they in particular would be on the receiving end of God's judgment within the historical time period that was about to unfold. Later Jewish apocalyptic literature is similar to Paul in expanding the metaphor to apply not just to a particular nation but to the people of all nations at the end of time. For example, the noncanonical book of 1 Enoch[2] uses the metaphor in this way. Talking about all the kings and rulers of the earth, not just a particular nation, it says, "And pain will come upon them as upon a woman in labor, for whom giving birth is difficult when her child enters the mouth of the womb, and she has difficulty giving birth" (1 Enoch 62:4). Here the difficulty of labor is emphasized to represent the trauma of the end times.

The New Testament Gospels use the metaphor in a way that seems to combine the prophetic use (applying to a particular nation in a historical period) and the apocalyptic use (applying to all nations at the end of time). In Mark 13, Jesus predicts that the temple in Jerusalem will be torn down. Some of the disciples ask him to tell them more about what he means—when it will happen and what the signs will be that it is about to happen. Jesus replies, "Many will come in my name and say, 'I am he!' and they will lead many astray. When you hear of wars and rumors of wars, do not be alarmed; this must take place, but the end is still to come. For nation will rise against nation and kingdom against kingdom; there will be earthquakes in various places; there will be famines. This is but the beginning of the birth pangs" (Mark 13:6–8). It is very hard to sort out in this passage, and in what follows in the rest of the chapter, whether Jesus is referring to the future destruction of the temple by the Romans (which would be a prophetic use of the metaphor), or if he is referring to an end-of-the-world scenario (which would be an apocalyptic use of the metaphor). Both seem to be in view at once. At any rate, Jesus, as recorded in Mark's Gospel, is also drawing on Jewish literary tradition when he uses the birth pangs metaphor to refer to cataclysmic future events that would involve particular nations (such as Rome) but also have wider implications.[3]

What was Paul trying to communicate to his readers by using the birth pangs metaphor? When read in the context of 1 Thessalonians 5, we can see that Paul uses the birth pangs metaphor to emphasize the suddenness, the suffering, and the inevitability associated with the end times. First, the unknown timing of the end is compared to the beginning of labor—a pregnant woman knows *that* labor is coming, but she doesn't know *when*. Similarly, Paul wants to say, we know that God's new age of peace and justice is coming, but we can't predict the exact day or hour it will arrive. In that sense, it will feel sudden even though it is expected. The beginnings of labor may take a woman by surprise, but once it begins there are two things we can know for sure. First, there will be pain, which is why Paul uses childbirth as a metaphor for the suffering associated with the end times, referred to in 1 Thessalonians 5:3 as "destruction." And the second thing we can know for sure is that once labor starts, there is no stopping it—it must proceed to some kind of conclusion. Ideally this conclusion is the birth of a healthy infant to a healthy mother, but unfortunately this is not always the case, especially in the ancient world. But whether the conclusion is a happy or a heart-wrenching one, either way, when labor begins, the woman cannot put it off or reschedule it for another time. So, Paul says, no one will be able to escape from or put off the changes that are coming to the world.[4]

ALL CREATION IN LABOR TOGETHER (ROM. 8:18-25)

As described in the section above, we could say that Paul's use of the birth pangs metaphor in 1 Thessalonians 5 was conventional. He drew on the image as used in Jewish prophetic and apocalyptic literature and didn't make any radical shifts away from how the metaphor had been used by other writers. In Romans 8 Paul again uses birth imagery when considering the future end of time as we know it. But in this instance his use of the metaphor is less conventional and more creative. Here Paul does not use the metaphor to emphasize the suddenness of the end or how judgment will come to other nations or enemies in the future. Rather, in Romans 8 Paul is talking about the current suffering that the people in his communities are already experiencing as the end is approaching. The image here is not one of division but of solidarity. In 1 Thessalonians 5 Paul says that those outside the Christian community will be surprised by "sudden destruction" when the end comes upon them like birth pangs on a pregnant woman (5:3), but that the Thessalonian community (the insiders) will not be surprised (5:4). As "children of light" (5:5) they are destined not for wrath or destruction but for salvation (5:9). This sense of there being insiders and outsiders that is present in 1 Thessalonians 5 is distinctly absent from Romans 8:22. Here, the sufferings that the Roman Christian community is experiencing are part of the suffering that all creation is currently experiencing. Christian and non-Christian, human and nonhuman, all are in the same predicament as Paul describes it in Romans 8:22.

In chapter 8 Paul has been talking about what life lived according to the Spirit of God looks like. Among other things, those who live by the Spirit recognize that they are God's heirs, and this has implications for how Jesus followers look at the future: those who are "joint heirs with Christ" suffer in the present but have hope of future glorification (8:14–17). In this context, Paul writes,

> I consider that the sufferings of this present time are not worth comparing with the glory about to be revealed to us. For the creation waits with eager longing for the revealing of the children of God, for the creation was subjected to futility, not of its own will, but by the will of the one who subjected it, in hope that the creation itself will be set free from its enslavement to decay and will obtain the freedom of the glory of the children of God. We know that the whole creation has been groaning together as it suffers together the pains of labor, and not only the creation, but we ourselves, who have the first fruits of the Spirit, groan inwardly while we wait for adoption, the redemption of our bodies. (Rom. 8:18–23)

In verse 22, Paul has taken the Greek verbs that mean "to groan" and "to suffer labor pains" and put a prefix on them that means to do something together—similar to the English prefix "co-." Paul writes that the whole creation has been co-groaning and co-laboring in the past and up to the present time—and we have, too, alongside creation and as part of creation. In that sense the birth metaphor in Romans 8 becomes an image of solidarity rather than an image of judgment and impending doom, as it had been in 1 Thessalonians 5 and other Jewish prophetic and apocalyptic writings. All creation is experiencing the same hardship and longing together for God's future of redemption.

Paul describes creation in this passage as "enslaved to decay" and as "subjected to futility." This expresses the idea that all is not currently right with the world, and that is why we need God to intervene to bring about a new age of peace and well-being. This ancient perspective is something I think modern readers can relate to as well. For example, since ancient times people have looked around and seen a world in which the wolf eats the lamb, and they have longed for a world in which the wolf and the lamb dwell in peace together (Isa. 11:6–9). People have looked around at a world in which the poor are trampled by the wealthy as the wealthy seek even greater wealth, and they have longed for a world in which everyone has enough. People have looked around at a world filled with violence and disease and longed for a world of health and peace. These longings are the soil out of which apocalypticism grows. Everyone who experiences hunger, suffering, disease, grief, violence, or pain can understand something of this longing for a better world expressed in Paul's letters and in other Jewish apocalyptic literature. This is where the hope comes in—the idea that a better world is possible, and God will bring it about. This is how the birth pangs image in Romans 8 creates such a beautiful picture of solidarity—it expresses the idea that all of creation, human and nonhuman, is experiencing suffering together, but experiencing it with a sense of hope. Because labor pain is not pointless pain. It is not empty pain. It is pain that represents the hard work of bringing forth new life. This labor pain is what the process feels like when God's new age of peace and justice is on the way.

Although this image of creation giving birth resonates universally, as I've been discussing, it also resonates in particular ways for those who, like Paul, consider themselves to be followers of the crucified one. Jesus's ministry led him to his own suffering on the cross, and he called on his followers to shoulder their own crosses (Mark 8:34). Paul expected suffering to be a part of life as a Jesus follower, and, indeed, this is what he encountered continuously according to his letters (see, for example, 2 Cor. 11:21b–29). He also warned his communities that they could expect to suffer as well, as a result of the countercultural shape of their life together as Jesus-following communities (see, for example, 1 Thess. 3:4). But what if all this suffering experienced by Paul, his coworkers, and his community members was not pointless suffering but rather a participation in the birth pangs of all creation, as it labors to bring forth new creation?[5] If this is the case, then Paul's ministry among the churches can be viewed as a participation in the labor of all creation. If Paul views all creation as being in labor, and he views his own ministry as a participation in that labor, then we may not be surprised to find Paul portraying himself as a woman in labor, as he does in Galatians 4:19, to which we will turn next.

Mother Paul

PAUL AS A WOMAN IN LABOR (GAL. 4:19-20)

In Galatians 4:19 Paul again uses a birth metaphor, but this time it is not enemies, nations, unbelievers, or even all creation that is in labor, but Paul himself. In this metaphor, Paul is pregnant with the Galatians and currently experiencing the process of labor. In his letter to the Galatians, Paul is distressed and angry about the fact that there are teachers among the Galatians arguing that gentile believers in Christ must be circumcised and keep other aspects of the Jewish law, such as food laws and Sabbath-keeping, to fully be members of the Christ-following community. Remember that Christianity emerged from within Judaism, and nearly all members of the church in the very earliest period were Jewish. As more gentile believers came in though the ministry of Paul and others, one of the earliest hot-button issues that the church dealt with was whether these new gentile converts needed to also convert to Judaism, or at least adopt some limited Jewish practices. After all, Jesus was Jewish and did not abandon the faith in which he was raised. Since this issue has been long settled for modern Christians, it is easy to forget how challenging an issue it would have been for early believers. For Jews, the Torah was their way of life and the way they showed their faith in and loyalty to God. Why should this change just because they now believed in Jesus as their Jewish Messiah? And why shouldn't gentile converts be invited to participate in this ancient way of life that they believed was God's will for humanity?

Nevertheless, Paul is insistent that not only should gentile believers not be forced to be circumcised and adopt other Torah practices, but they should not do so even if they wanted to. While Paul himself remained Jewish his entire life, he believed that Christ's death and resurrection had altered the role and relationship of Torah to the life of the people of God. Christ's death was the beginning of God's new age, which would be fully inaugurated with Christ's return in the near future. Though the Torah had served an important role in the old age, everything was now new and different because of what God did in Christ. Now, through faith, *all nations* were being brought into the blessing of God's promise to Abraham. They did not need to become Jews first. This was no ordinary religious conversion, but an invitation to come as they were to be part of God's people. In Paul's view, if you are in Christ, this makes you a descendant of Abraham; no circumcision required.

All this is to say that Paul viewed the issue of law observance being debated in Galatia not just as a personal choice or preference. Rather, Paul viewed the Galatian community as being in danger of falling away from the heart of the gospel message that he had preached to them. It is within the context of this argument that Paul uses the image of himself as a woman in labor. He writes, "My little children, for whom I am again in the pain of childbirth until Christ is formed in you, I wish I were present with you now and could change my tone, for I am perplexed about you" (Gal. 4:19–20). Paul uses the metaphor of birth to reflect on his founding of the community and the nature of this ongoing relationship with them. He originally gave birth to them back when he had first shared the gospel with them and established the Christian community. Now Paul feels that the situation in the Galatian church is so dire that it is like he has to give birth to them all over again.

This metaphor is complex in a couple of different ways. First, the image itself is complex. Paul is pregnant with the Galatians, but it is not that he is pregnant with them until they are formed in him and birthed through him—it is that he is pregnant with them until Christ is formed in them. So Paul is pregnant with the Galatians as they become pregnant with Christ! The second way that it is complex is that it is what Beverly Gaventa calls a "metaphor squared."[6] First of all, Paul has represented the founding of the community metaphorically as an act of giving birth. And then, to "square" the metaphor, the reader must further imagine that it is a man doing what only a woman can do in real life. Gaventa calls this "metaphorizing the metaphor."[7]

I will talk more about the significance of a first-century man presenting himself metaphorically as a woman later in the chapter. For now, I just want to connect this image to Paul's ministry and the apocalyptic nature of his thought. Paul views his ministry among the Galatians as maternal in nature, both in the sense that he "birthed" the community by founding it and in the sense that he has on ongoing role with the Galatians that is one of nurture, correction, and protection, which are all motherly roles. At the same time, we should recall here that in Romans Paul views all creation as experiencing labor pains as it anticipates and longs for God's new age. Is there a connection between those labor pains and the labor pains of Paul? Though Paul doesn't make the connection explicitly, it makes sense within Paul's theological thought world to imagine the hardships of gospel ministry as a participation in the birth pangs of all creation. Paul engaged in this labor with the Galatians so that Christ would be formed in them—that is, so that they might be conformed to the image of Christ, united with his death, having life through the Spirit, and living in hope of God's coming new age. This was Mother Paul's deepest wish for his children.

A BIRTH AND AN APOSTLE OUT OF SYNC (1 COR. 15:8)

A birth metaphor of a very different kind appears in 1 Corinthians 15:8. This is the only birth metaphor in Paul's letters that doesn't focus on the pain or process of labor, but rather on the circumstances or timing of a birth. In 1 Corinthians, Paul addresses a wide variety of theological and social issues that are plaguing the divided community of Christ followers in Corinth. One of the last major topics he addresses in the letter is the resurrection of the dead, which apparently was a matter of debate in the Corinthian community (see 1 Cor. 15:12–19). Paul wants to bolster their faith in Christ's resurrection and affirm the connection between Christ's resurrection and their own future resurrection from the dead. As part of his strategy to accomplish this, Paul rehearses what he had taught them about Christ's resurrection, including the stories that had been handed on to him about Christ's appearances to various apostles and followers after he was raised from the dead. Paul gives a list of people to whom Christ appeared in the order he appeared to them, beginning with Peter, called by his Aramaic nickname, Cephas (15:3–7).[8] At the end of this list, Paul writes, "Last of all, as to one untimely born, he appeared also to me" (1 Cor. 15:8). The Greek word that the NRSVue translates as "untimely born" is *ektrōma*. This word is difficult to translate into English because there is no single English word that corresponds to its meaning. It refers to a birth in which the baby exits the womb before the normal period of gestation is complete; this could be because of an abortion, a miscarriage, or preterm labor. Since we do not have a single term in English that can cover all three of those scenarios, the NRSVue translates it as "untimely born."

Ektrōma, however, always refers to a baby born or taken from the womb too soon, never to one born late, which makes it seem an odd image for Paul to choose, considering his point is that his apostleship came later than others. The word seems to express the opposite of what he is trying to say. But this may be a case where the image is meant to evoke an impression or feeling, and we should not press the details of the image too much. Paul here compares his apostleship to one born at the wrong time, as a way of showing himself to be an apostle whose apostleship began out of sync with all those who had seen Christ in the immediate aftermath of his resurrection. Paul's apostleship was out of sync with the others both because it began a bit later and because Paul was not already a follower of Jesus prior to the resurrection. This is why Paul calls attention to the fact that he had been a persecutor of the church, rather than a disciple of Jesus, prior to his experience of the risen Christ (15:9; see also Acts 8:1–3; 9:1–19).

Paul's use of this word might remind us once again how dangerous pregnancy and birth were in the ancient world, and how often things could go wrong. It may also be difficult to read for people who have experienced abortion, miscarriage, or premature labor. People sometimes have a sanitized view of the Bible and what it contains, but the messiness and pain of life are often on display in our Scriptures.

PAUL THE NURSING MOTHER (1 THESS. 2:5-8)

We will turn now from Paul's birth metaphors to his breastfeeding metaphors. The first of these is found in the second chapter of 1 Thessalonians.[9] This letter was written to a small community living in Macedonia that was young in faith. This little community of newly converted gentiles was struggling because of the local persecution they were experiencing and because some of the members of their community had died. Paul wrote to them to comfort them and to strengthen their faith. One of the ways that Paul felt he could strengthen their faith was to strengthen their connection to him as the one who had preached the gospel to them. So Paul does some relationship building in this letter. As part of this, Paul spends some time defending his own conduct and that of his coworkers when they were in Thessalonica founding the community. If Paul can show them that the good news of Christ had been preached to them in an upright manner, he hopes that this will renew their trust in the message itself, and they will be strengthened to endure the trials they are suffering and remain faithful to God.

It is with this aim in mind that Paul writes, "As you know and as God is our witness, we never came with words of flattery or with a pretext for greed, nor did we seek praise from mortals, whether from you or from others, though we might have made demands as apostles of Christ. But we were gentle among you, like a nurse tenderly caring for her own children. So deeply do we care for you that we are determined to share with you not only the gospel of God but also our own selves, because you have become very dear to us" (1 Thess 2:5–8). There are a few problems with this NRSVue translation. First, where the text reads "gentle," it is translating the Greek word *ēpioi*. However, the oldest and most reliable ancient Greek manuscripts of 1 Thessalonians that we have access to have a different Greek word in that spot—*nēpioi*. The difference between the two words in Greek is just one letter on the front, but *ēpioi* means "gentle" while *nēpioi* means "infants." Paul either originally wrote *ēpioi* and that was later changed by a scribe to *nēpioi*, or the other way around. For many centuries all manuscripts of the Bible were handwritten, and small changes like this were common, sometimes made accidentally and sometimes intentionally. A compelling case can be made that what Paul originally wrote was *nēpioi* ("infants"), not *ēpioi* ("gentle").[10]

The other problem with the NRSVue translation is that the way the text is punctuated does not fit well with the grammatical structures of the Greek text.[11] Ancient Greek manuscripts were not punctuated. Therefore, modern translators must decide how to punctuate the text. Punctuation is interpretation! Using the reading "infants" and punctuating the text in alignment with the Greek grammar results in this translation:

> For we never came with flattering words (just as you know), nor with a motive of greed (as God is witness), nor seeking honor from human beings, whether from you or from others (though we could have insisted on our own importance as apostles of Christ), but we were infants in your midst. Like a wet nurse tenderly caring for her own children, in the same way, longing for you, we were pleased to share with you not only the gospel of God, but also our very selves, because you had become beloved to us. (1 Thess 2:5–8, my translation)[12]

In this passage Paul first talks about what he and his coworkers were *not* like—they didn't use flattery, they were not greedy, and they didn't seek honor. All this Paul refutes with the infant metaphor, implying their innocence of all these potential charges. Next Paul expresses what he and his coworkers *were* like—they were like a wet nurse with her own children. That was the level of affection he felt for the community—he was willing to share himself with them as a breastfeeding mother does with her infant.

As I said above, Paul is doing some relationship building in this letter. The nursing mother metaphor is part of that strategy. With it, Paul paints a picture of tender intimacy between himself and the community. Today we associate breastfeeding not only with nourishment but also with comfort for the infant and bonding between the mother and child. The same was true in the ancient world.[13] Paul's readers would have understood the image as a tender, intimate, and comforting one. Paul seeks to comfort them in their current distress and also remind them of the ways he had nourished them with the gospel. And the nourishment was not just with an intellectual telling of the gospel message but came through Paul and his coworkers sharing "their very selves" with the Thessalonians, as a nursing mother feeds her infant from her own body. Paul and his coworkers were not cold and standoffish with the Thessalonians but gave themselves to the Thessalonians "without reservation."[14] This is part of Paul's strategy to strengthen their faith by "strengthening their connection to their faith's foundation," assuring them "that both the messengers and the message were upstanding and trustworthy."[15]

Paul doesn't use the word "mother" in this metaphor, but rather the word for "wet nurse." Wet nurses in ancient Roman times were enslaved or lower-class women who breastfed the infants of other women. This was a fairly common practice in the ancient world for a variety of reasons, including the lifestyle preferences of wealthy women, the need for lower-class women to return to work, and high maternal mortality rates.[16] The recognition that the woman in this metaphor is a wet nurse increases the intimacy and affection of the image even more, because of the words "her own" in verse 7. Wet nurses were often slaves and would not normally have any say over which babies they nourished. Even a free nurse would probably feel obligated to take whatever employment she could find to survive. But now, in this metaphor, a woman who usually breastfeeds the infants of other women has the opportunity to nourish *her own* children. That is the strength of affection Paul claims to have for the Thessalonians. It is an image that contains no sense of compulsion. With the wet nurse's own children is where her deepest joy and deepest loyalty lie. This image expresses that it is not a burden or obligation for Paul to care for the Thessalonians, but something he is pleased to do.

This book has noted several times already that suffering was associated with motherhood in the ancient world due to the dangers of childbirth for the mother and high infant and child mortality rates. Even in this intimate, tender, affectionate nursing mother image, a level of suffering is present. The metaphor expresses not just Paul's love and care for the Thessalonians but also his anguish about their situation and his worry for them. In this image, we might say that Paul is a nursing mother who is currently separated from her children. We can hear this especially in his use of the word "longing" in verse 8. Although in verse 8 Paul is primarily talking about the time when he was with the Thessalonians, we can easily imagine that that longing is only intensified now that Paul is no longer with them, and they are experiencing distress in his absence.

Yet even though Paul is away from them, he wants them to understand that they still have each other. They ought to be comforting one another and relying on one another. The metaphor plays into this idea as well, since, if Paul is the nursing mother to all of them, that makes them brothers and sisters to each other! If they begin to see one another as family, they can be strengthened to endure their current hardships, especially if they are being "disenfranchised from their families of origin" because of their faith.[17]

One final aspect of the nursing mother metaphor worth exploring is the way both intimacy and authority are present in it at the same time. We have already discussed the level of affection present in the metaphor and the fact that, in it, Paul associates himself with a lower-class female figure. And yet, this is not just an image of lowliness, because a nursing mother has authority over her children.[18] As I have previously written, "This metaphor plays on a delicate balance between intimacy and authority. On the one hand, Paul wishes to portray a sense of closeness with the community from which he is remote in physical distance but not in heart. On the other hand, Paul also seeks to maintain his position as the one who taught them the gospel, the one who still has much to teach them, and the one who can serve as a role model for them. With the image of a nursing mother, Paul can accomplish both of these goals at once."[19] The image presents Paul as a leader who teaches by example, cares for and loves those he teaches, is willing to endure suffering to benefit those in his care, and is not afraid to be associated with humility, weakness, and suffering. But it also reminds them that Paul is the one from whom they received the gospel; he is the source of their life together and the source of the message that gives them hope for the future. In that sense the metaphor does not compromise Paul's authority in the community but presents his authority as authoritative rather than authoritarian[20]—it is an authority that is trustworthy and affectionate and has their best interest at heart.

FEEDING WITH MILK (1 COR. 3:1-3)

While the Thessalonians were suffering and struggling with the persecution that resulted from the countercultural nature of their faith in Christ, it seems the Corinthians were enjoying life in their city to a much greater extent, not seeing a conflict between their faith and their culture, and priding themselves on being "spiritual" people who were full of wisdom and knowledge.[21] Paul is at pains in 1 Corinthians to remind the community that they are supposed to be focused on a life that is characterized by humility, weakness, and self-sacrifice, as modeled by the cross of Christ. Taking the way of the cross as your way of life was always countercultural in Paul's view. People living comfortable lives that were honorable by the world's standards could not possibly be living the way of the cross that Paul had taught them.

While the Corinthians considered themselves spiritually mature people, Paul says that they were in fact "infants in Christ," both when he had originally preached the gospel to them and at the time that he was writing the letter. Within this section, Paul uses a breastfeeding metaphor: "And so, brothers and sisters, I could not speak to you as spiritual people but rather as fleshly, as infants in Christ. I fed you with milk, not solid food, for you were not ready for solid food. Even now you are still not ready, for you are still fleshly. For as long as there is jealousy and quarreling among you, are you not fleshly and behaving according to human inclinations?" (1 Cor. 3:1-3). The Corinthians had heard and accepted the gospel of Christ, but they were failing to understand its implications. Because of this, they were thinking too highly of themselves and their own wisdom, and their community was also characterized by conflict and division. These divisions revealed that those who considered themselves to be spiritually mature were in fact spiritual infants.

Because they were like infants, Paul says that he had to feed them with milk rather than solid food. While we might think today of feeding an infant with a bottle, in the ancient context this is clearly a breastfeeding image, since that was the only common way to feed infants in the ancient world (hence the need for wet nurses when the mother was deceased or otherwise unavailable or unwilling to feed her infant). Paul was their nursing mother, nourishing them with the basics of the gospel since they weren't yet ready for the "meatier" subjects. "Paul as mother in 1 Corinthians is the one who knows better than her children what they need, and feeds them with the right kind of food for their maturity level."[22] The Corinthians probably did not particularly enjoy hearing this metaphor, since they considered themselves mature already. According to Paul, they had seriously misunderstood their own maturity level when it came to understanding the way of life Christ called them to.

I said in the previous section that while the 1 Thessalonians breastfeeding metaphor was mostly about comfort and affection, it also contained a level of authority. The authority implied by the breastfeeding metaphor in 1 Corinthians is more pointed. In this image Paul is a mother with the authority to decide what kind of food her children eat and when they eat it. She is the one with the authority to reprimand them and teach them the right way to behave. The difference between the gentle authority of the 1 Thessalonians image and the more direct authority of the 1 Corinthians image is one of context: "The Thessalonians were primarily in need of comfort; the Corinthians were primarily in need of correction."[23] A good mother knows that different children have different needs at different times, and which parental strategy to adopt depends on the context. It is significant for understanding Christian leadership and ministry that, according to Paul, "apostles are not only like farmers and builders (3:6–15) but are also like mothers giving milk to their children, then urging them on to solid food when the time is right."[24]

PRECEDENTS FOR PAUL'S MATERNAL LANGUAGE

The metaphors in this chapter in which Paul refers to himself as a mother are particularly striking. There are three of these—the breastfeeding images in 1 Thessalonians and 1 Corinthians and the birth image in Galatians 4. It was highly unusual for a man in the ancient world to employ such language for himself. Ancient male writers occasionally used mothers and nurses as examples in their writings, but almost never identified themselves as being like mothers or nurses. No doubt ancient male writers would not be keen to portray themselves in this way because it was considered shameful for men in ancient Greco-Roman culture to be too closely associated with women or to have attributes that were culturally associated with femaleness. For men, the maintenance of one's masculinity was important to one's honor, because women were considered physically and intellectually deficient in comparison to men.

Paul was unusual as a first-century man for applying female and maternal images to himself, but he was not entirely unique. There are a small number of examples of ancient men or male figures describing themselves with maternal language. For example, the Old Testament occasionally portrays God as giving birth. Many modern people are accustomed to thinking of God as "beyond gender," but in a world filled with the worship of a variety of gods and goddesses, the ancient Israelites would have conceived of their God Yahweh as a male deity. Yet this God, who is always referred to with masculine pronouns and almost always given masculine titles and depicted with culturally masculine attributes, is occasionally described as giving birth. Deuteronomy 32:18, Job 38:29, Isaiah 45:10–11, and Isaiah 46:3–4 depict God as giving birth to the people of Israel or to the world. This imagery is used in Isaiah 42:14 in a way that is particularly relevant to Paul's use of the birth metaphor for himself. This portion of the book of Isaiah is focused on God's promise to enact the return of the people from the Babylonian exile. The voice of God speaks in the text, saying that for a long time he had been quiet and inactive (i.e., he let the exile of the people occur without intervening), but now he will begin to act and bring them home. This action is depicted as God experiencing labor pain:

> For a long time I have held my peace;
> I have kept still and restrained myself;
> now I will cry out like a woman in labor;
> I will gasp and pant. (Isa. 42:14)

God had previously given birth to the people of Israel when they were founded as a people (Deut. 32:18 and Isa. 46:3–4); now it was time for him to bring them to birth again by bringing them home from exile and renewing their life in the land. This idea of giving birth to a community of people a second time might remind us strongly of Paul's image of being in the pain of childbirth again with the Galatians.

Another interesting passage that implies that God both gave birth to the people of Israel and nursed them is Numbers 11:11–12. The context for this passage is the time the Israelites spent in the wilderness after God had brought them out of Egypt. Both God and Moses become angry at the people when they complain about the hardships of their life in the wilderness and express their longing for the food of Egypt. Moses then says to God, "Why have you treated your servant so badly? Why have I not found favor in your sight, that you lay the burden of all this people on me? Did I conceive all this people?

Did I give birth to them, that you should say to me, 'Carry them in your bosom as a wet nurse carries a nursing child, to the land that you promised on oath to their ancestors'?" Here we have an interesting parallel to Paul's maternal metaphors because it is a passage in which a male leader (Moses) imagines himself as potentially the one who birthed and nursed the people. And yet, this is a role that Moses rejects. He is unwilling, at least at this point in the narrative, to be the mother of the people. In that sense this passage contrasts with the nursing image in 1 Thessalonians 2:7, in which Paul is "pleased" to be the nursing mother of the community. Moses's annoyance, though perhaps not his unwillingness, might remind us a bit more of Paul's nursing image in 1 Corinthians 3:2, in which Paul has to feed them with milk but thinks that they ought to be beyond the need for baby milk by now.

But Moses's rejection of the role of mother to the people strongly implies that someone else is their real mother. Numbers 11:12 contains two emphatic uses of the Hebrew word for "I," which we can show in English using italics: "Did *I* conceive all this people? Did *I* give birth to them?" Moses's insistence that *he* didn't give birth to the people strongly implies that God is the one who did. God is the one who conceived and gave birth to them, so now it ought to be God who carries and feeds them.[25] So we have again a case where a deity usually portrayed in masculine terms is pictured not only as giving birth, but also as the one who ought to breastfeed the people. Numbers 11:12 is not the only OT passage that refers to God breastfeeding. In Deuteronomy 32:13, God is depicted not just as the one who *ought* to breastfeed the people, but as the one who actually did breastfeed them.

While Moses rejects the role of nurse to the people, Paul is not the only man in the ancient world to embrace the role of nursing mother or wet nurse to a group of people. There is an interesting parallel to Paul's nursing metaphors in the Dead Sea Scrolls. The Hodayot, or Thanksgiving Scroll, is a book of hymns used by the community at Qumran, who were probably Essenes and lived near the Dead Sea from about 100 BCE to 68 CE. Some of these hymns, called the "Hymns of the Teacher," contain a striking first-person perspective as the leader of the group reflects on his position and relationship to the rest of the community.[26] In one of these Teacher Hymns we find these words addressed to God:

> You set me as a father to the sons of kindness
> and as a wet nurse to the men of portent.

> And they opened their mouths like a suckling babe [at the breast
> of its mother]
> and like a child taking delight in the bosom of its wet nurse.
>
> (1QHa XV 23b–25a)[27]

Here we have an example strikingly similar to Paul's nursing metaphors in 1 Thessalonians and 1 Corinthians. God gave the leader his position in the community, and the transmission of knowledge from the leader to the community is represented metaphorically by breastfeeding. In that it is related to the transmission of knowledge, the similarity to 1 Corinthians 3:2 is particularly striking, since there also the metaphor related primarily to the transmission of the gospel message from Paul to the Corinthians. However, the Hodayot passage is a very positive image, and in that way it is more similar to the image in 1 Thessalonians 2:7. In both the Hodayot passage and 1 Thessalonians, the leader is pleased to be the wet nurse of the community, whereas 1 Corinthians 3:2 implies that Paul has to be their nurse only because they have not yet reached the maturity level that they ought to have. "In 1 Thessalonians and Qumran, no shame is implied in being identified as an infant; in 1 Corinthians the community is exhorted to grow up."[28] The meanings and connotations that are implied by biblical breastfeeding metaphors depend greatly on the context in which they are used.[29]

WHY MATERNAL IMAGES?

The precedents for Paul's maternal metaphors described in the section above are the only few examples that can be found in all of ancient Jewish, Greek, and Roman literature. Therefore, although not entirely unique, Paul's metaphors can still be considered highly unusual. Such metaphors were rare because it was considered shameful for men to associate themselves with womanly attributes. Paul risked bringing shame on himself when he portrayed himself as being in labor or engaging in breastfeeding.[30] So if this is the case, why would Paul choose to use these metaphors? Paul does not tell us why, of course, but three reasons present themselves as plausible suggestions.

The first reason Paul may have chosen to use maternal images is simply how appropriate these images are for the message he was trying to convey. When Paul wanted to talk about end-of-time issues, what image could be better than birth for describing a painful experience that is nevertheless full of hope and leads to new life? When Paul wanted to talk about his authority in the communities but convince them that his authority was characterized by intimacy and affection, what better image than that of a nursing mother with her children? Paul may have employed maternal images simply because they conveyed his message better than anything else he could think of.

The second reason Paul may have chosen to use maternal images relates to the difference between how fathers and mothers were viewed in the ancient world. Fathers were associated with instruction and discipline while mothers were associated with nurture and comfort.[31] When Paul wanted to express instruction and discipline, he would have been more likely to choose a paternal metaphor (as he does in 1 Thess. 2:11–12), but when he wanted to express nurture and comfort, he would be more likely to choose a maternal metaphor. Mother and father metaphors were not interchangeable in his cultural context. Related to this, Margaret Aymer points out another reason Paul may have used maternal imagery more often than paternal: Fathers had legal power over their children, but mothers had to rely on influence and persuasion.[32] In that sense Paul's relationship to his communities was more like a maternal one than a paternal one—he had no legal authority over these communities but was continually trying to persuade them to listen to him and follow his advice.[33]

The third reason Paul may have chosen to use maternal images relates to the radical nature of his gospel message. It may be true that he risked being shamed because of these metaphors, but Paul did not shy away from shame. The message he preached turned the values of the world upside down by eschewing worldly power and domination and focusing on the weakness and suffering of the cross. This is what Paul means in 1 Corinthians 1:27 when he writes that "God chose what is foolish in the world to shame the wise; God chose what is weak in the world to shame the strong." When Paul kept his focus on the cross as the way of life that he was called to, it sometimes allowed him to break out of cultural norms in surprising ways, including by portraying himself as a laboring and nursing mother. And this shows us the promise of the gospel to break down gender barriers, even if this was not fully realized in Paul's own ministry or lifetime.[34] As Calvin Roetzel writes, Paul "becoming female in this metaphorical world was an act of denying both the self and the power constructions of the social world."[35]

CONCLUSION

Paul wrote about childbirth but never gave birth himself and likely never witnessed a birth directly. He used infant metaphors but likely was never involved in the day-to-day, hour-to-hour care of an infant. He wrote about nursing but certainly never breastfed a child himself. We've talked about some of the reasons Paul probably chose to use maternal imagery, but it is still striking to see a first-century male employ it. What do these metaphors say about Paul and about the gospel he preached?[36] Readers respond to Paul's maternal metaphors in a variety of ways. Some take a very positive view of them and of what they tell us about Paul's character—specifically that they show his humility and his rejection of social hierarchy. For example, Carolyn Osiek writes in response to Galatians 4:19, "Perhaps a man willing to use such an image is not as alienated from women's experience as Paul is often made out to be."[37] And Calvin Roetzel writes that Paul's maternal metaphors are his "renunciation of the superordinancy socially prescribed for males."[38] But other readers view the metaphors as a co-opting of women's experience—taking images from women's lives and using them to increase his own dominating power in the communities. For example, Margaret Aymer writes that Paul's breastfeeding metaphor in 1 Corinthians 3:2, far from being an egalitarian image, "suggests the dependency of the entire assembly on Mother-Mammy Paul for its existence and sustenance."[39] Aymer also writes in relation to all of Paul's maternal metaphors that Paul "is playing on two recognized themes: the virtuous mother and the gentle but persuasive mammy/nurse. But he retains the right to be mother and to define motherhood; not every mother counts in Paul's family."[40]

While I myself take a more positive view of Paul and the metaphors than Aymer does, her critiques are important. The metaphors discussed in this chapter are not just sweet little decorations of Paul's letters. He uses these metaphors to say important things about his view of the cosmos, his role as an apostle, and the nature of his relationship to his communities. In my view, these metaphors do not show us that Paul is either egalitarian or authoritarian. Rather, they show a man who viewed himself as having a position of authority, but one he tried to exercise in the community's best interest. In all things, Paul's model was the cross. "The cross is power, but it is power expressed through weakness, through humility, and through love."[41] When looked at through the lens of the cross, the maternal metaphors are also examples of power expressed through weakness, humility, and love. Paul chooses not to use the more powerful figure of the father in the ancient family associating himself instead with mothers and even with slave nurses, using the metaphors to express his deep care and concern for his communities. Aymer is right to point out that the metaphors enhance rather than diminish Paul's authority in the communities. Nevertheless, these metaphors remain striking examples of the gospel message empowering a first-century man to break down the cultural and hierarchical stereotypes of his day. To witness that may inspire us to do the same.

DISCUSSION QUESTIONS

1. What are the similarities and differences between the ways that birth imagery is employed in 1 Thess. 5:2–3, Rom. 8:18–25, and Gal. 4:19–20?
2. How does the nursing mother metaphor in 1 Thess. 2:7 serve the purposes Paul is trying to accomplish in the letter?
3. What do the birth and breastfeeding metaphors in the section "Precedents for Paul's Maternal Language" contribute to our understanding of Paul's use of this type of metaphor?
4. What does a study of Paul's maternal metaphors contribute to our understanding of the gospel message Paul was trying to communicate to the churches?
5. What do you think Paul's maternal metaphors show us about his character in relation to his communities? As described in the chapter's conclusion, do you agree more with Osiek's and Roetzel's evaluation of Paul's character, or with Aymer's evaluation?

11

SAVED THROUGH CHILDBEARING?

Mothers in the Later Pauline Letters

The previous two chapters considered mothers and motherhood in the letters that most scholars agree Paul himself wrote. In this chapter, we will turn to the letters that many scholars think Paul did not write but rather were written in his name after his death—Colossians, Ephesians, and the Pastoral Epistles (1 and 2 Timothy and Titus).[1] Authorship questions complicate our interpretations of these letters because uncertainty about authorship also means uncertainty about when they were written. If we do not know when they were written, we do not know the historical context in which their content should be understood. If we think Paul wrote the passages that we will be analyzing in this chapter, we might understand and interpret them differently than if we think they were written by someone else at a later time. This is why the question of authorship matters. It doesn't matter for the canonical status of these passages, but it does matter for knowing how to interpret them well.

The disputed epistles have a lot to say about women in general, but in this chapter we will stay focused on motherhood. I'll begin this chapter with a discussion of authorship issues to explain why I will be reading these letters as coming from a late first-century context rather than Paul's lifetime. Then we will put the disputed epistles in historical context to help us interpret them well. Finally, the chapter will explore the passages relevant to motherhood in these letters.

Saved Through Childbearing?

AUTHORSHIP OF THE DISPUTED LETTERS

It is important for modern readers to understand that if Paul did not write the disputed letters (or did not write some subset of them), this does not make them invalid or deceitful. We have to take into account the fact that writing practices were different in the ancient world than they are today. The ancient world had no copyright laws and no sense of intellectual property. Authorship was often a more communal endeavor than it is today, with people revising and building on earlier works without specifically giving credit to previous authors. We see this in the Synoptic Gospels, where Matthew and Luke incorporate Mark and other sources into their work without including citations. The Gospel of John is also thought to have been composed of sources and to have been revised by multiple hands over time, without credit being given to individual authors along the way.

For understanding the letters of the New Testament, even more important is the fact that pseudonymity was regularly practiced in the ancient world. By "pseudonymity" we simply mean one person writing in the name of another person. Typically, an unidentified author would write in the name of a famous person from the recent or distant past. This was done for a variety of reasons, including to honor the legacy of the revered figure from the past, to show that the present writing is in line with the ideas of the revered figure, to extend the ideas of the revered figure to comment on the issues of a new generation, and to gain an audience for one's writing. We have numerous examples of both Jewish and Greco-Roman pseudonymous writings from the ancient world contemporaneous to the New Testament. This includes the Jewish Pseudepigrapha—numerous Jewish writings written within a couple of centuries before to a couple of centuries after the New Testament, which bear the names of Enoch, Noah, Moses, Ezra, and others. But it is quite clear that these writings come from a time much later than those figures would have lived. Similarly, during the first three centuries of the Christian church, many writings appeared bearing the names of Paul, Peter, James, John, and other famous early church leaders. Many of these are clear examples of pseudonymity, including those usually categorized as "Gnostic Gospels." There is no question that early Christians produced pseudonymous writings. The question is, are any of the *New Testament* books pseudonymous? This point is debated by scholars, but most biblical scholars think that at least some of the writings bearing the name of Paul in the New Testament were written later by people who considered themselves the inheritors of Paul's legacy.

Scholars consider a variety of criteria when making the argument that Paul either did or did not write one of the disputed letters. One group of criteria relates to language: scholars see significant differences between the undisputed and disputed epistles in terms of vocabulary, writing style, and use of grammatical constructions. Related to this, the disputed letters seem to have a less intimate, less personal tone when compared to the undisputed epistles. They also seem to be more general in the issues they address, compared to the very specific issues and details dealt with in the undisputed letters. Finally, some scholars feel the disputed letters are dealing with theological and social issues of a later time, after Paul's life was over.

The debate about the authorship of Paul's letters is ongoing within biblical scholarship. It is beyond the scope of this book to go over detailed arguments. Interested readers can consult introductory New Testament textbooks or individual commentaries on the disputed letters to learn more.[2] The truth is there is no way we can know with certainty whether Paul wrote the disputed epistles. However, as I see it, the evidence is weighted more toward the disputed letters being pseudonymous. It does seem that the disputed epistles present us with a different perspective and a different historical setting than we saw in the undisputed letters of Paul. In addition to significant differences in writing style from Paul's undisputed letters, these letters have numerous other characteristics that are quite different: They reflect a higher level of church organization than we would expect in Paul's lifetime, they do not seem to expect that Jesus will return soon, they are not concerned with the relationship between Jews and gentiles in the church, they are concerned with the social respectability of the church, and they describe the role of women in the church very differently. Therefore, I will interpret the disputed epistles in this chapter as pseudonymous letters written after Paul's lifetime. I assume that the authors of these letters considered themselves to be inheritors of Paul's legacy and wanted to update some of Paul's ideas for new circumstances.

READING THE DISPUTED EPISTLES IN THEIR SOCIAL AND HISTORICAL CONTEXT

It is hard to overemphasize the importance of reading texts in context. That includes their historical context. An author's view of their subject matter will be influenced by the time and place they live—their culture and the particular events that are occurring in their world. For interpreting what the New Testament authors say about women, it is crucial to understand both their broader cultural context and the particular issues and problems that they may have been responding to when they wrote. This includes the view of women that was prevalent in Greco-Roman society at the time these letters were written.

Greco-Roman philosophers, physicians, and social commentators considered women to be inferior to men physically, intellectually, and emotionally. Gender stereotypes are rampant in these writings, which portray men as naturally strong, assertive, dominant, and intelligent, and women as naturally weak, passive, dependent, and gullible. It was considered shameful for either group to behave in ways that went against these stereotypes (e.g., for a man to behave passively or for a woman to behave assertively). Households typically had a man as the head of household, and he was supposed to govern his household with unquestioned authority over his wife, children, and, if he owned them, slaves. Households were viewed as the building blocks of society, so instability in the household was viewed as dangerous for society. Proper hierarchies were believed to ensure the stability of the household and therefore the stability of society. Because it was a patriarchal society, the honor of men was tied to the chastity of the women of their household, and so women were encouraged to dress modestly, talk to men they were not related to as little as possible, and refrain from participation in male-dominated discourse in public marketplaces and assembly halls.

Some early Christians were countercultural when it came to these Greco-Roman gender norms. Paul, for example, believed that the cross had upended social hierarchies: "There is no longer Jew or Greek; there is no longer slave or free; there is no longer male and female, for all of you are one in Christ Jesus" (Gal. 3:28). Rather than masculine traits like strength, assertiveness, and competitiveness, Paul urged his communities to embrace a way of life modeled on the cross—one that was characterized by humility, service, and self-sacrifice. Also, as we saw in chapter 10, Paul portrayed himself as metaphorically female in 1 Thessalonians 2:7, 1 Corinthians 3:2, and Galatians 4:19, even though for a man to associate himself with women or femininity would be considered shameful. Paul also promoted celibacy for women (1 Cor. 7:7–8, 25–40), which could potentially allow them to live outside of traditional household authority structures, and he advocated mutuality for those who did get married (1 Cor. 7:3–4). He honored women as his coworkers in the gospel (Phil. 4:2–3; Rom. 16:3–5a) and did not object to them speaking aloud to the gathered community during worship services (1 Cor. 11:5). Presumably, Paul was not the only early Christian who held these views.

There is evidence that this unconventional thinking related to gender was part of what was causing the persecution that the early church was experiencing. Outsiders would not have thought of these unusual views of mutuality in the household and in religious gatherings as a harmless difference of opinion. Rather, outsiders would have thought of these ideas as threatening the stability of the household and therefore as being a danger to the safety and security of society. Thus, the behavior of women in Christian groups was a particular focus of Greco-Roman critics of Christianity. Several ancient authors criticized Christianity for being particularly associated with women and expressed the view that the foolishness and gullibility of women tainted the whole Christian movement.[3]

As a result of this, the behavior of women also became a focus for some Christian leaders in the later parts of the first century and into the second century. Since Jesus had not returned as soon as expected, Christian leaders now had to think about the future of the church and how it was going to survive within Greco-Roman society. So that the church could survive to the next generation and continue to grow, they wanted to keep it from being discredited in the eyes of the world. The author of 1 Timothy states this as the goal behind the advice given in the letter: "that we may lead a quiet and peaceable life in all godliness and dignity" (1 Tim. 2:2). First Timothy and the other disputed epistles encourage behaviors and practices that would allow the church to live peaceably in society moving forward. This draws attention to the behavior of Christian women and how it is viewed by outsiders. The behavior of women was one of the things that was preventing the church from having a "quiet and peaceable" life. The authors of the disputed epistles want women to behave in more traditional ways so that the church can survive in the society in which it is embedded. With that in mind, we will turn now to the texts that are relevant to motherhood in the disputed epistles.

THE HOUSEHOLD CODES IN COLOSSIANS AND EPHESIANS

Greco-Roman writers were fond of talking about household relationships and the hierarchies that they felt should govern those relationships for the sake of the stability of society. In that sense, the household codes that we find in

Colossians 3:18–4:1 and Ephesians 5:21–6:9 are not unusual or surprising. In line with many non-Christian writings of their time, the biblical household codes call on wives, children, and slaves to be obedient to their husbands, fathers, and masters. But the Colossians and Ephesians codes do give these common household expectations a theological basis. The authors seem to be asserting that these hierarchical expectations are no longer just cultural norms but are now also proper Christian behavior. For example, Colossians 3:18 reads, "Wives, be subject to your husbands, *as is fitting in the Lord*" (emphasis mine). Nevertheless, the directives of the household codes are clearly heavily influenced by the norms of Greco-Roman culture, and so the reader should not assume that these directives ought to apply universally to all times and places.

The Colossians and Ephesians household codes are androcentric. All household members are described in relation to the father of the family. There is no description of the relationship between the women and slaves of the household or between the children and slaves, and very little discussion of the relationship between women and their children. The picture of the household that the codes paint centers on the father. Though children are told to obey their parents (Col. 3:20 and Eph. 6:1; *goneusin* in Greek), it is only fathers who are told how to behave in relation to their children (Col. 2:21 and Eph. 6:4; *pateres* in Greek). The only other place motherhood is mentioned in the codes is Ephesians 6:2–3, which quotes the Ten Commandments in calling on children to honor their fathers and mothers (see Exod. 20:12 and Deut. 5:16). Children are supposed to obey their mothers, but no more is said about the role of mothers or the relationship of mothers to their children. Thus, motherhood is largely eclipsed in the codes in favor of a focus on husbands and fathers.

MOTHERS IN THE PASTORAL EPISTLES

The epistles 1 and 2 Timothy and Titus are known as the Pastoral Epistles. These three letters are usually studied together because of significant similarities in their language and content. They are called the Pastoral Epistles because they are addressed to individual church leaders rather than to communities, and they give advice related to how those leaders should guide and govern the churches. These three letters mention women and their behavior with some regularity, but motherhood is not frequently a focus. It is sometimes mentioned incidentally, such as when the author of Titus instructs older women to encourage younger women to be self-controlled and submissive, and to love their husbands and love their children (Titus 2:3–5). Two passages in the Pastoral Epistles merit particular attention in relation to mothers and motherhood: 1 Timothy 2:8–15, and 1 Timothy 5:3–16.

Salvation through Childbearing

First Timothy 2:8–15 is among the most challenging passages in the whole Bible for those interested in women's leadership and participation in the church. It is also relevant to the topic of this book because it discusses an Old Testament mother (Eve) and ends with a direct reference to motherhood. The passage begins, "Therefore, I want the men to pray in every place, lifting up devout hands without wrath and dispute" (2:8).[4] Whenever a passage starts with a word like "therefore," it is a good idea to check what comes before it! The section that comes right before this passage is the one I referenced above that names the main goal of the advice given in 1 Timothy: that prayers should be made for all "so that we may lead a quiet and peaceable life in all godliness and dignity" (2:2). And further, this should be the goal because it is right in God's eyes, because God "desires everyone to be saved and to come to the knowledge of the truth" (2:4). These are the twin goals of 1 Timothy: a peaceful life for the church and the effectiveness of its mission (that all come to a knowledge of the truth). Indeed, these two goals are directly related. The church needs a peaceful life in society *so that* it can have an effective mission. If the church is viewed as completely unacceptable to society, very few people will listen to its message. If there is constant and unending persecution, mission will be less effective. These twin goals, then, govern all the advice in the letter, including the words about women we are about to read. That's important for us to keep in mind for good interpretation: the quietness and obedience of women that the letter encourages is so that the church can lead a peaceful life with an effective outreach within its cultural context. Those who do not live in the ancient Greco-Roman world should ask whether following this advice today would still serve this goal. Does the silencing and subservience of women in Christian communities still lead to a peaceful life and an effective outreach today?

The passage continues, "Likewise, I want women to adorn themselves in appropriate attire, with modesty and moderation, not with braided hair and gold jewelry or pearls or expensive clothing, but, as is fitting for women who profess godliness, through good works. Let a woman learn in quietness, with complete submission. I do not permit a woman to teach or give orders to a man, but she should be quiet" (2:9–12). After being encouraged to dress modestly, women are instructed in behavior in the church community in relation to learning and to the church's leadership. Women should learn the content of the Christian faith quietly, submitting to male authority and not becoming teachers themselves. This advice is in line with expectations for women in the Greco-Roman world. However, as the passage continues, this advice is given a theological justification rather than just a cultural one.

The author supports his instructions with reference to Scripture, in particular the story of Adam and Eve: "For Adam was formed first, then Eve. And Adam was not deceived, but the woman, having been thoroughly deceived, had come into transgression" (2:13–14). The word "for" links these sentences directly to what came before. The reason women are not permitted to teach and should remain quiet is both because Adam was created first and because Eve was the one who was deceived and transgressed. These words send the reader back to Genesis 2–3. One could argue with 1 Timothy's author about his interpretation of the Genesis story. For example, nothing in Genesis 2–3 indicates that Eve is inferior to Adam because she was created later. She is created to be his partner and is celebrated by Adam as "at last . . . bone of my bones and flesh of my flesh" (2:23). Additionally, Genesis 3:6 says that Adam was "with" Eve when she ate the fruit and that he ate of it alongside her. Nowhere else in the Hebrew Bible or New Testament does it indicate that Eve was the only one or the primary one who transgressed. In fact, in Romans 5:12 Paul writes that "sin came into the world through one man" (Adam). Frances Taylor Gench calls 1 Timothy 2:8–15 a "highly selective reading of Genesis."[5] But 1 Timothy uses the story of Adam and Eve to call particular attention to Eve's deception by the serpent and seems to claim that this means all women of all times are more easily deceived than men, and therefore should not be teachers.

The passage concludes with a verse that is very difficult to understand and interpret: "But she will be saved through the bearing of children, if they remain in faith and love and holiness, with moderation" (2:15). Does "she" refer only to Eve, or to all women? What is meant by "saved" in this context? Why do the pronouns change from "she" to "they"? To whom does "they" refer—the women? The women and their husbands? The children born to the women? What can it mean that she/they are saved through the bearing of children? Interpreters have long wrestled with the meaning of this verse and have proposed different solutions to its various conundrums. We will consider three of these proposed interpretations.[6]

The first interpretation we'll consider is perhaps the most straightforward—that women are untrustworthy due to inheriting the sin of Eve and her easily deceived nature, but they can be saved (i.e., forgiven, redeemed) by becoming good wives and mothers. This reading may be the most straightforward reading of the grammar of the verse, but it is theologically problematic. This is a letter in the Pauline tradition—what happened to faith being what saves us? Gench understands the passage according to this first interpretation and is troubled by it. She writes that the passage "is unique in the New Testament in suggesting that salvation for women is different from that of men, requiring adherence to domestic, maternal roles."[7] This interpretation of the text leaves us asking a very significant question—do women have to be mothers to be saved? This idea obviously stands in tension with our modern sensibilities, but it also stands in tension with much of the rest of the Bible, which nowhere else makes motherhood a requirement for salvation.

A second interpretation that has been proposed is that the text should be translated "she will be saved through childbirth," and that the childbirth that is referenced is the birth of Jesus. In other words, Mary's action of giving birth to Jesus has redeemed Eve's act of disobedience. This interpretation is much less troubling theologically, but does it fit with the grammar, content, and context of the verse? Dorothy Lee proposes a translation to illustrate this interpretation: "But she [Eve] will be saved through the Child-bearing, if they [Christian women] abide in faith and love and holiness with wisdom."[8] I would argue that a translation that requires multiple instances of explanatory brackets and unusual capitalization to make its meaning clear may be reading into the text more than what is really there. Certainly, if the author of 1 Timothy had wanted to refer to Mary's bearing of Jesus, he could have done so much more explicitly. Why be so enigmatic?

A third interpretation to consider is to rethink what is meant by "saved" and combine that with knowledge of the historical context. Westfall takes this approach, arguing that the text means that women will be kept safe (that is, not die) in childbirth if they are faithful to God.[9] Artemis was the goddess whom Greco-Roman women typically prayed to for safety in childbirth. According to this line of argument, the author of 1 Timothy was trying to get women to trust in the one true God rather than in Artemis when it came time for them to give birth. This understanding of "saved" is in line with the use of the word elsewhere in the Bible. Modern readers tend to read the word "saved" as referring to our destination in the afterlife, but often in the Bible the word refers to much more earthly types of rescue, deliverance, or healing. Though it is entirely possible that we should understand "saved" in this more earthly way in this passage, this interpretation is problematic in other ways. First, it is theologically problematic. Women did not stop dying in childbirth in the ancient world once they started to trust in the God of Israel instead of Artemis, and it would be a false promise for the author of 1 Timothy to say that they would. It is also problematic because it implies that, if a woman dies in childbirth, she must have failed at having enough faith. In addition to being theologically problematic, I find this interpretation unlikely literarily as well, since the problem of women dying in childbirth is never mentioned in the passage. Up to this point, the passage has been about women's clothing and whether they can be teachers with authority over men. If the author wanted to talk about women dying in childbirth, he could have explained that a lot more clearly. Again, why be so enigmatic?

All three of these interpretive possibilities are problematic in some way. I don't think we can be certain what the author meant by this verse or how his first readers would have understood it. However, the interpretation I find most likely is closest to the first interpretation above, but with a less individualistic flavor. Western Christians are accustomed to thinking of biblical texts very individualistically. If there is mention of women and salvation, we tend to assume that the text is talking about how an individual woman is saved, in terms of her eternal destiny. But I'm not convinced that is what this text is about. I think the author is talking about women as a group, not as individuals. I doubt that the author would say that an individual woman has to be a mother to be saved, but I do think he might believe that, generally speaking, motherhood is womankind's salvation. Womanhood, tainted by association with Eve, can be redeemed through a focus on the domestic roles of wife and mother, practiced in quietness and obedience. This is the way that women can reverse what, in the author's mind, Eve started.

Mothers in the Later Pauline Letters

Widowed Mothers and Church Ministry

In 1 Timothy 5 we find this passage:

> Do not speak harshly to an older man, but speak to him as to a father, to younger men as brothers, to older women as mothers, to younger women as sisters—with absolute purity. Honor widows who are really widows. If a widow has children or grandchildren, they should first learn their religious duty to their own family and make some repayment to their parents, for this is pleasing in God's sight. The real widow, left alone, has set her hope on God and continues in supplications and prayers night and day, but the widow who lives for pleasure is dead even while she lives. Give these commands as well, so that they may be above reproach. And whoever does not provide for relatives, and especially for family members, has denied the faith and is worse than an unbeliever. (1 Tim. 5:1–8)

At the start of this passage we see a theme we have already encountered elsewhere in the New Testament—that church members are to relate to one another as family. In that way church members should regard all the older women of the congregation as their mothers. The text goes on to talk about widows. We see from clues in this text that the early church was supporting widows who had no means to support themselves. However, it seems this was placing a burden on the church, and the author of this letter wants to make sure that widowed mothers are being cared for by their adult children when possible, rather than relying on the church's charity. The author wants church support to be saved for widows who truly have no one else to care for them.

But this seemingly straightforward text about the church's support for destitute widows becomes more complicated as the passage continues: "Let a widow be put on the list if she is not less than sixty years old and has been married only once; she must be well attested for her good works, as one who has brought up children, shown hospitality, washed the saints' feet, helped the afflicted, and devoted herself to doing good in every way" (1 Tim. 5:9–10). This does not sound like a list of qualifications for receiving charity; it sounds like the qualifications for church leaders described in 1 Timothy 3. If this passage is really about supporting widows in a charitable sense, can it be that the church will only support a widow if she is well attested for good works, is a mother, has shown hospitality, and has served the poor? Would a widow who has not done all of those things be left to starve? That's why many interpreters think this passage is not just about charity but also about a kind of ministry that some widows were engaged in. The idea here is that ministry was not just something done for widows in the early church, but also something done by them. There are some references in early church writings to a group of people called "the widows," so there is some support for the idea of an order of widows in the early church. These women may have lived together and engaged in various kinds of ministry, prayer, and service. This "order of widows" may have been open to celibate women who were not widows as well, as indicated by a greeting in a letter from Ignatius of Antioch to "the virgins who are called widows" (*Epistle to the Smyrnaeans* 13 [Ehrman, LCL]). Young unmarried women (virgins) and widows may have banded together to devote themselves to ministry and service, free to do so because they were free from household duties. After all, the freedom to spend time serving the Lord was one of Paul's reasons for advocating celibacy (1 Cor. 7:32–35). It seems that some women of the early church had taken up this calling as described by Paul.

The idea of women being free of husbands and household duties, and therefore relatively free of constraints, is exactly what worries the author of 1 Timothy about this group of widows. He wants to restrict this group of women to those over sixty years old who have no family to support them and therefore need the church's charity. He goes on to describe his reasons for prohibiting younger widows from being part of this group:

> But refuse to put younger widows on the list, for when their sensual desires alienate them from Christ, they want to marry, and so they incur condemnation for having violated their first pledge. Besides that, they learn to be idle, gadding about from house to house, and they are not merely idle but also gossips and busybodies, saying what they should not say. So I would have younger widows marry, bear children, and manage their households, so as to give the adversary no occasion to revile us. For some have already turned away to follow Satan. If any believing woman has relatives who are widows, let her assist them; let the church not be burdened, so that it can assist those who are real widows. (1 Tim. 5:11–16)

The author's first problem with young widows choosing to live this life of celibate ministry is that he believes they will change their minds about the celibacy part due to sexual desire. His second problem with young widows choosing this life is that, without household duties, they will simply have too much time on their hands, which he believes they will fill with idleness and gossip. He describes the women going from house to house—likely something they did as part of their ministry of service and possibly as a way of spreading the gospel. But the author views it as the activity of idle busybodies.

The author of 1 Timothy is worried that this kind of behavior is going to bring trouble upon the church from outsiders. Therefore, he encourages the younger widows to remarry, have children, and spend their time on their household duties (5:14). Note that this advice, that it is best for widows to remarry, is the opposite of the advice that Paul gave in 1 Corinthians 7:8, which says that it is best for widows to remain unmarried. Notice also the words "so as to give the adversary no occasion to revile us" in 5:14. "The adversary" is probably a reference to Satan, but if Satan wants to attack the church, he is likely to do so though hostile outsiders. So we see here the Pastoral Epistles' concern for the church's reputation. The author of 1 Timothy is worried that the behavior of unsupervised women is going to bring disgrace on the church. Therefore, he wants them to remarry and be reincorporated into the authority structures of the household. Motherhood, in this case, is a way to rein these women in—to keep them busy with maternal duties and bring them back under the authority of a husband. Motherhood, in this case, serves as a form of social control.

"Real" Mothers in Action

The previous sections considered what the Pastoral Epistles have to say about women and mothers in general. But there are also a few specific women named in the Pastoral Epistles. This includes two women who are explicitly identified as mothers. Second Timothy 1:5, addressing Timothy, says, "I am reminded of your sincere faith, a faith that lived first in your grandmother Lois and your mother Eunice and now, I am sure, lives in you."[10] Here in the midst of the Pastoral Epistles, which can be so restrictive of women's lives and behavior and ministry, we have an acknowledgment that Timothy has the faith he has because of his mother and grandmother. These women were the ones who shaped and guided him in his faith life, leading him to dedicate his life to the ministry of the church. Of course, as Ross Kraemer writes, it may be that the author praises Lois and Eunice because they are the kind of women he approves of—devout, quiet women who educate their children at home but do not make any kind of splash in public.[11] Nevertheless, their mention in the text is a reminder of the power of motherhood to the shape the next generation, even in circumstances that are quite restrictive. The author of 2 Timothy may have wanted to restrict women from teaching the faith to men, but it was Lois and Eunice who did the most to shape the faith of the church leader named as the recipient of this letter.

CONCLUSION

The most helpful light in which to understand the disputed epistles is as representing a transition in the life of the church from movement to organization. What had been a loosely structured movement has to become an organization in order to survive and move forward into the future. Additionally, the church is facing increasing hostility from the surrounding culture and the threat of local persecution, and the behavior of women in the church is one of the things driving that hostility. The authors of these letters want the church to find a place to fit in society and to have to the respect of society so that it can survive and have an effective mission. Therefore, they promote behavior for women that is consistent with the traditional gender roles of Greco-Roman society. In interpretation of these texts, we must consider that our context is very different from the context in which these guidelines were originally given. Additionally, as we read the Pastoral Epistles, we can remember Lois and Eunice and the many other named and unnamed women who are commended in the New Testament for their ministries. No matter how we interpret the disputed epistles' words about women, we know that women, including mothers, were active participants in the life of the early church.

DISCUSSION QUESTIONS

1. Do you think the words about women in the disputed epistles could have been written by Paul? Why or why not?
2. What difference does it make for interpretation to understand something about the Greco-Roman context of these letters?

3. What do you think the author of 1 Timothy means by "she will be saved through childbearing"?
4. Why do you think 1 Cor. 7:8 encourages widows to remain unmarried but 1 Tim. 5:14 encourages them to marry? Why the difference?
5. Considering the similarities and differences between your own culture and ancient Greco-Roman society, in what way do you think the passages explored in this chapter apply to churches and families today?

12

FOREMOTHERS AND SPIRITUAL MILK

Mothers and Motherhood in Hebrews and the General Epistles

If mentions of mothers are few and far between in Paul's letters, they are mentioned even less in the rest of the letters of the New Testament (the books of Hebrews through Jude). In fact, women in general, whether mothers or not, are infrequently mentioned in this portion of the New Testament. Nevertheless, these letters do make use of maternal metaphors, including birth imagery, breastfeeding imagery, and the idea of the church as mother. In this chapter we will consider these images and then explore the parts of the letters in which Old Testament mothers are mentioned. As we'll see, mothers and motherhood, even if infrequently mentioned, become important themes used by the authors of these letters to define the identity of those who belong to Christ.

GOD GIVING BIRTH

Birth imagery, found in James, 1 Peter, and 1 John, functions as a creator of community in the later letters of the New Testament. Images of birth are images of connection, implying a relationship between the mother and the child and also between children born to the same mother. When the metaphor is used in these three letters, God is the one giving birth (rather than a human leader like Paul). Therefore, these images create a sense of identity for the people as children of God and siblings to one another.

Mothers and Motherhood in Hebrews and the General Epistles

The book of James is an example of wisdom literature, focusing on teaching a way of life rather than teaching beliefs about God or Jesus. Though Jesus is not frequently mentioned in the book (only in 1:1 and 2:1), nevertheless the author focuses on teachings that will create a community of Jesus followers in the midst of Greco-Roman society that focuses on faith in God, good works, just treatment of the poor, patience in suffering, and the power of prayer. James describes this community in 1:18 as being birthed by God: "In fulfillment of his own purpose he gave birth to us by the word of truth, so that we would become a kind of first fruits of his creatures." This birth is in sharp contrast to the birth described a few verses earlier, in which desire conceives sin, "and sin, when it is fully grown, gives birth to death" (1:15). According to James, when temptations and desires are allowed to control our actions, then sin is our mother and death the result. But when God is our mother, then we are characterized by faithfulness, compassion, and wisdom. The metaphor is an identity-creating one: to recognize that God is your mother is to find your place among your siblings in this justice-oriented community of Jesus followers.

The letter of 1 Peter identifies its author as the apostle Peter, but the letter is thought by some scholars to be pseudonymous. No matter who the author was, the letter was written to give encouragement to small communities of suffering Christians living in Asia Minor sometime during the first century, calling them to live holy lives in the midst of hardship. In an image very similar to that found in James 1:18, this community, the author says, was birthed by God: "By his great mercy he has given us a new birth into a living hope through the resurrection of Jesus Christ from the dead and into an inheritance that is imperishable, undefiled, and unfading, kept in heaven for you, who are being protected by the power of God through faith for a salvation ready to be revealed in the last time" (1:3b–5). Through birth, children are connected to the identity and status of their parents, and so by being born of God, the community receives an inheritance—an imperishable one that will be revealed at the end of time. This is an inheritance of hope. The community is currently suffering, but, as children of the God who gave birth to them, they can endure, knowing that their future is secure and their suffering will end. Eugene Boring also connects this imagery of rebirth to the idea of chosenness in the letter. Being born of God means the creation of the community was a result of God's initiative and choice; those who are born do not make the decision to be born.[1] This connects to the language a little later in the letter in which the community

Foremothers and Spiritual Milk

is identified as "a chosen people, a royal priesthood, a holy nation, God's own people" (2:9). So, in addition to their future being secure, in the present their identity is not in doubt. They are God's chosen, beloved people. This is what it means to be born of God.

The letters 1–3 John focus on God's love, the identity of Jesus, and church conflict. 1 John 4:7 contains an image of birth: "Beloved, let us love one another because love is from God; everyone who loves is born of God and knows God." This idea of the community being born of God is similar to James 1:18 and 1 Peter 1:3, discussed above, though different in emphasis. Once again the metaphor is identity-creating, but whereas James focuses on a community of justice and wisdom, and 1 Peter focuses on hope in suffering, 1 John focuses on love. The following verse states that "God is love" (4:8). Therefore, those who are born of God should also be characterized by love. This is both the love that community members have for God and the love that they have for one another (4:7, 11, 21). For this author, to be a child of God is to be like God, and love is God's primary characteristic. Therefore, the language of birth establishes the community as a community of love.

BREASTFEEDING IMAGERY

When we looked at breastfeeding imagery in Paul's letters (chapter 10) we saw that the metaphor could be used in both a positive and a negative sense. When Paul identified himself as the nursing mother of the Thessalonians, it was an intimate image of caring and connection (1 Thess. 2:7). But when he used the metaphor with the Corinthians, it was a reprimand—he was still needing to give them milk when they ought to have been ready for solid food (1 Cor. 3:2). Similarly, in the later letters of the New Testament, we find a negative use of the metaphor in Hebrews 5:12 and a positive use of it in 1 Peter 2:2.

Hebrews is the source of many famous images and ideas, including Jesus as our high priest, believers as pilgrims, and the great cloud of witnesses. After expounding on the idea of Jesus as the great high priest in 4:14–5:10, the author focuses on his audience and writes, "About this we have much to say that is hard to explain, since you have become sluggish in hearing. For though by this time you ought to be teachers, you need someone to teach you again the basic elements of the oracles of God. You need milk, not solid food, for everyone who lives on milk, being still an infant, is unskilled in the word of righteousness.

But solid food is for the mature, for those whose faculties have been trained by practice to distinguish good from evil" (Heb. 5:11–14). This is very similar to 1 Corinthians 3:2. In both passages the author reprimands the audience for their lack of maturity, still needing mother's milk when they ought to be mature enough for solid food. There are differences of emphasis between the two passages, however. In 1 Corinthians, Paul is focused on behaviors and how the community members were treating each other: their divisions and quarrels were a sign of their immaturity and a sign that they were still in the early stages of learning to live according to the gospel. In Hebrews, the message seems to be more knowledge-focused than behavior-focused. The author cannot explain the idea of Christ as the high priest with the level of depth he wishes because the community is stuck at a basic level of knowledge and understanding of the Christian message. Nevertheless, knowledge and behavior are never entirely divorced from one another in Christian practice—the author of Hebrews identifies maturity as the ability to distinguish good from evil, something that surely has implications for community life and behavior (5:14).

A very different breastfeeding image occurs in 1 Peter 2:2. In contrast to both Hebrews 5:12 and 1 Corinthians 3:2, here milk is viewed positively, as something that the community should long for: "Like newborn infants, long for the pure, spiritual milk, so that by it you may grow into salvation—if indeed you have tasted that the Lord is good" (2:2–3). In addition to the milk being viewed positively, another difference with this version of the metaphor is who is doing the breastfeeding. In Hebrews and 1 Corinthians it is a human leader who is pictured in the role of nursing mother. In 1 Corinthians 3:2 Paul is explicit about this: "I fed you with milk." In Hebrews it is not spelled out in that fashion, but it is implied that it is the author or other human leaders who are having to breastfeed the letter's recipients: "You need someone to teach you . . . you need milk" (5:12). By contrast, in the 1 Peter metaphor the author does not claim to be the one feeding the community with milk, and there is no mention of human teachers directly connected to the metaphor or in the surrounding context. Rather, the milk they receive will help them grow into salvation, and what they will taste when they drink it is that "the Lord is good." This would seem to imply that the milk is the gospel message, or the word of the Lord, which would imply that the Lord is the one nourishing them with it. When a woman breastfeeds an infant, she is feeding the infant from what her own body produces. Therefore, if the community tastes the goodness of the Lord when they receive the spiritual milk, this implies that the Lord is their nursing mother.

The word "Lord" here could be understood as a reference to God, especially since "you have tasted that the Lord is good" is a paraphrase of Psalm 34:8. In the Psalm, the word "Lord" refers to Yahweh, the God of Israel. However, in the New Testament this word "Lord" typically refers to Jesus, and so that is likely to be the case in 1 Peter. The idea that the Lord referred to is Christ is strengthened by the fact that the very next verse says, "Come to him, a living stone, though rejected by mortals yet chosen and precious in God's sight" (2:4). To receive the milk that will help them grow into salvation, the community members should come to Christ, the living stone rejected by humans but chosen and precious to God. In this way we could understand 1 Peter as encouraging its readers to nurse at the breast of Christ.

As breastfeeding metaphors often are, this is an identity-shaping image. If the community views itself as nursing at the breast of Christ, then they are intimately connected both to Christ and to each other. A struggling and suffering community can be consoled and strengthened by such an image—they do not belong to the forces of empire, but to Christ—Christ cares for them and nourishes them with his own body. Furthermore, the image is a hopeful one, especially when combined with the image of the living stone that immediately follows it. The stone was "rejected by mortals yet chosen and precious in God's sight" (2:4). Therefore, since they themselves are currently suffering rejection from the society around them, they might dare to hope that, if they are rejected like Christ was, they are also "chosen and precious in God's sight," as Christ is. Things may look bleak for them based on the world's viewpoint, but there is a deeper reality at play for them. Though others cannot see it, they are in fact "a chosen people, a royal priesthood, a holy nation, God's own people" (2:9). They are the people nursed at the breast of Christ.

THE CHURCH AS MOTHER

While the metaphor of "the church as our mother" became commonly used in Christianity, especially in Roman Catholicism, this metaphor does not appear in a full-fledged form in the New Testament. There are places it is hinted at, such as when the church is referred to as the bride of Christ (2 Cor. 11:2 and Eph. 5:22–23). Presumably, if the church is the bride of Christ, she could be understood by extension as the mother of believers, even if these passages do not explicitly say so. New Jerusalem, a concept that is often closely associated with the church or the community of believers, is also pictured in the New Testament as the bride of Christ and as our mother (Gal. 4:26 and Rev. 21:2).

The closest the New Testament comes to the full-fledged metaphor of the church as our mother may be 2 John 1. Here the opening salutation states that the letter is from someone named "the elder," and it is being written to "the elect lady and her children." It is possible that "the elect lady" refers to a specific first-century woman who was a member of the church community being written to, but most scholars consider it much more likely that this is metaphorical language, with the church community being addressed as a lady (in which case her children would be the individual members of the community). There are a couple of reasons this is most likely the case. First, the second-person pronouns and verbs in the original Greek text are singular from verse 1 through verse 5, then they switch to plural for verses 6–13, before returning to singular for the closing of the letter in verse 13. This makes it seem likely that the author began the letter with the metaphor of the church as a singular lady, then dropped the metaphor in the middle of the letter, switching to address the community in the plural, and then finally returned to the metaphor and its singular grammar in the final verse. The second reason the elect lady is probably metaphorical is the content of that final verse: "The children of your elect sister send you their greetings." While it is theoretically possible the author is sending a real woman greetings from her real nieces and nephews, it seems to me that this is a clear case of the author referring to the church he is writing from as the sister of the church he is writing to. Different churches in different places are described as related to each other through a sister relationship, and furthermore referred to as the mothers of their respective members.

This is still not a full-fledged version of the later church-as-mother metaphor, because the later metaphor often refers to the universal church as the mother of all the faithful, whereas the metaphor in 2 John refers only to individual church communities as different mothers. Nevertheless, we can see this church-as-mother metaphor beginning to develop here in 2 John. As with the other metaphors we have discussed in this chapter, the introduction of maternal language here strengthens the identity of the community. If the church is their mother, then church members derive their identity from her, and are also siblings to each other. If they view the church as their mother, they will be defined by the values of Christ, not the values of the world, and if they view one another as siblings, they will keep Jesus's commandment to "love one another" (John 13:34–35; 15:12, 17; 1 John 3:11, 23; 4:7, 11, 12; 2 John 5).

One final consideration related to this passage is the word used for this metaphorical woman in the original Greek. The word "lady" used in the NRSVue (and nearly all other English translations) is not translating the Greek word for "woman" (*gynē*) but the word *kyria*, which is the feminine version of *kyrios*. *Kyrios* is usually translated "lord" and is commonly used in the New Testament to refer to Jesus. This explains the ubiquitous translation "lady" in English, because "lady" is the traditional counterpart to "lord" in English. In Greek it is even easier to see the connection between this lady and the Lord because they are *kyria* and *kyrios*. In one sense, this endows the church with some authority—this is not a lower-class woman, but a high born lady. *Kyria* would have been the term used to refer to the lady of a large, wealthy household, in charge of the running of the household, including directing the slaves. In that sense we could also say that the church here is "mistress" of the community of faith. On the other hand, though the language of *kyria* endows the woman with some authority, she is still subordinated to the *kyrios*. And it may be that the "elder" who writes the letter claims the authority to speak on behalf of the *kyrios* and give instruction to the *kyria*. Thus, as Gail O'Day points out, language like this could be "the beginning of patriarchal structures of governance in which the elder becomes 'lord' over lady church."[2] It is important to remember that just because female images are used, it does not mean that real women were endowed with authority. As the church grew and developed beyond the New Testament period, the metaphor of the church as mother would also develop more fully, but this church that was referred to as mother would also largely shut women out of official positions of leadership for millennia to come. Patriarchal systems can easily adopt feminine imagery and metaphors for their own purposes.

OLD TESTAMENT MOTHERS IN HEBREWS AND THE GENERAL EPISTLES

In addition to the metaphorical uses of motherhood discussed above, the section of the canon from Hebrews to Jude also contains mentions of a few Old Testament mothers. As we'll see, Sarah and Rahab are most prominent, being mentioned more than once and the only ones mentioned by name.

The Foremothers of Hebrews 11

Hebrews 11 is probably one of the best-known passages in this section of the New Testament. The chapter begins with a definition of faith: "Now faith is the assurance of things hoped for, the conviction of things not seen" (11:1). Then it proceeds to a litany of remembrance that celebrates the ancient heroes of faith, with the repeated words "by faith": "By faith Abel offered . . . by faith Abraham obeyed . . ." (11:4, 8). Numerous Old Testament figures are mentioned, and their ability to do what they did in the old stories is attributed to their faith in God. The vast majority of faith heroes mentioned in this chapter are men. But four women or groups of women do make the list, all of whom are mothers.

Sarah

Sarah is mentioned in 11:11–12, a passage that is notoriously difficult to translate, due to variant readings in the manuscripts and ambiguous grammar. Consider the differences between these three English translations of 11:11, all of which come from the same translation tradition:

> By faith Sarah herself received power to conceive, even when she was past the age, since she considered him faithful who had promised. (RSV)

> By faith he received power of procreation, even though he was too old—and Sarah herself was barren—because he considered him faithful who had promised. (NRSV)

> By faith, with Sarah's involvement, he received power of procreation, even though he was too old, because he considered him faithful who had promised. (NRSVue)

Notice how in the oldest translation, it is Sarah who has faith, but in the other two, it is Abraham who has faith, though Sarah is involved. Unfortunately for those who would like to see a woman's faith highlighted, it does seem that something along the lines of the NRSV or NRSVue is more likely to be the original textual reading and the better interpretation of the verse's grammar. It is also more consistent with the story in Genesis, which portrays Abraham as having faith that God's promise would be fulfilled (Gen. 15:6), but does not portray Sarah as having faith.[3] She first takes matters into her own hands by giving her slave Hagar to Abraham to produce an heir for him (Gen. 16:1–6), and then later laughs in seeming unbelief when the divine or angelic visitors say that she will conceive a son (Gen. 18:9–15). Nevertheless, though neither Genesis nor Hebrews points directly to Sarah's faith, it cannot be denied that Sarah was involved in the fulfillment of God's promise to Abraham! It was her body that bore the promised son, Isaac. Genesis may say that Abraham believed and Sarah laughed, but Abraham also was skeptical and laughed at one point (Gen. 17:17–18), and Sarah celebrated Isaac's birth with a different kind of laughter altogether and an acknowledgment that it was God who had done this for her (Gen. 21:6–7). Perhaps we can celebrate Sarah for her faith after all.

Moses's Biological and Adoptive Mothers

Hebrews 11:23–28 highlights Moses for his faith, making mention of both mothers in his life. Verse 23 says, "By faith Moses was hidden by his parents for three months after his birth, because they saw that the child was beautiful, and they were not afraid of the king's edict." When we look back at Exodus 2:1–4, we see that Exodus attributes these actions only to Moses's mother, not his father. Though not named in Hebrews 11 or Exodus 2, she is identified as Jochebed in Exodus 6:20. Though the pharaoh had ordered that all male infants of the Hebrews be killed, Exodus 2:2–4 says that Jochebed hid the infant Moses for three months, and then when she felt she could hide him no longer she put him in a basket among the reeds at the edge of the river, and his sister Miriam kept an eye on him there. According to Hebrews it was "by faith" that Jochebed did these things. Like the midwives in Exodus 1, Jochebed defied Pharaoh's orders in favor of faithfulness to God. She also used the courage her motherhood gave her to find a way to save her son's life.

After Moses is left in the basket, another mother enters his life: Pharaoh's daughter comes down to the river to bathe and finds the baby. She immediately realizes he must be a Hebrew. Surely she is aware that her father has ordered the death of all male Hebrew infants, but nevertheless she has compassion for Moses and readily agrees to Miriam's clever offer to go find a Hebrew woman to nurse him. Thus it is that Jochebed gets to nurse and care for her son Moses during his early childhood. After that she brings him to Pharaoh's daughter, who becomes his mother (Exod. 2:5–10). Hebrews 11:24–25 mentions Pharaoh's daughter, but only to highlight Moses's rejection of her: "By faith Moses, when he was grown up, refused to be called a son of Pharaoh's daughter, choosing rather to share ill-treatment with the people of God than to enjoy the fleeting pleasures of sin." Exodus does not explicitly mention Moses's rejection of Pharaoh's daughter as his mother, but it does show him choosing to identify with the suffering of the Hebrews rather than with the Egyptians (Exod. 2:11–15).

Though Hebrews mentions Pharaoh's daughter only in a negative light, as rejected by Moses, surely as his adoptive mother she bears some responsibility for the kind of man he grew up to be. We see something of her character in Exodus 2 when she saves Moses's life and adopts him as her son, despite that this meant going against her father's orders regarding Hebrew infants. How could being raised by a woman such as this have no effect on who Moses came to be? Both Moses and his adoptive mother are people who put their own safety and security on the line to come to the aid of those who are vulnerable and suffering. All of this is not to deny the influence also of Moses's biological mother Jochebed. We may imagine that she also influences the development of his character, since she is able to nurse and nurture him when he is young. Perhaps it is the kindness and courage of Jochebed that Moses remembers as an adult when he chooses to identify with the suffering Hebrew people rather than the household of Pharaoh. As mothers, both Jochebed and Pharaoh's daughter are powerful influences on Moses's life.

Rahab

Hebrews 11:31 highlights the faith of Rahab, the prostitute in Jericho who hides the Israelite spies (Josh. 2:1–24). She not only keeps the spies safe but also professes faith in the God of Israel (Josh. 2:11). As a reward she and her family are spared when Jericho is defeated, and they become part of the people of Israel (Josh. 6:22–25). Although neither Joshua nor Hebrews identifies Rahab as a mother, as discussed in chapter 2 of this book, Matthew's genealogy identifies her as the mother of Boaz and the great-great-grandmother of David. Although the story in Joshua does not mention her motherhood, it does portray her as a strong woman whose brave actions are responsible for saving her entire family. And, according to Hebrews, it was "by faith" that she was able to do this.

Women Who Received Their Dead by Resurrection

Hebrews 11 mentions one more set of mothers—the women who "received their dead by resurrection" (11:35a). The verse does not identify which stories this refers to, but interpreters commonly identify 1 Kings 17:8–24 and 2 Kings 4:8–37 as the only Old Testament stories that fit this description. 1 Kings 17:8–24 tells the story of Elijah raising the son of the widow of Zarephath, and 2 Kings 4:8–37 tells the story of Elisha raising the son of the Shunammite woman. In both stories the prophet brings the boy back to life through prayer and by lying on top of the body (1 Kings 17:19–22; 2 Kings 4:32–35). Also in both stories, the mothers express faith in God, which is what the author of Hebrews would most want us to notice. The widow of Zarephath shows faith by serving Elijah before herself and her son with the little bit of food she has left (1 Kings 17:13–16) and by saying to Elijah after her son is raised, "Now I know that you are a man of God and that the word of the LORD in your mouth is truth" (1 Kings 17:24). The Shunammite woman shows faith by believing that Elisha is a man of God who can raise her son—she goes to him as soon as her son has died and refuses to leave until he comes with her (2 Kings 4:9, 22, 30). Although these stories are given only the briefest possible mention by the author of Hebrews, when we dig deeper we see in them themes related to motherhood that we have encountered before: the suffering that was associated with motherhood in the ancient world, and the willingness of mothers to go to great lengths to get help for their children.

The Hidden Mothers of Hebrews 11

The four passages mentioned above are the only places Hebrews 11 explicitly mentions women. However, there are many other places in the chapter where we can bring to light the hidden presence of women in general and mothers in particular. Verse 7 mentions that Noah saved his household with the ark—this household would include the woman who was his wife and the mother of his children (Gen. 7:6–7). Verse 9 mentions that Isaac and Jacob lived in tents while waiting for the promise of a land of their own—we might remember that Rebecca, Rachel, Leah, Zilpah, and Bilhah did, too (Gen. 29–30). Verse 21 mentions Jacob's blessing of the sons of Joseph—we might note that those sons also had a mother, an Egyptian woman named Asenath (Gen. 41:45, 50).

Verse 29 mentions the people passing through the Red Sea on dry land—how many mothers were in that multitude (Exod. 14:22)?

Toward the end of the litany of faith heroes, the author of Hebrews writes in 11:32, "And what more should I say? For time would fail me to tell of Gideon, Barak, Samson, Jephthah, of David and Samuel and the prophets." He reminds his readers that there are so many men of faith who have come before us that there is not time to talk of them all in detail. But what of the other women of faith that he has also not had time to mention? How many other mothers might we remember that we could learn faith lessons from? Would time fail us to tell of Hagar, a woman who gave God a name and whom God saved and provided for (Gen. 16:1–16; 21:8–21)? What about Tamar, whose unconventional but righteous actions move the story of God's people to the next generation (Gen. 38:1–30)? Then there is Zipporah, the mother of Moses's children (Exod. 2:21–22), who saves her family with some quick thinking in a very strange story in Exodus 4:18–26. The author of Hebrews mentions Barak, but what about Deborah, the one in that story with the most wisdom, faith, and courage (Judg. 4)? Judges 5:7 says the people prospered because Deborah "arose as a mother in Israel." Then we might remember the faithful Ruth, loyal to her mother-in-law and her mother-in-law's God (Ruth 1:16). And what about Hannah, who by faith received the son she requested from the Lord (1 Sam. 1:1–2:11)? All these mothers and many other women are also part of the "great cloud of witnesses" surrounding us (Heb. 12:1).

Other Mentions of Sarah and Rahab

Sarah and Rahab are the only two women mentioned by name in Hebrews 11. Interestingly, they are also the only two women mentioned by name elsewhere in the section of the canon from Hebrews through Jude. Sarah is mentioned in 1 Peter 3:6, and Rahab is mentioned in James 2:25. These two women seem to have captured the imaginations of early Christian writers in ways that other Old Testament women did not.[4]

Sarah is mentioned in 1 Peter 3:6 as the one named example of the "holy women" of old who hoped in God and were submissive to their husbands. This is part of a household code in which Christian women are encouraged to let purity and respect define their behavior, so that, if they are married to unbelievers, their unbelieving husbands might be "won over" to the Christian way by their wives' "gentle and quiet spirit" (3:1–4). There is much we could say about the context of 1 Peter and why the author might feel compelled to give wives this advice. But here I just want to focus on the use of Sarah for this purpose. According to the author, "Sarah obeyed Abraham and called him lord" (3:6a). One might ask if this is a revisionist history, considering all we know of Sarah's character. "Gentle and quiet" might not be the first words that come to mind to describe her, much less "submissive." As Cynthia Briggs Kittredge writes, "The Old Testament narratives portray Sarah as a complex figure, resourceful, jealous, and harsh, and twice God tells Abraham to obey her."[5] Though there may be some tension between how 1 Peter portrays Sarah and how Genesis portrays her, the second half of 1 Peter 3:6 reveals the author's purposes in portraying Sarah this way: "You have become her daughters as long as you do what is good and never let fears alarm you." The main purpose is not to discuss Sarah's character in Genesis but to present her as a model for the way the author wants women in the first-century community to behave. We have already seen in this chapter how the author of 1 Peter used maternal images to shape the identity of the community, using birth imagery in 1:3 and breastfeeding imagery in 2:2. Here we have another maternal metaphor—if the women of the community behave in the way the author describes, then they will have Sarah as their mother, and they will derive their identity from her rather than from the norms of the Greco-Roman culture surrounding them.

Finally, Rahab is also mentioned in James 2:25. In this section of the letter James has been arguing that "faith by itself, if it has no works, is dead" (2:17). He is arguing against the idea that belief in God is all that is needed for salvation, and it doesn't matter what a person does. What he argues against may have been a distortion of Paul's theology surrounding faith and works.[6] To support his argument that both belief and actions matter, James cites two examples from the Old Testament. First, he mentions Abraham, whom he says was justified by his works when he was willing to sacrifice his son Isaac to God (Gen. 22:1–19). And second, he mentions Rahab: "Likewise, was not Rahab the prostitute also justified by works when she welcomed the messengers and sent them out by another road?" (James 2:25). It is interesting that James, when he only cites two examples of faith and action from the whole of the Old Testament, chooses to reference Abraham and Rahab. Abraham we expect, since he is the founding patriarch of the Israelite people. But why Rahab? It is hard to say for sure, but it may be that she was a key figure for several New Testament writers because she was originally a foreigner and would have worshiped Canaanite gods, but then she embraced the God of Israel and became part of the nation of Israel. New Testament authors may have felt that this made her a fitting example for gentiles who had turned from the worship of Greco-Roman deities and embraced the worship of the God of Israel by becoming Christians.

CONCLUSION

Identity issues swirl around the mothers and maternal imagery in this section of the New Testament. One thing all the authors in this part of the New Testament have in common is that they are trying to get their readers to view their identity as grounded first and foremost in Christ and the Christian community. The small, beleaguered, persecuted churches of the late first century need encouragement and strength. If they don't receive it, they may be in danger of falling away from the faith. The authors of the New Testament believe that these church communities will receive the strength they need by banding together with one another and by identifying with Christ. A big part of a person's identity is derived from the identity of their mother. To have been born of God means that one is part of God's family and inherits the values of God rather than the values of Greco-Roman society. To nurse at the breast of Christ is to be nourished and sustained by the gospel. It also means that one is intimately connected to Christ and to all the other people who nurse at this breast. To have Sarah as your mother is to know who you are, even if you struggle because of the ways you are trying to live differently from your neighbors. To identify with Rahab is to be secure in the knowledge that, no matter what happens, you are forever part of God's family, just as Rahab and her descendants became part of Israel perpetually (Josh. 6:25). Old Testament mothers and metaphorical uses of motherhood were invaluable resources for New Testament authors to use as part of their identity-shaping message.

DISCUSSION QUESTIONS

1. This part of the canon contains multiple references to being "born of God" or God giving birth to us, yet readers often fail to make the connection that if we are born of God, then God is our mother. What difference does it make

theologically and spiritually to not just talk about being "born of God" but to speak of God as Mother?
2. The chapter argued that birth and breastfeeding images in the later letters of the New Testament have an identity-shaping purpose. Could such images be effective ones for shaping the identity of Christians today as well?
3. How much influence do you think each of Moses's mothers had on the man he grew up to be?
4. Which Old Testament mothers would you include if you were going to create a list of faith heroes modeled on Hebrews 11? What would you say about their faith?
5. Why do you think that Sarah and Rahab in particular (more than other Old Testament women) were important to the authors of this part of the New Testament canon?

13

A DRAGON IN THE DELIVERY ROOM

Mothers and Motherhood in Revelation

Revelation has always been a challenging and mysterious book. There were debates in the early church about whether it should be included in the canon of the New Testament.[1] In the fourth century the great church scholar Jerome said of Revelation that "it has as many mysteries as words." He did not mean to insult the book but rather exult in the many meanings that "lie hidden in its every word" (Letter LIII.9 [Fremantle]). Revelation can be off-putting to the casual reader with its confusing symbolism and violent imagery, but it rewards diligent study by opening up an imaginative world of apocalypse and promise.[2] In Revelation, someone named John[3] sees visions in which God responds to the suffering of creation and the oppressed people within it by transforming creation (in the end) into a place of peace and justice.[4] In saying this, I do not mean to deny that many parts of Revelation are violent and disturbing. Revelation presents modern readers with many challenges. Nowhere is this more true than when it comes to the ways in which women are portrayed in the book. Revelation has long been critiqued by feminist interpreters for portraying female figures in stereotypical ways and even glorifying violence against women.[5] In this chapter we will explore the passages in the book that feature women and female figures, with special focus on motherhood. As with other aspects of the book, we'll find that, when it comes to women and motherhood, Revelation presents us with many promises and many challenges.

A Dragon in the Delivery Room

READING AND INTERPRETING REVELATION

The average church-going Bible reader is probably most familiar with a "futuristic" approach to reading Revelation. This approach interprets the book as a description of the future end of the world and is usually concerned with looking for people, places, and events in the modern world that might correlate to passages in Revelation. When these are identified, it is believed to be a sign that "the end is near." Most biblical scholars do not read the book in this way, but rather engage in a "historical" approach to Revelation. This approach does not seek to identify the signs and symbols of Revelation with things in the modern world; rather, it seeks to understand the content of Revelation in its original, historical context—to uncover what the signs and symbols of Revelation would have been likely to mean to its original readers. When the book is read in this way, it quickly becomes clear that many of the symbols of Revelation relate to the Roman Empire. The author of Revelation views the Roman Empire as evil because it promotes the worship of false gods, persecutes God's people, and oppresses the poor. The book of Revelation envisions an end to the Roman Empire and all other empires of any kind that usurp God's place and oppress and persecute God's people.

REVELATION AND THE VIRGIN-WHORE DICHOTOMY

The virgin-whore dichotomy is a term that is used to refer to the ways that patriarchal cultures pigeonhole women and their sexuality into one of two categories: pure virgins admired for their chastity and obedience, or shameless whores indulging in illicit activity. Patriarchal culture doesn't allow for the richness of portraying women in their full humanity but defines them only in relation to men and places them in one of these two categories based on how well their behavior conforms to patriarchal norms and expectations. Although the term is usually called the *virgin*-whore dichotomy, the "virgin" category can be extended to include chaste married women who engage in sexual activity only with their husbands and primarily for the purposes of procreation and pleasing their husbands rather than for their own gratification. In extreme forms of patriarchy, to be a mother is the only acceptable way to be nonvirginal without being put in the whore category. For this reason, it is interesting to note that the three symbolic female figures in Revelation are a virgin, a whore, and a mother. This is not a coincidence. These three ideas of what women can be are deeply embedded in the ancient patriarchal culture out of which Revelation arises.[6]

THE MOTHER (THE WOMAN CLOTHED WITH THE SUN)

The book of Revelation begins with an introduction and an initial vision of Christ (chapter 1), followed by letters to seven churches in Asia Minor (chapters 2–3), and a vision of the throne room of God (chapter 4). Following this, the seven seals of a scroll are opened, and seven trumpets are blown (chapters 5–11). The opening of the seals and the blowing of the trumpets in heaven results in all kinds of calamities on earth, such as violence, famine, and disease. After this, John sees a vision of a woman in the heavens who is "clothed with the sun, with the moon under her feet, and on her head a crown of twelve stars" (12:1). Of all the figures in the book of Revelation, this woman is one of the most mysterious. She is usually identified either as the Virgin Mary or as representing Israel or the church. The author of Revelation does not identify her for us, so we are left to make educated guesses based on the clues in her story.

The woman is pregnant, and when we meet her, she is in labor, crying out in pain. As she experiences her birth pangs, the narrator draws our attention to another figure that has appeared—"a great red dragon, with seven heads and ten horns and seven diadems on his heads" (12:3). In Revelation, the dragon represents Satan (he is identified explicitly as such in 12:9). The dragon sweeps a third of the stars of heaven down to earth with its tail and then stands in front of the woman in labor, waiting to devour her child as soon as it is born. In a scene terrifying to imagine, the woman gives birth to a son as the dragon waits nearby, poised to strike. The child born is the one "who is to rule all the nations with a scepter of iron," a reference to Psalm 2:8–9 and usually interpreted as a reference to the Messiah (12:5). Though threatened by the dragon upon his birth, the baby is immediately "snatched away" by (and to) God, leaving the woman to flee alone into the wilderness, where God has prepared a place for her to be nourished. While she is there, the angel Michael leads an angelic army in battle against the dragon and his angels. Michael is victorious, and the dragon and his angels are thrown down to earth. This is good news for those in the heavens but bad news for those on earth because Satan is now among them (12:12).

When the dragon finds himself thrown down to earth he begins to pursue the woman who had given birth. She is given wings like an eagle's so that she can fly from the dragon to her place of nourishment in the wilderness. But the dragon does not relent, seeking to sweep the woman away with a flood of water coming from his mouth. This time, the earth itself comes to the woman's aid, opening its mouth to swallow the river of water before it reaches her. Frustrated, the dragon finally stops pursuing the woman, and instead heads off to make war on the woman's other children, whom the text identifies as "those who keep the commandments of God and hold the testimony of Jesus" (12:17). This is the end of the woman's story.

One of the biggest interpretive questions related to this story is the woman's identity or what she represents. The first thing to note is that her "celestial garb" and her location in the heavens associate her with various ancient goddesses who could each be called the "queen of heaven."[7] The woman's story has particular resonances with the Greek myth in which the goddess Leto gives birth to Apollo and Artemis. Hera, jealous that Leto is pregnant by Zeus, sends the great serpent Python to pursue Leto and keep her from giving birth. Leto eventually finds a safe place and gives birth. Although twins are born, the myth focuses particularly on Apollo, because he will be the one to pursue and slay Python in revenge for the trouble caused to his mother. In both Revelation and the Leto myth, a pregnant or laboring mother is in danger from a serpentine monster, and the son who is born will grow up to be the one responsible for the monster's destruction. Although the Revelation story does not describe this as directly as the Leto myth, the dragon is said to be defeated "by the blood of the lamb" (12:11), so if we interpret the son who is born to the woman as Jesus, then it is by this son that the dragon will be defeated. In yet another connection between the two stories, in the Leto myth the monster Python is the child of Gaia, the personification of the earth. The personified earth also plays a role in Revelation 12, when it opens its mouth to swallow the river of water that the dragon sends to sweep the woman away.

In addition to the Leto myth, the Woman Clothed with the Sun is also similar to other ancient goddesses, perhaps most notably Isis, who is described in Egyptian mythology as the queen of heaven, and who had to flee while pregnant with her son Horus to protect him from being killed by her brother Set. These resonances with the stories of Leto, Isis, and other ancient mythologies are unmistakable and can hardly be coincidental. And yet, of course,

Revelation is not a book of Greco-Roman or Egyptian mythology. And so, while the author clearly draws on mythological imagery to create this figure, we can assume that he does not intend for the reader to think that the Woman Clothed with the Sun *is* Leto or Isis. So, if she is not Leto or Isis, who is she? Since she gives birth to a son with messianic associations, it has been common for readers to identify her with the Virgin Mary, especially in Roman Catholic interpretation. Protestant interpreters, hesitant to accord Mary the status of queen of heaven, have more often interpreted the woman as an entirely symbolic figure, representing either Israel or the church. The woman's crown of twelve stars may associate her with Israel and its twelve tribes, and the idea that she gives birth to the Messiah also strengthens this connection with Israel, since the Messiah is Israel's. Other interpreters see her as the church, because she is said to be the mother not just of the one infant born in the story, but also of all those on Earth who keep God's commands and "hold the testimony of Jesus." In other words, she is portrayed as the mother of all Christians.

Mary, Israel, and the church each fit some aspects of the woman's story but not others. It may be that we are not actually meant to figure out the one person or entity that the woman represents, but rather to explore the multiple associations her story evokes. The most important question may not be who the woman is, but rather what effect her story is meant to have on its readers. The original audience for the book of Revelation was Christians living in Asia Minor in the late first century experiencing hardships and persecutions as they sought to live out their faith as a small, powerless group of people in one corner of a vast, powerful empire. These readers would likely have understood themselves to be the rest of the woman's children (12:17), who were now being attacked by the dragon. This identification would help them explain their current distressing circumstances and give them hope—though the dragon was currently attacking them, his days were numbered. He had already been defeated in heaven and would one day soon be defeated on the earth.[8] Their role, then, was to persevere and continue their brave testimony about Jesus. Mitchell Reddish suggests that this message for Revelation's first-century readers is also helpful for Christian readers today who may "need to be reminded that in spite of how dominant and pervasive evil may appear, evil carries with it a mortal wound."[9]

No matter which person, group, or nation we associate the woman with, one of the most central things about her is that she is a mother. When I read her story through the lens of motherhood, a dramatic story becomes even

A Dragon in the Delivery Room

more dramatic. Imagine the terror of giving birth while a dragon waits to devour the child. The experience of labor and delivery is painful and nerve-racking enough without the addition of a murderous, serpentine creature threatening to strike as soon as the child emerges from the womb! Looking at the story through the lens of motherhood also heightens the sadness of the story. Though the woman is saved from the dragon, she is also separated from her son as soon as he is born, and the text never describes a reunion between the two. The story ends with her in the wilderness, protected but alone. This is not a very satisfying end. But in her story and in its ending we see themes related to motherhood that we have already encountered elsewhere in this book—the association of motherhood with danger and suffering.

THE WHORE (BABYLON THE GREAT)

After we leave the Woman Clothed with the Sun in the wilderness, chapter 13 introduces a new symbolic figure—a beast rising out of the sea with seven heads and ten horns. The dragon, waiting on the shore, gives its power to this beast (13:2). The beast represents the Roman Empire, and so Revelation is making the bold claim that Satan (the dragon) is the power behind the Roman Empire (the beast). We can see that the beast represents the Roman Empire because it is given authority over all peoples and makes war on the followers of Jesus (13:7), and because the description of the beast in 13:1–4 is based on the way that other apocalyptic literature describes empires and their rulers (e.g., Dan. 7:1–8). Furthermore, all the people of the earth (other than faithful Jesus followers) worship the beast, a reference to the imperial cult (13:8). The book of Revelation is adamantly opposed to the imperial cult—that is, the honoring of the emperor and empire through religious rituals—viewing it as an insidious form of idolatry. After some further visions of the Lamb and various angels in chapter 14, and bowls of God's wrath being poured on the earth in chapters 15 and 16, the beast reappears in chapter 17, this time with a rider—the Whore of Babylon.

The Whore of Babylon is less mysterious than the Woman Clothed with the Sun, but she is equally striking. The Greek word used to describe her is *pornē*, translated as "whore" in the NRSVue and sometimes also translated as "harlot" or "prostitute." While prostitute is the more neutral term for translating *pornē* into English, there is good reason to choose the translation whore. As I write this chapter, my word processing software keeps underlining the word whore and suggesting I change it, because the word might be offensive to my readers. I could change whore to prostitute to be more polite, but the text of Revelation is not trying to be polite. The text wants you to find this woman offensive—so offensive that you resolve to have nothing to do with her. Revelation wants you to take sides and to choose Jesus rather than the whore. Therefore, the more offensive term in English is truer to the meaning of the text. When we move from the Woman Clothed with the Sun to the Whore of Babylon, we have definitely switched to the other side of the virgin-whore dichotomy.

The whore is wearing expensive clothing and jewelry, is holding "a golden cup full of abominations and the impurities of her prostitution," is seated on the beast with "blasphemous names," and is drunk with the blood of the saints (17:1–6). Her name is written on her forehead: "Babylon the great, mother of whores and of earth's abominations" (17:5). An angel explains to John that the seven heads of the beast are the seven mountains on which the woman is sitting (17:9), and she is also said to be sitting on "many waters," which represent many peoples and nations (17:1, 15). Altogether, the way the whore is depicted bears striking resemblance to the goddess Roma, the deification of the city of Rome, who is depicted on ancient Roman coins seated on the seven hills of Rome with the river Tiber flowing by.[10] In this way the whore seems to represent the city of Rome, while the beast represents the empire as a whole. Clinching this identification of the whore with Rome, 17:18 says that she is "the great city that rules over the kings of the earth." It was common in ancient literature for cities to be personified as female, and in the Hebrew Bible Israel, Jerusalem, and other cities and nations are personified as prostitutes and adulterous women who "cheat" on Yahweh with their sexually depraved behavior. This is their way of portraying idolatry—the worship of false gods (see, for example, Ezek. 16 and 23 and Hosea 1–3). The Whore of Babylon fits squarely in this motif, her prostitution with the kings of the earth (17:2) representing the idolatry of the city of Rome.

If the woman represents Rome, why is her name Babylon? This is symbolic as well. The ancient empire of Babylon destroyed the first temple in Jerusalem in 586 BCE; in 70 CE, the Roman Empire destroyed the second temple. Thus "Babylon" became a code name for Rome in some Jewish and Christian writings after the year 70. And just as Babylon had forced many of the residents of Judah into exile, so the Roman Empire had forced many Jews to leave their homeland and now, according to the Book of Revelation, was also persecuting Christians. The sin of Rome as portrayed in Revelation 17 goes beyond idolatry to include the violent persecution of God's people. These two sins, along with a third, the economic oppression of the poor, are all visually illustrated in the image of the whore in Revelation 17. We see idolatry in the beast's blasphemous names and in the woman's acts of prostitution, violence and persecution in the fact that the woman is drunk on the blood of the saints, and the oppression of the poor represented by the woman's sumptuous clothing and expensive jewelry.[11]

In addition to Babylon, the woman is also called "mother of whores and of earth's abominations" (17:5). While the woman is not depicted with any literal children, she is presented to us as a metaphorical mother. This is a way of indicating that her influence extends beyond herself—not only has she engaged in these behaviors, but she has also encouraged others to do so. This could be a way of indicating that idolatry, violence, and oppression were not only problems in the city of Rome itself, but also throughout the empire, wherever Rome's influence extended.[12] In this sense the Whore of Babylon as mother represents the influence mothers have over their children, far and near. Her motherhood can also remind us that while Revelation's first readers would have identified the woman with Rome, the text is not limited to that interpretation. The Whore of Babylon can be read to represent the oppressive forces of empire wherever and whenever they arise in our world.[13] She is the mother of all idolatry, violence, and oppression.

In the Old Testament passages I referenced earlier in which Israel and Jerusalem are represented by prostitutes or adulterous women, such as Ezekiel 16 and 23 and Hosea 1–3, the women are punished for their behaviors by being stripped naked and attacked, often by the very men that they had been committing adultery with (Ezek. 16:35–43; 23:9–10; 22–35; Hosea 2:3, 9–10). We should not be surprised, then, that a similar fate awaits the Whore of Babylon. Though she has been riding the beast and seems to be almost unified with it throughout most of chapter 17, the beast (and its horns in particular) will turn on the woman at the end of chapter 17. The beast and the horns will "make her desolate and naked; they will devour her flesh and burn her up with fire" (17:16). In 18:1–19:8 we learn that different groups have different reactions to the downfall of the Whore of Babylon. Angels and other unidentified voices from heaven rejoice at her downfall, urging those carrying out the attack against her to "render to her as she herself has rendered, and repay her double for her deeds; mix a double dose for her in the cup she mixed" (18:6). They watch her burn and rejoice that "the smoke goes up from her forever" (19:3). However, not all rejoice at her destruction. The kings, merchants, and sailors, seeing the same smoke, lament the end of the great city, for they are the ones who had been enriched by her (18:9–19).

Just as the participants in the apocalyptic drama of Revelation's narrative have different reactions to the downfall of the Whore of Babylon, so do readers. On the one hand, the woman represents idolatry, violence, and oppression, so some readers feel she receives a fitting end. It is evil that is being punished. But other readers find this imagery very disturbing. Despite what the woman represents, it can still be very troubling to read an account of a woman's body being stripped naked, feasted upon, and burned, with a prolonged celebration over her burning body. It is true that the Whore of Babylon is not a real woman; she is a symbolic figure. And yet language such as that found in Ezekiel 16:35–43, Ezekiel 23:9–10, Hosea 2:3–4, and Revelation 17:16 can normalize violence against women, leading to real-world consequences, including the idea that "women are sometimes deserving of such violence."[14] Mitzi Smith has observed that "women who are socially constructed as whores can be subjected to violence—verbal, emotional, spiritual, and physical abuse.... Whores can be subject to violence because they are whores."[15] In other words, from a patriarchal perspective, those who have been labeled whores cannot be victims, because they are, by definition, deserving of the punishment they are receiving, no matter how severe. The reader of a text like Revelation 17:16 has to face the question whether to align themselves with that patriarchal worldview.

The challenge for the modern reader is to find ways to receive the important message of the text regarding idolatry and oppression without reinscribing the ancient text's patriarchal worldview in our modern lives. This may be easier said than done, but the undertaking is worth the effort. Too often people take the view that there are only two options when reading challenging biblical texts—either reject the text altogether or accept it uncritically. It is simply not true that these are the only options. Faithful readers of Scripture have been wrestling with its more challenging passages for as long as Scripture has existed. To reject and to read uncritically are both very surface-level ways of reading. As Ellen Davis writes, if it seems like a biblical text has nothing of value to offer us, then "we are not reading deeply enough; we have not probed the layers of the text with sufficient care."[16] Concurring with Davis, Frances Taylor Gench argues that "wrestling with Scripture is an act of faithfulness, an act of taking the text with the utmost seriousness."[17] We take Revelation seriously when we read its theological and social message in the context of the time and culture in which it was created, allowing its core message to speak to us and to our world, but resisting harmful readings that uncritically impose ancient patriarchal views and practices on our very different world today.

THE VIRGIN BRIDE (NEW JERUSALEM)

The third symbolic female figure in Revelation is the Bride. We will not spend long on her because she is the only female figure in Revelation who is not portrayed as a mother, but we must say at least a bit about her since she is presented as the opposite of the whore. She is best known for her appearance in Revelation 21:2, to which we will return in a moment, but she is introduced for the first time in 19:7 at the end of the celebration over the whore's downfall. In fact, the end of the celebration of the death of the whore blends seamlessly into the beginning of the celebration of the marriage of the Lamb to the Bride. The contrast between the Whore of Babylon and the Bride could not be more clear. While the last wisps of smoke are still rising from the woman who represents everything debased and depraved, the heavenly multitudes turn toward the woman who represents everything pure and holy: "For the marriage of the Lamb has come, and his bride has made herself ready" (19:7). In contrast to the purple and scarlet dress of the whore, the Bride is clothed "fine linen, bright and pure," representing "the righteous deeds of the saints" (19:8). The contrast between these two women is the virgin-whore dichotomy on full display.

After this brief introduction of the Bride, Revelation narrates the story of the final battle between Christ (who now takes the form of a rider on a white horse) and the dragon and the beast, followed by the resurrection and judgment of the dead. After this, the Bride is reintroduced: "Then I saw a new heaven and a new earth, for the first heaven and the first earth had passed away, and the sea was no more. And I saw the holy city, the new Jerusalem, coming down out of heaven from God, prepared as a bride adorned for her husband" (21:1-2). A little later in the chapter an angel gives John a tour of this city, "the bride, the wife of the Lamb" (21:9-22:7). Both the Whore of Babylon and the Bride represent cities—one a city of idolatry and violence and the other a city of radiance in which God dwells. The virgin-whore dichotomy is a very useful cultural tool for the author of Revelation to use to express this contrast. We can recognize the reasons the author made this choice while simultaneously decrying the negative effects that such stereotypical language can have on the lives of women. Garrett draws attention to the way Revelation categorizes women as "wholly good" or "wholly bad," and argues that the "wholly good" are those women "whose sexuality is effectively controlled," and the "wholly bad" are those women "whose sexuality escapes male management and manipulation."[18] The purity requirements of patriarchal culture are harmful to the lives of women, and such a binary does not encapsulate the richness of real women's lives in their full complexity.

All three of the female figures we have looked at so far are symbolic figures. Even if we understand the Woman Clothed with the Sun to be Mary, it is still a highly symbolic narrative, not a historical description of Mary's life. It is time now to turn to the only historical woman in Revelation and see if she will be portrayed in her full humanity, or if she will be similarly pigeonholed by the virgin-whore dichotomy.

JEZEBEL

In this chapter we have traveled through the text of Revelation from beginning to end, pausing to analyze in detail the female figures presented in the narrative. Now we are going to return to the beginning of the book, which, after some introductory material and an initial vision of Christ in chapter 1, presents letters from Jesus to seven churches in Asia Minor in chapters 2–3. In the letters, each church is commended or reprimanded for how faithful they have been in their devotion to God and their dedication to the truth. The fourth letter is to the church in the city of Thyatira (2:18–29). This letter briefly commends church members for their faith and service, but then reprimands them for tolerating "that woman Jezebel, who calls herself a prophet and is teaching and beguiling my servants to engage in sexual immorality and eat food sacrificed to idols" (2:20). The author uses the name Jezebel to refer to a woman who was a leader in the church at Thyatira. Though she was most likely a real woman in the early church, Jezebel was likely not her actual name. The text gives her the name of the villain Jezebel from 1–2 Kings, the wife of Ahab and the enemy of Elijah. In the Old Testament, Jezebel was portrayed not only as evil herself, but also as leading the nation astray to the worship of other gods. This is what made her so dangerous. Labeling the woman of Revelation 2 with this name emphasizes that she is not just behaving improperly herself but is also influencing others to behave in these ways.

The Jezebel of Revelation is accused of sexual immorality. This is probably not because of anything related to her actual sexual life, but because, as we have seen, the author of Revelation draws on the metaphor of adultery and prostitution to describe idolatry, and Jezebel is accused of encouraging people to eat meat that had been sacrificed to idols. In other words, the accusation of sexual immorality and the accusation about idol meat are likely one single accusation rather than two—she is called sexually immoral because of her involvement in the idol meat issue. Meat that had been previously used in pagan religious rituals was regularly available for sale in the marketplaces of Greco-Roman cities and was also served at various social and business-related events. The question whether Christians could consume such meat was a hot-button issue in the first-century church. Some early Christians believed that meat involved in pagan rituals should never be eaten by Christians, while others believed that as long as you knew that the other gods weren't real, then there really wasn't any harm in eating this meat. It seems that Jezebel was probably in the latter camp, while the author of Revelation was definitely in the former camp.[19] So Jezebel is accused of association with idol worship, which leads to accusations of sexual immorality as a metaphor for unfaithfulness to God. Those in the community who are influenced by Jezebel are said to be committing adultery with her (2:22).

I would suggest that it is not possible to say anything with confidence about this woman's actual sexual life. This is all symbolic language related to idol worship. But, at any rate, this accusation of sexual immorality places Jezebel in the "whore" category, even if she was not literally a whore. Her punishment will be that Christ will "throw her on a bed" (2:22). This is usually interpreted to mean a sickbed—that she will become ill. Yet I don't think it is a coincidence that the image of a bed is chosen, since she has been accused of sexual immorality. Mitchell Reddish has this to say in his commentary on Revelation, which I think is helpful for understanding this image: "The punishment is that God would strike her with an illness. The phrase has a double meaning, however, suggesting a sexual implication. She liked the bed so much that Christ would throw her into it. But this bed is not one of sexual (idolatrous) pleasures, but one of pain and suffering. This is an example of 'measure-for-measure' punishment in which the punishment suits the offense."[20] As Reddish notes, there is an appropriateness to the image—the punishment fits the crime. And yet, I would add that we also need to be cautious about what we do with texts that shame women using sexual language. The sexual overtones to Jezebel's punishment have the potential to normalize sexual violence against women, in a similar way to the passages from Ezekiel 16 and 23, Hosea 2, and Revelation 17, discussed above. This also is a text to be wrestled with.

The final thing to note about Jezebel is that she is also described as a mother. Part of her punishment will be that Christ "will strike her children dead" (2:23). Again, this is most likely metaphorical language, with the "children" of Jezebel being those who followed her and were persuaded by her teachings. Whether she was literally a mother is impossible to say. But once again we see Revelation turning to the metaphor of motherhood to describe the influence a woman has over others (similar to Babylon being described as the "mother of whores"). Jezebel was a powerful leader in the church and those who were influenced by her became her "children."

Mothers are a powerful force in the lives of their children. The character of a child's mother is very important for the child's development, beliefs, and morality. Normally one has no control over who their mother is. But in the world of Revelation, believers have the power to choose their spiritual mother. Revelation urges its readers to choose to be a child of the Woman Clothed with the Sun, rather than a child of the Whore of Babylon or Jezebel. This is the major purpose of the shaming language directed toward the Whore of Babylon and Jezebel—that readers would want to distance themselves from these women and instead become faithful children of the Woman Clothed with the Sun, also associating themselves with the pure Bride of Christ.

CONCLUSION

In many ways, what we find in Revelation when it comes to women and mothers is not a pretty picture. The virgin-whore dichotomy is on full display. The Woman Clothed with the Sun vanishes abruptly at the end of her short but terrifying story. The Whore of Babylon is presented stereotypically and then disposed of through graphic violence. The only historical woman in the book, Jezebel, is insulted, vilified, and threatened. Yet the antidote to these problems that the book causes can be found within the book itself. Revelation promises its readers a world in which oppression ceases and justice reigns. Surely if this became a reality it would be a world in which women are no longer defined by patriarchal sexual norms and vilified or threatened. The way Revelation portrays women is heavily influenced by the patriarchal culture in which it was written. Yet the deeper theological streams running underneath it point us toward a world that provides safety and wholeness for women and all people. May we work toward making that vision of the world a reality.

DISCUSSION QUESTIONS

1. What was your experience with the book of Revelation before reading this chapter? Were your ideas about Revelation confirmed or challenged by a closer look at the female figures in the book?
2. Have you seen or experienced the virgin-whore dichotomy in places other than the Bible? What affect does this phenomenon have on the lives of women and on our ways of reading texts?
3. Who or what do you think the Woman Clothed with the Sun is supposed to represent? How does motherhood play into her story? What do you think we are meant to learn from it?
4. Do you think the punishment of the whore is a fitting and appropriate end for her, or do you find it disturbing? What experiences in your life cause you to react to the text in the way you do?
5. The chapter argues that rejecting difficult texts and reading them uncritically are both surface-level ways of reading. Do you agree? What does it look like to wrestle faithfully with a difficult passage of Scripture?
6. What does motherhood signify in the book of Revelation?

CONCLUSION

In this book we have explored diverse presentations of mothers and motherhood in the New Testament. As we draw this study to a close, in this chapter I will summarize the recurring themes related to motherhood that we have seen throughout the book, and then consider the implications of this study—why does a study of the mothers of the New Testament matter?

MATERNAL THEMES IN THE NEW TESTAMENT

The passages analyzed in this book did not all look at motherhood from the same perspective or engage it for the same rhetorical goals. For example, in 1 Thessalonians 2:7, the intimacy between mother and child was used to express Paul's care for the community, while the connection and loyalty between mother and child was viewed as potentially detrimental to a faith commitment by the Synoptic Gospels' authors. The influence of mothers was viewed positively in the case of Mary's raising of Jesus, but negatively when it came to Herodias's interactions with her daughter. Mothers' advocacy on behalf of their children was admirable in the case of the Syrophoenician woman but critiqued in the case of the mother of the sons of Zebedee. Within the Bible's pages are multiple viewpoints on the place and role of motherhood in society, the family, and religious communities. Nevertheless, within this diversity, there were several themes swirling around motherhood that surfaced again and again in our study. These themes can provide us with the big picture of motherhood in the New Testament, even if not every mother in its pages fits every theme. The most significant themes we have seen in this exploration are motherhood's association with new life, suffering, identity, caregiving, and influence.

New Life

This theme has a literal and a figurative dimension. In a literal sense, biological mothers give birth to new human beings. That is one of the most central ways that families and nations grow. This was a focus in the Old Testament, since mothers were how the people of Israel came into existence and therefore how God's plans were moved forward. The New Testament continues this theme, especially in the early chapters of Matthew and Luke. Matthew's genealogy reminds us of the mothers who were part of Israel and the lineage of Abraham and David. Then Matthew launches us into a new story of a birth that furthers God's plans for the world—the birth of Jesus to Mary and Joseph. Luke's opening chapters also play on Old Testament maternal themes, especially with the barrenness of Elizabeth, and portray the birth of Jesus to Mary as a part of God's salvation plan.

The New Testament also uses the idea of birth in a figurative sense to represent the new life that people are given in Christ and will be given in the future restoration of all things. This theme is especially prominent in John, with images of believers being born of God and born from above, water flowing from the womb of Jesus, and Jesus birthing the church at the cross. We also see the theme used in the apocalyptic parts of the New Testament, with birth pangs describing the end times experience in 1 Thessalonians 5:2–3 and Mark 13:8, and labor pain symbolizing the solidarity of all creation as it moves toward God's future in Romans 8:18–23. Additionally, birth language symbolizes new life in James, 1 Peter, and 1 John.

Suffering

Childbirth was a dangerous endeavor in the ancient world. Not only was it painful, with no option for pain medication, but it also so often resulted in the death of the infant, the death of the mother, or both. This danger and pain surrounding childbirth plays into the New Testament's birth metaphors. The pain of the birth process, but also the joy that may come at the end of it, is

Conclusion

emphasized in the apocalyptic metaphors in 1 Thessalonians 5:2–3 and Romans 8:18–23, and in the childbirth parable in Jesus's farewell discourse in John 16:20–22. Danger and the threat of suffering associated with motherhood also do not end when childbirth is over. In Luke, Mary is warned by Simeon that her experience of motherhood will be like a sword piercing her soul (2:35), and she is filled with anxiety when Jesus goes missing as a twelve-year-old boy (2:48). The threat of mothers possibly being separated from their children heightens the drama of some biblical narratives, such as Mary and Jesus being threatened by Herod in Matthew and the story of the Syrophoenician/Canaanite woman, who is desperate to get help for her unwell daughter.

Sometimes the New Testament portrays not just the threat of separation between mother and child but actual separation, by death or other means. In a poignant scene in Matthew, the mothers of Bethlehem expressing grief over their murdered children are pictured as "Rachel weeping for her children" (2:18). Mary endures the death of Jesus at the foot of the cross in John. In the figurative realm, the Woman Clothed with the Sun is separated from her son as soon as he is born (Rev. 12:5). The reality of this kind of heartbreak also heightens the emotional impact of New Testament stories in which mothers' lost children are returned to them. Because the pain of separation was so real, readers rejoice all the more to hear of the raising of the widow of Nain's son (Luke 7:11–17) and the raising of Jairus's daughter (Mark 5:21–43). These stories show the reader the power of the new life that Christ offers.

Identity

Motherhood in the New Testament is often associated with connection, and connection to others relates to the identity of individuals as part of the community of God's people. A connection between Mary and Jesus is established in Matthew's birth story with the repeated use of the phrase "the child and his mother" (2:11, 13, 14, 20, 21). Luke also connects Mary closely to Jesus through her thoughtful contemplation of the significance of the events surrounding his birth and her role in raising him. John's Gospel also establishes this connection with Mary present at the beginning and end of Jesus's ministry. The connection between Mary and Jesus is an example of the connection of biological family. This kind of connection is so strong that we see the Synoptic Gospels express-

Conclusion

ing ambivalence about it and urging Jesus followers to prioritize relationships in the faith community over relationships with biological family.

Themes of motherhood and connection expressing identity are also present elsewhere. Paul uses the image of himself as a nursing mother with the Thessalonians to strengthen his connection to them and their connection to the Christian community. Birth imagery in James, 1 Peter, and 1 John identifies believers as those who have God as their mother, with implications for what that means for life together. These themes also encourage readers to associate themselves with God and the believing community rather than with outsiders. For example, Paul urges the Galatians to consider Sarah their mother rather than Hagar, and the author of Revelation wants readers to see themselves as children of the Woman Clothed with the Sun rather than of Babylon, "mother of whores." Children derive a large part of their identity from their mothers, so these images of motherhood in the New Testament become powerful means by which the authors seek to establish the identity of the church.

Caregiving

By the term "caregiving" I mean to include all the things that mothers do in raising their children, including feeding, nurturing, comforting, protecting, and advocating for them. These activities are associated with motherhood time and again in the Bible. Mary cares for and protects Jesus when he is small. The mother of the sons of Zebedee and the Syrophoenician/Canaanite woman advocate for their children. The caregiving activities mothers engage in can also extend to those who are not their biological children—Simon's mother-in-law serves a meal to Jesus and the disciples, the mother of John Mark provides hospitality for the community, and Rufus's mother cares for Paul in a way that makes Paul think of her as a mother to him. Because mothers are associated with protection and advocacy, readers are sometimes surprised to find mothers not behaving in this way, such as the mother of the man born blind in John, who tries to be involved with her son's situation as little as possible, and Herodias, who subjects her daughter to a gruesome experience to fulfill her own goals.

Because of these strong associations between motherhood and nurture and protection, the Bible sometimes turns to maternal metaphors when it wants to

Conclusion

attribute these kinds of caregiving activities to men or to God. Paul becomes a nursing mother when he wants to express care for the Thessalonians or be the one to make decisions about the Corinthians' "food." 1 Peter imagines Christ in the role of breastfeeding mother, nourishing the community with the milk that leads to salvation. And Jesus pictures himself as a mother hen as he seeks to comfort and protect the city of Jerusalem.

Influence

Mothers teach their children, have authority over them, and influence them in various ways. We see this in Jesus's obedience to his parents in Luke and in the way Mary is a catalyst for Jesus's public ministry in the Cana story in John. We also see it in the way that Timothy's mother and grandmother are credited with giving him his faith. The idea of maternal influence is also used in various metaphors in the New Testament. Paul pictures himself as a mother in labor when he is seeking to influence the thinking of the Galatians and as a nursing mother when he is trying to guide the Corinthians. Woman Wisdom is the mother of Jesus and John the Baptist when they are walking in her ways. Recognizing the power that mothers and maternal figures have over people, some of the authors of the New Testament warn their readers to choose their mother figures carefully—do not have the Whore of Babylon or Jezebel as your mother!

WHY IT MATTERS

Motherhood is a topic that impacts everyone. Every human being enters this world through the body of a mother. And who that mother is (her social status, her ethnicity, her personality, her parenting style, etc.) can affect a child throughout their lifetime—even after the mother has died. This is true for me, it is true for you, and it was true for Moses, for the Syrophoenician woman's daughter, and for Jesus. This alone makes motherhood in the Bible a worthy topic of study. I would also propose three further reasons that a study of motherhood in the Bible matters: it helps us combat androcentrism, it highlights various social and family-related issues, and it illuminates the heart of the gospel.

Conclusion

Combating the Androcentrism of the Bible and Its Interpreters

The Bible is androcentric. It primarily contains male perspectives and focuses on the stories of men much more than the stories of women. But there are a lot of women in the Bible and an intriguing variety of female metaphors and images. Biblical scholars and preachers have not always highlighted this fact. Many have taken the easy path of sticking with dominant narratives and failing to explore the Bible's submerged streams and counternarratives—or even, in many cases, intentionally burying those submerged streams even further, so that many church-goers are unaware of the role of Woman Wisdom in both Testaments, or the birth imagery in the Gospel of John, or the story of the sassy Syrophoenician woman, or countless other fascinating texts. Since many of the Bible's women are mothers and many of the Bible's female metaphors are maternal, studying the mothers of the New Testament is one effective method of counteracting the ways that women and women's concerns have been excluded within traditional biblical scholarship and within the preaching and Bible studies of many parts of the church.

Highlighting Social and Family Issues

In Mark 1:31 Simon's mother-in-law serves Jesus and the others in the house. But the only reason she is able to do so is because Jesus has just healed her of her fever. Mothers provide food and clothing, give love and comfort, and protect and guide their own children and other people. But these activities become immensely harder when there is illness, poverty, or lack of support. Mothers give help, and they also need it. A look at motherhood in the Bible can lead us to look more closely at the ways that social and family systems work. In what ways did patriarchy affect the lives of mothers in the ancient world? What kind of work did mothers do? In what ways were family relationships both valued and marginalized in Christian communities and the larger Greco-Roman society? Exploring these kinds of questions for the ancient world can also lead us to reflect on the health of social and family systems in our own time and place. In what ways are mothers and children supported, and in what ways are we failing to provide support? What do our family systems say about our values and about our faith? A look at motherhood in the Bible can be an avenue into these and many other questions.

Conclusion

Expressing the Heart of the Gospel

Sally Douglas writes this about connecting her own experience of motherhood to the theology of the church: "There is something profound about feeding a tiny baby from your very own body. In my experience, and I suspect in the experience of many, this awoke an entirely different way into the language of the liturgy: 'This is my body given for you.' There are unmistakable overlaps in the themes of self-giving and sustenance in both breastfeeding and in the Eucharistic liturgy."[1] Douglas is making two important points. First, that motherhood themes and experiences are powerful ways of expressing what the heart of the Christian message is about. And second, that if we want to see this, it helps to have mothers as participants in doing theology and interpreting the Bible. You do not have to be a farmer to read and interpret Jesus's agricultural metaphors, but it might be helpful to have people with farming experience as part of the conversation. Similarly, you do not have to be a mother to read and interpret the Bible's maternal metaphors, but it might be helpful to have mothers as part of the conversation. The greater the diversity we have within the community of Bible scholars and interpreters, the better we will be able to understand and probe the depths of our sacred texts.

Maternal language in the Bible is not just decorative. It is one avenue of expressing the heart of the Bible's theological message. What is God like? According to the Bible God is not just like a father but also like a mother. How does God relate to humanity? Many biblical images show God as the one who gives birth to us, breastfeeds us, carries us, gives us food, and protects us like a mother. How should we characterize the meaning of Jesus's life, death, and resurrection? Images and ideas about this abound but include the ideas that Jesus is our mother hen, a manifestation of Mother Wisdom, and the one who gave birth to the church from the cross. How should we live together as Christian community? According to Paul, servant leaders should be like nursing mothers to the community, and community members should relate to one another as siblings nursed at the same breast. The author of 1 Peter would remind us that the breast we nurse at is really the breast of Christ. If we pay attention to the maternal metaphors the Bible uses, we will be able to go deeper into the text's theological expression of who God is, how God relates to humanity, and how we ought to relate to each other.

CONCLUSION

In this book we have explored a great variety of mothers and maternal images: The varied role of Mary in Jesus's life in the different Gospels (chapters 2–4); the mothers who seek Jesus's help, engage him in dialogue, and are characterized in various ways by the Gospel writers (chapters 5–6); the maternal imagery used for Jesus in the Gospels (chapter 7); brief glimpses of motherhood in Acts and the undisputed letters of Paul (chapters 8–9); maternal metaphors in Paul's writings (chapter 10); challenging texts about mothers in the disputed Pauline letters (chapter 11); images of birth and breastfeeding in Hebrews and the General Epistles (chapter 12); and striking apocalyptic images of motherhood in Revelation (chapter 13). While diverse, these characters and images also coalesce around the themes of new life, suffering, identity, caregiving, and influence. These themes are not peripheral to the text but express the heart of the New Testament's theological message about Christ, as its authors call their readers to faithful life together "under her wings."

DISCUSSION QUESTIONS

1. Which mother or maternal image in this book interested you the most? Why?
2. The chapter talked about new life, suffering, identity, caregiving, and influence as the maternal themes emphasized in the New Testament. Would you add anything to that list? What else did you notice about what motherhood signifies in the New Testament?
3. In your view, what are the implications of this study for faith and for life?

ACKNOWLEDGMENTS

I'm grateful to everyone at Eerdmans for making this book a reality, and especially to Trevor Thompson for showing interest in this project and to Laurel Draper for bringing it to fruition.

My students at St. Mary's Ecumenical Institute and United Lutheran Seminary have been excellent conversation partners over the years as I have refined my approach to reading many of the passages in this book. I am particularly appreciative of the students in the Ecumenical Institute class Mothers in Jewish and Christian Scripture and Tradition in the fall of 2019 who, along with my coteacher Rabbi Nina Beth Cardin, helped me refine my thinking about mothers in biblical literature.

I am also thankful for the members and friends of New Hope Lutheran Church who joined my discussion group and contributed to the improvement of these chapters in many ways. Some only came a few times and some stuck with it for more than two years, but all contributed to making this book better. Thank you, Alexa, Aruna, Amanda, Carol, Colleen, Deborah, Ellen, Jeanne, Judy, Kate, Kathleen, Leah, Louise, Marg, Sangeetha, and Sea.

Thank you to my father, Dave, and my sister Patty. You've been part of my unwavering support system for my entire life and your presence in my life has made many things possible.

To my sons, Justin and Sam—without you this book would probably not exist, since, if I had not become a mother, I probably would not have written

Acknowledgments

it! Thank you for taking the puppy for so many walks so that I could get some writing done.

Thanks are always due to my husband, Tim, who supports me as a friend, a partner, and also an excellent proofreader! Your support makes what I do possible, and I'm grateful.

Finally, this book is dedicated to my mother, Judy Houston. Mom, you've done more than anyone else to shape my faith, and you have shown me by your example what a good mother is. Thank you.

NOTES

CHAPTER 1

1. Leila Leah Bronner, *Stories of Biblical Mothers: Maternal Power in the Hebrew Bible* (Lanham, MD: University Press of America, 2004), ix.
2. See Bronner, *Stories of Biblical Mothers*, 106–15.
3. Bronner, *Stories of Biblical Mothers*, 115.
4. For my fuller treatment of this topic, see Jennifer Houston McNeel, *Paul as Infant and Nursing Mother: Metaphor, Rhetoric, and Identity in 1 Thessalonians 2:5–8*, Early Christianity and Its Literature (Atlanta: SBL Press, 2014), 62–80. See also Carolyn Osiek, Margaret Y. MacDonald, and Janet H. Tulloch, *A Woman's Place: House Churches in Earliest Christianity* (Minneapolis: Fortress, 2006); Beryl Rawson, *Children and Childhood in Roman Italy* (Oxford: Oxford University Press, 2003); and Suzanne Dixon, *The Roman Mother* (Norman: University of Oklahoma Press, 1988).
5. Osiek, MacDonald, and Tulloch, *A Woman's Place*, 20.
6. Valerie French, "Birth Control, Childbirth, and Early Childhood," in *Civilizations of the Ancient Mediterranean*, ed. Michael Grant and Rachel Kitzinger, vol. 3 (New York: Scribner's, 1988), 1357.
7. World Health Organization, "Maternal Mortality," April 26, 2024, https://www.who.int/news-room/fact-sheets/detail/maternal-mortality.
8. Rawson, *Children and Childhood*, 103–4.
9. See Keith R. Bradley, "Wet-Nursing at Rome: A Study in Social Relations," in *The Family in Ancient Rome: New Perspectives*, ed. Beryl Rawson (Ithaca, NY: Cornell University Press, 1986), 201–29.

Notes to Pages 12–30

10. Lynn H. Cohick, *Women in the World of the Earliest Christians: Illuminating Ancient Ways of Life* (Grand Rapids: Baker Academic, 2009), 146.

11. For a fuller treatment of the ideas in this paragraph, see Alicia D. Myers, *Blessed Among Women? Mothers and Motherhood in the New Testament* (New York: Oxford University Press, 2017), 18–41.

CHAPTER 2

1. We do not know who wrote the New Testament Gospels—the authors did not include their names as a part of their writings. I will follow the convention of calling the authors of the Gospels by the names that church tradition assigned to them.

2. Beverly Roberts Gaventa, *Mary: Glimpses of the Mother of Jesus* (Minneapolis: Fortress, 1999), 37.

3. For a strong argument in favor of this view, see Richard Bauckham, *Gospel Women: Studies of the Named Women in the Gospels* (Grand Rapids: Eerdmans, 2002), 17–46.

4. Amy-Jill Levine, "Gospel of Matthew," in *Women's Bible Commentary: Revised and Updated*, ed. Carol A. Newsom, Sharon H. Ringe, and Jacqueline E. Lapsley, 3rd ed. (Louisville: Westminster John Knox, 2012), 467.

5. Jennifer Houston McNeel, "Praying to Learn, Learning to Pray: Reading the Lord's Prayer in Context," *Review and Expositor* 118, no. 4 (2021): 508.

6. To see how Matthew uses the word righteousness, see 1:19; 3:15; 5:6, 10, 20, 45; 6:1, 33; 10:41; 13:43; 21:32; 23:28, 35; 25:37, 46.

7. "Played the whore" is the translation in the original NRSV.

8. We, of course, will have a different view from our very different perspective. In my view, David's actions in this story are vile and a violation against Bathsheba herself. However, in the eyes of ancient patriarchal culture, the violation was not against Bathsheba but against Uriah. When David has Bathsheba brought to him, he takes what only Uriah had rights to.

9. Levine, "Matthew," 467.

10. Gaventa, *Mary*, 43.

CHAPTER 3

1. Cohick, *Women in the World*, 152.

2. Barren matriarchs include Sarah (Gen. 16:1–3), Rebekah (Gen. 25:21), and

Rachel (Gen. 30:1). Barrenness also plays a major role in the later narrative of Hannah (1 Sam. 1:1–8).

3. In the Genesis story Sarah also expresses skepticism (Gen. 18:12). In Luke, we are not told anything about Elizabeth's thoughts prior to her pregnancy.

4. Recall that when God forms Adam in Gen. 2:7, it is when he breathes into him that Adam becomes a living being. So the "breath" as life-force is found in Jewish tradition as well as Greco-Roman medical traditions.

5. For more information on ancient understandings of conception and their implications for New Testament texts about Mary, see Myers, *Blessed Among Women?*, 44–51.

6. Jaime Clark-Soles, *Women in the Bible*, Interpretation (Louisville: Westminster John Knox, 2020), 150.

7. Clark-Soles, *Women in the Bible*, 150.

8. F. Scott Spencer, *Salty Wives, Spirited Mothers, and Savvy Widows: Capable Women of Purpose and Persistence in Luke's Gospel* (Grand Rapids: Eerdmans, 2012), 55–58.

9. Spencer, *Salty Wives*, 72.

10. Gaventa, *Mary*, 54.

11. Gaventa, *Mary*, 54.

12. Spencer, *Salty Wives*, 73.

13. Gaventa, *Mary*, 55.

14. Stephanie Buckhanon Crowder, *When Momma Speaks: The Bible and Motherhood from a Womanist Perspective* (Louisville: Westminster John Knox, 2016), 78–79.

15. Crowder, *When Momma Speaks*, 82.

16. Prophets in the Bible are not primarily people who foretell the future. Rather, prophets are people called by God to speak on God's behalf to the people of God. They point out injustice, call the people to repentance, and provide visions of what life could be like if the community would live according to God's will. Luke portrays Jesus as a prophet in his ministry and in his death.

17. Barbara E. Reid, *Wisdom's Feast: An Invitation to Feminist Interpretation of the Scriptures* (Grand Rapids: Eerdmans, 2016), 54–55.

18. Reid, *Wisdom's Feast*, 56.

19. There is a star in Matthew's story, but it leads the magi to a house, not a stable. In the noncanonical Protoevangelium of James, Mary does ride a donkey but then gives birth in a cave, not a stable, and there is no mention of an inn or innkeeper. The star leads the magi to the cave.

20. Walter Bauer et al., "κατάλυμα," *A Greek-English Lexicon of the New Testament and Other Early Christian Literature*, 3rd ed. (Chicago: University of Chicago Press, 2000), 521.

21. I mentioned earlier that families would bring their animals inside to shelter overnight. However, that was only the case with peasant families owning a small number of animals. The wealthy who owned large flocks would not bring them inside overnight but could afford to pay shepherds to watch over the animals outside at night.

22. Bauer et al., "συντηρέω," *A Greek-English Lexicon*, 975.

23. Bauer et al., "συμβάλλω," *A Greek-English Lexicon*, 956.

24. Bonnie J. Miller-McLemore, "'Pondering All These Things': Mary and Motherhood," in *Blessed One: Protestant Perspectives on Mary*, ed. Beverly Roberts Gaventa and Cynthia L. Rigby (Louisville: Westminster John Knox, 2002), 106.

25. Miller-McLemore, "'Pondering All These Things,'" 107–8.

26. Miller-McLemore, "'Pondering All These Things,'" 108.

27. See Mark 3:33, Matt. 12:48, and Luke 8:21. We will explore this story in more depth in chapter 6.

28. Gaventa, *Mary*, 68.

29. Cohick, *Women in the World*, 143–44.

30. Clark-Soles, *Women in the Bible*, 148–61.

31. For a treatment of what Mary taught Jesus that goes beyond the themes of the Annunciation and Magnificat, see James F. McGrath, *What Jesus Learned from Women* (Eugene, OR: Cascade, 2021), 17–45.

32. Miller-McLemore, "'Pondering All These Things,'" 109.

33. Gaventa, *Mary*, 69.

34. The first passage is when Mary and her other children come to visit Jesus, and Jesus responds, "Who are my mother and my brothers?" In the second passage, a woman blesses the womb and breasts of Jesus's mother. I will discuss both passages in more detail in chapter 6.

CHAPTER 4

1. Cohick, *Women in the World*, 148; Dixon, *Roman Mother*, 202–3.

2. Gaventa, *Mary*, 89.

3. Frances Taylor Gench, *Encounters with Jesus: Studies in the Gospel of John* (Louisville: Westminster John Knox, 2007), 15.

4. Bruce J. Malina and Richard L. Rohrbaugh, *Social-Science Commentary on the Gospel of John* (Minneapolis: Fortress, 1998), 66.

5. Gaventa, *Mary*, 84. See also her discussion of the various meanings expressed by different English translations, similar to my discussion that follows.

6. Clark-Soles, *Women in the Bible*, 169.

7. Raymond E. Brown, *The Gospel According to John (I–XII)*, Anchor Bible (Garden City, NY: Doubleday, 1966), 99.

8. See, for example, Mark 3:31–35 and Luke 11:27–28. These and similar passages will be discussed in more detail in chapter 6.

9. Brown, *John*, 105.

10. Christian traditions that believe in the perpetual virginity of Mary, such as the Roman Catholic Church, believe that these siblings of Jesus are either cousins or Joseph's children from a previous marriage. Most Protestants believe that Jesus's siblings are children that Mary and Joseph had together after Jesus was born.

11. Clark-Soles, *Women in the Bible*, 171; Gench, *Encounters with Jesus*, 14. Contrary to the view expressed here, Beverly Gaventa argues that what is going on in this story is that Jesus is separating himself from all his earthly connections to return to the Father: "Just as he is stripped of his clothing, he divests himself of his mother and his Beloved Disciple" (Gaventa, *Mary*, 91).

12. Gail R. O'Day, "Gospel of John," in Newsom, Ringe, and Lapsley, *Women's Bible Commentary*, 3rd ed., 527.

13. Clark-Soles, *Women in the Bible*, 168.

CHAPTER 5

1. The only place in the New Testament where Peter's wife is directly mentioned is 1 Cor. 9:5. In this passage Paul is talking about certain "rights" he has as an apostle that he has chosen to forgo. One of these rights is the right to be accompanied in his ministry by a wife. He indicates that other apostles, including Cephas, are accompanied by wives. "Cephas" is yet another name for Peter in the New Testament, so this verse is an indication that Peter was married at the time Paul wrote 1 Corinthians. This may or may not be the same wife whose mother was sick with a fever in the Gospels, since remarriage after the death of a spouse was common in the ancient world, and 1 Corinthians was written a couple of decades after the healing event described in the Gospels would have taken place.

2. Susan E. Hylen, *Women in the New Testament World* (New York: Oxford University Press, 2019), 84.

3. Hylen, *Women*, 84.

4. I have given examples from Mark, but see also Matt. 20:25–28; 23:11; and Luke

22:24–27. For more on the idea of both women and men being called to serve at table in the Gospels, see Spencer, *Salty Wives*, 114–19.

5. None of the Gospels specifies exactly where this story takes place, though Mark seems to indicate that it is somewhere on the western shore of the Sea of Galilee, because Jesus has just crossed back over the sea from the other side (Mark 5:21).

6. Frances Taylor Gench, *Back to the Well: Women's Encounters with Jesus in the Gospels* (Louisville: Westminster John Knox, 2004), 6.

7. Gench, *Back to the Well*, 4.

8. Gench, *Back to the Well*, 4.

9. Gench, *Back to the Well*, 4.

10. Levine, "Matthew," 474.

11. Jesus feeds five thousand Jews before meeting the Canaanite woman (Matt. 14:13–21). Right after his encounter with the Canaanite woman, Jesus heals and then feeds a crowd of four thousand. This crowd of four thousand is likely a gentile crowd, because they are said to "praise the God of Israel" (15:31). In Mark's narrative Jesus also moves through gentile areas after his encounter with the Syrophoenician woman. For more on what Jesus learned from this woman and how it affected his ministry, see McGrath, *What Jesus Learned*, 101–5.

12. Mitzi J. Smith, *Womanist Sass and Talk Back: Social (In)Justice, Intersectionality, and Biblical Interpretation* (Eugene, OR: Cascade, 2018), 30.

13. Smith, *Womanist Sass*, 42.

14. Surekha Nelavala, "Smart Syrophoenician Woman: A Dalit Feminist Reading of Mark 7:24–31," *Expository Times* 118, no. 2 (2006): 69.

15. This does not mean women did not contribute economically to the household. They did so in crucial ways, such as by making clothing and food, managing the running of the household, and sometimes earning income through their own labor. A man without any women in his household would have needed help as much as a woman who had lost her male family members. Such a man would be unlikely to know how to feed himself or create or obtain new clothing or keep the house clean. The social system created interdependence between men and women and within families. Almost no one lived on their own in the ancient world. We should keep in mind, though, that interdependence does not mean equality. In terms of power and authority, gender hierarchy was firmly in place in ancient Greco-Roman and Jewish cultures.

CHAPTER 6

1. McGrath, *What Jesus Learned*, 22.
2. Bauer et al., "μισέω," *A Greek-English Lexicon*, 652–53.
3. Luke, for his part, eliminates the story altogether.
4. Crowder, *When Momma Speaks*, 96.
5. Crowder, *When Momma Speaks*, 98.
6. The only mother that could rival Herodias for the title of "worst mother in the New Testament" would be the symbolic figure of "Babylon, mother of whores" in Rev. 17. Her story will be analyzed in chapter 13.
7. F. Scott Spencer, *Dancing Girls, Loose Ladies, and Woman of the Cloth: The Women in Jesus's Life* (New York: Continuum, 2004), 56.
8. The incident is not described by any nonbiblical sources, leading many scholars to be skeptical of its historicity.
9. Regina Janes, "Why the Daughter of Herodias Must Dance (Mark 6.14–29)," *Journal for the Study of the New Testament* 28, no. 4 (2006): 443–67.
10. Janes, "Why the Daughter," 8–11.
11. Janes, "Why the Daughter," 10.

CHAPTER 7

1. A thorough exploration of Wisdom Christology is beyond the scope of this book, but an accessible place to begin further reading is Clark-Soles, *Women in the Bible*, 236–40. See also the resources for further reading she includes at the end of the chapter. For a book-length introduction that is accessible to the nonspecialist, see Sally Douglas, *Jesus Sophia: Returning to Woman Wisdom in the Bible, Practice, and Prayer* (Eugene, OR: Cascade, 2023).
2. Barbara E. Reid, "Wisdom's Children Justified (Mt. 11.16–19; Lk. 7.31–35)," in *The Lost Coin: Parables of Women, Work, and Wisdom*, ed. Mary Ann Beavis, The Biblical Seminar 86 (London: Sheffield Academic, 2002), 302–3.
3. Here I will focus only on the Gospel of John, but see chapter 10 for a brief look at birth pang imagery in the apocalyptic sections of Mark and Matthew.
4. Sandra M. Schneiders, *Written That You May Believe: Encountering Jesus in the Fourth Gospel*, rev. ed. (New York: Crossroad, 2003), 122–23, as quoted in Gench, *Encounters with Jesus*, 25.

5. Reid, *Wisdom's Feast*, 127.
6. Reid, *Wisdom's Feast*, 131.
7. Douglas, *Jesus Sophia*, 4.

CHAPTER 8

1. Rhoda was most likely a slave, despite the NRSVue's gentle and somewhat misleading translation, "maid." For an analysis of this story in connection with stories of other slave girls in Luke-Acts, see Spencer, *Dancing Girls*, 144–65. For a critique of the story for trying to get laughs at Rhoda's expense, see Margaret Aymer, "Outrageous, Audacious, Courageous, Willful: Reading the Enslaved Girl of Acts 12," in *Womanist Interpretations of the Bible: Expanding the Discourse*, ed. Gay L. Byron and Vanessa Lovelace (Atlanta: SBL Press, 2016), 265–89.
2. Although the Gospels are placed first in the canon, Paul's letters were written before they were composed.

CHAPTER 9

1. "The angel of the Lord" in the Old Testament is a mysterious figure, sometimes seeming to be a messenger sent by God and other times seeming actually to be God.
2. See Delores S. Williams, *Sisters in the Wilderness: The Challenge of Womanist God-Talk* (Maryknoll, NY: Orbis Books, 1993); Wilda C. Gafney, *Womanist Midrash: A Reintroduction to the Women of the Torah and the Throne* (Louisville: Westminster John Knox, 2017), 38–45.
3. See, for example, references to the "heavenly country" and "the city that is to come" in Heb. 11:16 and 13:14, and to "the holy city, new Jerusalem" coming down from heaven in Rev. 21:2.
4. David A. deSilva, *The Letter to the Galatians*, New International Commentary on the New Testament (Grand Rapids: Eerdmans, 2018), 400.
5. deSilva, *Galatians*, 400.
6. Carolyn Osiek, "Galatians," in Newsom, Ringe, and Lapsley, *Women's Bible Commentary*, 3rd ed., 574.
7. Raymond F. Collins, *First Corinthians*, Sacra Pagina (Collegeville, MN: Liturgical Press, 1999), 209.
8. Those who have read chapter 7 of this book may be interested to know that the word translated as "womb" in this verse is *koilia*.

CHAPTER 10

1. The ideas in this chapter owe a lot to the foundational work of Beverly Roberts Gaventa. See especially Beverly Roberts Gaventa, *Our Mother Saint Paul* (Louisville: Westminster John Knox, 2007). For my own fuller treatment of this topic, see McNeel, *Paul as Infant*. For another example of a study that interprets Paul's maternal metaphors as deeply connected to his theology, see Susan G. Eastman, *Recovering Paul's Mother Tongue: Language and Theology in Galatians* (Grand Rapids: Eerdmans, 2007).

2. The book of 1 Enoch contains writings from different time periods and is difficult to date, but various passages probably range in origin from the second century BCE to the first century CE.

3. See also the parallel use of the metaphor in a very similar context in Matt. 24:8.

4. I recognize that, in the modern day, some of what I have said about labor in this paragraph is not true. Today, people sometimes do know exactly when labor will start, because they schedule it to be induced. And sometimes premature labor can be stopped with medical intervention. But in the ancient world, women would not have known when labor would start, and in most cases they would not have been able to stop it once it began. To understand the metaphor as Paul uses it, we have to think about the ways that ancient people would have thought about and experienced labor rather than the ways modern people do.

5. Luzia Sutter Rehman, "To Turn the Groaning into Labor: Romans 8.22–23," in *A Feminist Companion to Paul*, ed. Amy-Jill Levine and Marianne Blickenstaff (Cleveland: Pilgrim, 2004), 84.

6. Gaventa, *Our Mother Saint Paul*, 4–5.

7. Gaventa, *Our Mother Saint Paul*, 5.

8. Conspicuously absent from this list is any mention of Mary Magdalene and the other women from the resurrection stories in the Gospels. All three Synoptic Gospels report that Mary Magdalene and a few other women were the first to hear the news of the resurrection from men or angels at the empty tomb (Matt. 28:5–6; Mark 16:6; Luke 24:5–7), and Matthew also reports that the women were the first to see the risen Jesus (Matt. 28:8–10). According to John, Mary Magdalene alone was the first to encounter and speak with the risen Jesus (John 20:11–17). It is unknown why Paul does not mention the women in this passage. Was he unfamiliar with the stories that featured women? Had he heard them but chose not to mention them here? We don't know.

9. For a much more detailed analysis of this passage, see my book McNeel, *Paul as Infant*.

10. For all the arguments in favor of *nēpioi*, see McNeel, *Paul as Infant*, 35–43.

11. McNeel, *Paul as Infant*, 43–47.

12. McNeel, *Paul as Infant*, 47–60.

13. McNeel, *Paul as Infant*, 104–8.

14. F. F. Bruce, *1 and 2 Thessalonians*, Word Biblical Commentary (Waco, TX: Word, 1982), 32.

15. Jennifer Houston McNeel, "Feeding with Milk: Paul's Nursing Metaphors in Context," *Review and Expositor* 110, no. 4 (2013): 563.

16. McNeel, *Paul as Infant*, 72.

17. Gaventa, *Our Mother Saint Paul*, 27.

18. Gaventa, *Our Mother Saint Paul*, 13–14.

19. McNeel, "Feeding with Milk," 567.

20. Victor Paul Furnish, *The Moral Teaching of Paul: Selected Issues*, 3rd ed. (Nashville: Abingdon, 2009), 52; Gaventa, *Our Mother Saint Paul*, 14.

21. See John M. G. Barclay, "Thessalonica and Corinth: Social Contrasts in Pauline Christianity," *Journal for the Study of the New Testament* 47 (1992): 49–74.

22. McNeel, "Feeding with Milk," 570.

23. McNeel, "Feeding with Milk," 571.

24. McNeel, *Paul as Infant*, 5–6.

25. McNeel, *Paul as Infant*, 110.

26. Esther G. Chazon, "Hymns and Prayers in the Dead Sea Scrolls," in *The Dead Sea Scrolls after Fifty Years: A Comprehensive Assessment*, ed. Peter W. Flint and James C. VanderKam, vol. 1 (Leiden: Brill, 1998), 266.

27. My translation, based on the Hebrew text in Hartmut Stegemann, Eileen Schuller, and Carol A. Newsom, *Qumran Cave 1.III: 1QHodayot a: With Incorporation of 1QHodayot b and 4QHodayot a–f*, vol. 40, Discoveries in the Judean Desert (Oxford: Clarendon, 2009), 199. The text in brackets is uncertain. I have taken this reading from Florentino Garcia Martinez and Eibert J. C. Tigchelaar, *The Dead Sea Scrolls Study Edition*, vol. 1 (Leiden: Brill, 1997), 178. For my fuller analysis and interpretation of this passage, see McNeel, *Paul as Infant*, 111–17. For my analysis of another passage in the Hodayot that describes God as a wet nurse, see McNeel, *Paul as Infant*, 117–21.

28. McNeel, "Feeding with Milk," 572.

29. See chapter 12 for more examples of breastfeeding and milk metaphors in the New Testament, found in Heb. 5:11–14 and 1 Pet. 2:2.

30. Gaventa, *Our Mother Saint Paul*, 13–14.

31. Trevor J. Burke, *Family Matters: A Socio-Historical Study of Kinship Metaphors in 1 Thessalonians*, Journal for the Study of the New Testament Supplement Series 247 (London: T&T Clark, 2003), 152.

32. Margaret Aymer, "'Mother Knows Best': The Story of Mother Paul Revisited," in *Mother Goose, Mother Jones, Mommie Dearest: Biblical Mothers and Their Children*, ed. Cheryl A. Kirk-Duggan and Tina Pippin, Semeia Studies 61 (Atlanta: Society of Biblical Literature, 2009), 195.

33. McNeel, *Paul as Infant*, 144–45.

34. I am indebted here to Sandra Hack Polaski's idea of feminist "trajectories"—that there are elements of Paul's thought that lead in liberating directions, and as modern people of faith we can follow these liberating directions further than Paul himself went. See Sandra Hack Polaski, *A Feminist Introduction to Paul* (St. Louis: Chalice, 2005), 4.

35. Calvin J. Roetzel, *Paul: A Jew on the Margins* (Louisville: Westminster John Knox, 1998), 16–17.

36. For my fuller treatment of what the metaphors say about Paul's character, see McNeel, *Paul as Infant*, 161–72.

37. Osiek, "Galatians," 426.

38. Roetzel, *Paul*, 17.

39. Aymer, "Mother Knows Best," 192.

40. Aymer, "Mother Knows Best," 197.

41. McNeel, *Paul as Infant*, 171.

CHAPTER 11

1. Second Thessalonians is also a disputed epistle but will not be explored in this book because it does not mention any women or have any content directly relevant to motherhood.

2. For one helpful introduction to the issues, see Patrick Gray, *Opening Paul's Letters: A Reader's Guide to Genre and Interpretation* (Grand Rapids: Baker Academic, 2021), 139–51.

3. For a detailed treatment of the ideas in this paragraph, see Margaret Y. Mac-

Donald, *Early Christian Women and Pagan Opinion: The Power of the Hysterical Woman* (Cambridge: Cambridge University Press, 1996).

4. The translation of 1 Tim. 2:8–15 in this section is my own. Translations of verses other than those in 2:8–15 are taken from the NRSVue.

5. Frances Taylor Gench, *Encountering God in Tyrannical Texts: Reflections on Paul, Women, and the Authority of Scripture* (Louisville: Westminster John Knox, 2015), 7.

6. For a few other possibilities in addition to the three I will describe here, see Cohick, *Women in the World*, 138–40.

7. Gench, *Encountering God*, 7.

8. Dorothy A. Lee, *The Ministry of Women in the New Testament: Reclaiming the Biblical Vision for Church Leadership* (Grand Rapids: Baker Academic, 2021), 128.

9. Cynthia Long Westfall, *Paul and Gender: Reclaiming the Apostle's Vision for Men and Women in Christ* (Grand Rapids: Baker Academic, 2016), 305–12.

10. Timothy's mother is also mentioned in Acts 16:1, and I discuss her briefly in chapter 8.

11. Ross S. Kraemer, "Eunice," in *Women in Scripture: A Dictionary of Named and Unnamed Women in the Hebrew Bible, the Apocryphal/Deuterocanonical Books, and the New Testament*, ed. Carol A. Meyers, Toni Craven, and Ross S. Kraemer (Grand Rapids: Eerdmans, 2000), 78–79.

CHAPTER 12

1. M. Eugene Boring, *1 Peter*, Abingdon New Testament Commentaries (Nashville: Abingdon, 1999), 61–62.

2. Gail R. O'Day, "1, 2, and 3 John," in Newsom, Ringe, and Lapsley, *Women's Bible Commentary*, 3rd ed., 623.

3. Victor C. Pfitzner, *Hebrews*, Abingdon New Testament Commentaries (Nashville: Abingdon, 1997), 159–60.

4. Both women are also mentioned in parts of the New Testament that I discussed in earlier chapters: Sarah in Rom. 4:19, Rom. 9:9, and Gal. 4:21–31, and Rahab in Matt. 1:5.

5. Cynthia Briggs Kittredge, "1 Peter," in Newsom, Ringe, and Lapsley, *Women's Bible Commentary*, 3rd ed., 618.

6. Contrary to some post-Reformation interpretations of Paul, when you read Paul's letters it is easy to see that he cared very much about what Christians did and

how they behaved! Justification is "by faith" in Paul's letters, but this "faith" does not only refer to beliefs but refers to a trusting relationship with God that is correlated to a way of life.

CHAPTER 13

1. Mitchell G. Reddish, *Revelation*, Smyth & Helwys Bible Commentary (Macon, GA: Smyth & Helwys, 2001), 1.

2. For an introduction to Revelation and apocalyptic literature and to the many ways Revelation has been interpreted through the centuries, see chapter 1 of Craig R. Koester, *Revelation and the End of All Things* (Grand Rapids: Eerdmans, 2001). See also my comments about apocalyptic literature in chapter 10 of this book.

3. Despite popular belief that this John is the apostle John and the author of the Gospel of John, in reality the book of Revelation does not identify which John this is, and most biblical scholars do not think that the Gospel of John and Revelation could have been written by the same author. For more on the authorship of Revelation, see Reddish, *Revelation*, 17–19.

4. For a helpful exploration of the ongoing relevance of Revelation for modern life, see Barbara R. Rossing, "Prophecy, End-Times, and American Apocalypse: Reclaiming Hope for Our World," *Anglican Theological Review* 89, no. 4 (2007): 549–63.

5. Susan R. Garrett, "Revelation," in *Women's Bible Commentary: Expanded Edition with Apocrypha*, ed. Carol A. Newsom and Sharon H. Ringe (Louisville: Westminster John Knox, 1998), 474. See also Tina Pippin, "Revelation/Apocalypse of John," in Newsom, Ringe, and Lapsley, *Women's Bible Commentary*, 3rd ed., 627–32.

6. Garrett, "Revelation," 469.

7. Garrett, "Revelation," 471.

8. Garrett, "Revelation," 472.

9. Reddish, *Revelation*, 248.

10. Garrett, "Revelation," 473.

11. Garrett, "Revelation," 473.

12. Reddish, *Revelation*, 326.

13. Reddish, *Revelation*, 334.

14. Garrett, "Revelation," 473.

15. Mitzi J. Smith, "Fashioning Our Own Souls: A Womanist Reading of the Virgin-Whore Binary in Matthew and Revelation," in *I Found God in Me: A Womanist Biblical Hermeneutics Reader*, ed. Mitzi J. Smith (Eugene, OR: Cascade, 2015), 174.

16. Ellen F. Davis, "Critical Traditioning: Seeking an Inner Biblical Hermeneutic," in *The Art of Reading Scripture*, ed. Ellen F. Davis and Richard B. Hays (Grand Rapids: Eerdmans, 2003), 164.

17. Gench, *Encountering God*, 12.

18. Garrett, "Revelation," 474.

19. See 1 Cor. 8:1–13 for Paul's position on the issue, which might be described as a moderating position between these two camps.

20. Reddish, *Revelation*, 65.

CONCLUSION

1. Douglas, *Jesus Sophia*, 72.

BIBLIOGRAPHY

Aristotle. *Nicomachean Ethics*. Translated by H. Rackham. Loeb Classical Library 73. Cambridge, MA: Harvard University Press, 1926.

Aymer, Margaret. "'Mother Knows Best': The Story of Mother Paul Revisited." Pages 187–98 in *Mother Goose, Mother Jones, Mommie Dearest: Biblical Mothers and Their Children*. Edited by Cheryl A. Kirk-Duggan and Tina Pippin. Semeia Studies 61. Atlanta: Society of Biblical Literature, 2009.

———. "Outrageous, Audacious, Courageous, Willful: Reading the Enslaved Girl of Acts 12." Pages 265–89 in *Womanist Interpretations of the Bible: Expanding the Discourse*. Edited by Gay L. Byron and Vanessa Lovelace. Atlanta: SBL Press, 2016.

Barclay, John M. G. "Thessalonica and Corinth: Social Contrasts in Pauline Christianity." *Journal for the Study of the New Testament* 47 (1992): 49–74.

Bauckham, Richard. *Gospel Women: Studies of the Named Women in the Gospels*. Grand Rapids: Eerdmans, 2002.

Bauer, Walter, F. W. Danker, W. F. Arndt, and F. W. Gingrich. *A Greek-English Lexicon of the New Testament and Other Early Christian Literature*. 3rd ed. Chicago: University of Chicago Press, 2000.

Boring, M. Eugene. *1 Peter*. Abingdon New Testament Commentaries. Nashville: Abingdon, 1999.

Bradley, Keith R. "Wet-Nursing at Rome: A Study in Social Relations." Pages 201–29 in *The Family in Ancient Rome: New Perspectives*. Edited by Beryl Rawson. Ithaca, NY: Cornell University Press, 1986.

Bibliography

Bronner, Leila Leah. *Stories of Biblical Mothers: Maternal Power in the Hebrew Bible*. Lanham, MD: University Press of America, 2004.

Brown, Raymond E. *The Gospel According to John (I–XII)*. Anchor Bible. Garden City, NY: Doubleday, 1966.

Bruce, F. F. *1 and 2 Thessalonians*. Word Biblical Commentary. Waco, TX: Word, 1982.

Burke, Trevor J. *Family Matters: A Socio-Historical Study of Kinship Metaphors in 1 Thessalonians*. Journal for the Study of the New Testament Supplement Series 247. London: T&T Clark, 2003.

Chazon, Esther G. "Hymns and Prayers in the Dead Sea Scrolls." Pages 244–70 in vol. 1 of *The Dead Sea Scrolls after Fifty Years: A Comprehensive Assessment*. Edited by Peter W. Flint and James C. VanderKam. Leiden: Brill, 1998.

Clark-Soles, Jaime. *Women in the Bible*. Interpretation. Louisville: Westminster John Knox, 2020.

Cohick, Lynn H. *Women in the World of the Earliest Christians: Illuminating Ancient Ways of Life*. Grand Rapids: Baker Academic, 2009.

Collins, Raymond F. *First Corinthians*. Sacra Pagina. Collegeville, MN: Liturgical Press, 1999.

Crowder, Stephanie Buckhanon. *When Momma Speaks: The Bible and Motherhood from a Womanist Perspective*. Louisville: Westminster John Knox, 2016.

Davis, Ellen F. "Critical Traditioning: Seeking an Inner Biblical Hermeneutic." Pages 163–80 in *The Art of Reading Scripture*. Edited by Ellen F. Davis and Richard B. Hays. Grand Rapids: Eerdmans, 2003.

deSilva, David A. *The Letter to the Galatians*. New International Commentary on the New Testament. Grand Rapids: Eerdmans, 2018.

Dixon, Suzanne. *The Roman Mother*. Norman: University of Oklahoma Press, 1988.

Douglas, Sally. *Jesus Sophia: Returning to Woman Wisdom in the Bible, Practice, and Prayer*. Eugene, OR: Cascade, 2023.

Eastman, Susan G. *Recovering Paul's Mother Tongue: Language and Theology in Galatians*. Grand Rapids: Eerdmans, 2007.

French, Valerie. "Birth Control, Childbirth, and Early Childhood." Pages 1355–62 in vol. 3 of *Civilizations of the Ancient Mediterranean*. Edited by Michael Grant and Rachel Kitzinger. New York: Scribner's, 1988.

Furnish, Victor Paul. *The Moral Teaching of Paul: Selected Issues*. 3rd ed. Nashville: Abingdon, 2009.

Gafney, Wilda C. *Womanist Midrash: A Reintroduction to the Women of the Torah and the Throne*. Louisville: Westminster John Knox, 2017.

Bibliography

Garcia Martinez, Florentino, and Eibert J. C. Tigchelaar. *The Dead Sea Scrolls Study Edition*. Vol. 1. Leiden: Brill, 1997.

Garrett, Susan R. "Revelation." Pages 469–74 in *Women's Bible Commentary: Expanded Edition with Apocrypha*. Edited by Carol A. Newsom and Sharon H. Ringe. Louisville: Westminster John Knox, 1998.

Gaventa, Beverly Roberts. *Mary: Glimpses of the Mother of Jesus*. Minneapolis: Fortress, 1999.

———. *Our Mother Saint Paul*. Louisville: Westminster John Knox, 2007.

Gench, Frances Taylor. *Back to the Well: Women's Encounters with Jesus in the Gospels*. Louisville: Westminster John Knox, 2004.

———. *Encountering God in Tyrannical Texts: Reflections on Paul, Women, and the Authority of Scripture*. Louisville: Westminster John Knox, 2015.

———. *Encounters with Jesus: Studies in the Gospel of John*. Louisville: Westminster John Knox, 2007.

Gray, Patrick. *Opening Paul's Letters: A Reader's Guide to Genre and Interpretation*. Grand Rapids: Baker Academic, 2021.

Hylen, Susan E. *Women in the New Testament World*. New York: Oxford University Press, 2019.

Ignatius. "To the Smyrneans." Pages 294–309 in vol. 1 of *The Apostolic Fathers I*. Translated by Bart D. Ehrman. Loeb Classical Library 24. Cambridge, MA: Harvard University Press, 2003.

Janes, Regina. "Why the Daughter of Herodias Must Dance (Mark 6.14–29)." *Journal for the Study of the New Testament* 28, no. 4 (2006): 443–67.

Jerome. "Letter LIII." Pages 96–102 in vol. 6 of *Nicene and Post-Nicene Fathers: Jerome: Letters and Selected Works*. Edited by Philip Schaff and Henry Wace. Translated by W. H. Fremantle. Second Series. Peabody, MA: Hendrickson, 1994.

Kittredge, Cynthia Briggs. "1 Peter." Pages 616–19 in *Women's Bible Commentary: Revised and Updated*. Edited by Carol A. Newsom, Sharon H. Ringe, and Jacqueline E. Lapsley. 3rd ed. Louisville: Westminster John Knox, 2012.

Koester, Craig R. *Revelation and the End of All Things*. Grand Rapids: Eerdmans, 2001.

Kraemer, Ross S. "Eunice." Pages 78–79 in *Women in Scripture: A Dictionary of Named and Unnamed Women in the Hebrew Bible, the Apocryphal/Deuterocanonical Books, and the New Testament*. Edited by Carol A. Meyers, Toni Craven, and Ross S. Kraemer. Grand Rapids: Eerdmans, 2000.

Bibliography

Lee, Dorothy A. *The Ministry of Women in the New Testament: Reclaiming the Biblical Vision for Church Leadership*. Grand Rapids: Baker Academic, 2021.

Levine, Amy-Jill. "Gospel of Matthew." Pages 465–77 in *Women's Bible Commentary: Revised and Updated*, by Carol A Newsom, Sharon H. Ringe, and Jacqueline E. Lapsley. 3rd ed. Louisville: Westminster John Knox, 2012.

MacDonald, Margaret Y. *Early Christian Women and Pagan Opinion: The Power of the Hysterical Woman*. Cambridge: Cambridge University Press, 1996.

Malina, Bruce J., and Richard L. Rohrbaugh. *Social-Science Commentary on the Gospel of John*. Minneapolis: Fortress, 1998.

McGrath, James F. *What Jesus Learned from Women*. Eugene, OR: Cascade, 2021.

McNeel, Jennifer Houston. "Feeding with Milk: Paul's Nursing Metaphors in Context." *Review and Expositor* 110, no. 4 (2013): 561–75.

———. *Paul as Infant and Nursing Mother: Metaphor, Rhetoric, and Identity in 1 Thessalonians 2:5–8*. Early Christianity and Its Literature. Atlanta: SBL Press, 2014.

———. "Praying to Learn, Learning to Pray: Reading the Lord's Prayer in Context." *Review and Expositor* 118, no. 4 (2021): 507–12.

Miller-McLemore, Bonnie J. "'Pondering All These Things': Mary and Motherhood." Pages 97–114 in *Blessed One: Protestant Perspectives on Mary*. Edited by Beverly Roberts Gaventa and Cynthia L. Rigby. Louisville: Westminster John Knox, 2002.

Myers, Alicia D. *Blessed Among Women? Mothers and Motherhood in the New Testament*. New York: Oxford University Press, 2017.

Nelavala, Surekha. "Smart Syrophoenician Woman: A Dalit Feminist Reading of Mark 7:24–31." *The Expository Times* 118, no. 2 (2006): 64–69.

O'Day, Gail R. "1, 2, and 3 John." Pages 622–24 in *Women's Bible Commentary: Revised and Updated*. Edited by Carol A. Newsom, Sharon H. Ringe, and Jacqueline E. Lapsley. 3rd ed. Louisville: Westminster John Knox, 2012.

———. "Gospel of John." Pages 517–35 in *Women's Bible Commentary: Revised and Updated*. Edited by Carol A Newsom, Sharon H. Ringe, and Jacqueline E. Lapsley. 3rd ed. Louisville: Westminster John Knox, 2012.

Osiek, Carolyn. "Galatians." Pages 570–75 in *Women's Bible Commentary: Revised and Updated*. Edited by Carol A. Newsom, Sharon H. Ringe, and Jacqueline E. Lapsley. 3rd ed. Louisville: Westminster John Knox, 2012.

Osiek, Carolyn, Margaret Y. MacDonald, and Janet H. Tulloch. *A Woman's Place: House Churches in Earliest Christianity*. Minneapolis: Fortress, 2006.

Pfitzner, Victor C. *Hebrews*. Abingdon New Testament Commentaries. Nashville: Abingdon, 1997.

Bibliography

Pippin, Tina. "Revelation/Apocalypse of John." Pages 627–32 in *Women's Bible Commentary: Revised and Updated*. Edited by Carol A. Newsom, Sharon H. Ringe, and Jacqueline E. Lapsley. 3rd ed. Louisville: Westminster John Knox, 2012.

Polaski, Sandra Hack. *A Feminist Introduction to Paul*. St. Louis: Chalice, 2005.

Rawson, Beryl. *Children and Childhood in Roman Italy*. Oxford: Oxford University Press, 2003.

Reddish, Mitchell G. *Revelation*. Smyth & Helwys Bible Commentary. Macon, GA: Smyth & Helwys, 2001.

Rehman, Luzia Sutter. "To Turn the Groaning into Labor: Romans 8.22–23." Pages 74–84 in *A Feminist Companion to Paul*. Edited by Amy-Jill Levine and Marianne Blickenstaff. Cleveland: Pilgrim, 2004.

Reid, Barbara E. "Wisdom's Children Justified (Mt. 11.16–19; Lk. 7.31–35)." Pages 287–305 in *The Lost Coin: Parables of Women, Work, and Wisdom*. Edited by Mary Ann Beavis. The Biblical Seminar 86. London: Sheffield Academic, 2002.

———. *Wisdom's Feast: An Invitation to Feminist Interpretation of the Scriptures*. Grand Rapids: Eerdmans, 2016.

Roetzel, Calvin J. *Paul: A Jew on the Margins*. Louisville: Westminster John Knox, 1998.

Rossing, Barbara R. "Prophecy, End-Times, and American Apocalypse: Reclaiming Hope for Our World." *Anglican Theological Review* 89, no. 4 (2007): 549–63.

Schneiders, Sandra M. *Written That You May Believe: Encountering Jesus in the Fourth Gospel*. Rev. ed. New York: Crossroad, 2003.

Seneca. "De Providentia." Pages 2–47 in volume 1 of *Seneca: Moral Essays*. Edited by G. P. Goold. Translated by John W. Basore. Loeb Classical Library 214. Cambridge, MA: Harvard University Press, 1998.

Smith, Mitzi J. "Fashioning Our Own Souls: A Womanist Reading of the Virgin-Whore Binary in Matthew and Revelation." Pages 158–82 in *I Found God in Me: A Womanist Biblical Hermeneutics Reader*. Edited by Mitzi J. Smith. Eugene, OR: Cascade, 2015.

———. *Womanist Sass and Talk Back: Social (In)Justice, Intersectionality, and Biblical Interpretation*. Eugene, OR: Cascade, 2018.

Spencer, F. Scott. *Dancing Girls, Loose Ladies, and Woman of the Cloth: The Women in Jesus's Life*. New York: Continuum, 2004.

———. *Salty Wives, Spirited Mothers, and Savvy Widows: Capable Women of Purpose and Persistence in Luke's Gospel*. Grand Rapids: Eerdmans, 2012.

Stegemann, Hartmut, Eileen Schuller, and Carol A. Newsom. *Qumran Cave 1.III:*

Bibliography

1QHodayot a: With Incorporation of 1QHodayot b and 4QHodayot a–f. Vol. 40. Discoveries in the Judean Desert. Oxford: Clarendon, 2009.

Westfall, Cynthia Long. *Paul and Gender: Reclaiming the Apostle's Vision for Men and Women in Christ*. Grand Rapids: Baker Academic, 2016.

Williams, Delores S. *Sisters in the Wilderness: The Challenge of Womanist God-Talk*. Maryknoll, NY: Orbis Books, 1993.

World Health Organization. "Maternal Mortality." April 26, 2024. https://www.who.int/news-room/fact-sheets/detail/maternal-mortality.

INDEX OF AUTHORS

Aymer, Margaret, 130, 131, 194n1, 197n32, 197nn39–40

Barclay, John M. G., 196n21
Bauckham, Richard, 188n3
Boring, Eugene, 149, 198n1
Bradley, Keith R., 187n9
Bronner, Leila Leah, 9–10, 187nn1–3
Brown, Raymond E., 191n7, 191n9
Bruce, F. F., 196n14
Burke, Trevor J., 197n31

Chazon, Esther G., 196n26
Clark-Soles, Jaime, 31–32, 42, 49, 53, 189nn6–7, 190n30, 191n6, 191n11, 191n13, 193n1
Cohick, Lynn, 12, 188n1, 188n10, 190n1, 190n29, 198n6
Collins, Raymond F., 194n7
Crowder, Stephanie Buckhanon, 34, 79, 189nn14–15, 193nn4–5

Davis, Ellen, 171, 200n16
deSilva, David, 103, 194nn4–5

Dixon, Suzanne, 187n4
Douglas, Sally, 183, 193n1, 194n7, 200n1

Eastman, Susan G., 195n1

French, Valerie, 187n6
Furnish, Victor Paul, 196n20

Gafney, Wilda C., 194n2
Garcia Martinez, Florentino, 196n27
Garrett, Susan R., 173, 199n5, 199nn6–8, 199nn10–11, 199n14, 200n18
Gaventa, Beverly, 16, 26, 33, 41, 46, 48, 119, 188n2, 188n9, 189nn10–11, 189n13, 190n28, 190n2, 190n33, 191n5, 191n11, 195n1, 195nn6–7, 196nn17–18, 196n20, 197n30
Gench, Frances Taylor, 62, 140, 141, 172, 190n3, 191n11, 192nn6–9, 193n4, 198n5, 198n7, 200n17
Gray, Patrick, 197n2

Hylen, Susan E., 191nn2–3

Janes, Regina, 81–82, 193nn9–11

Index of Authors

Kittredge, Cynthia Briggs, 160, 198n5
Koester, Craig R., 199n2
Kraemer, Ross, 146, 198n11

Lee, Dorothy, 141, 198n8
Levine, Amy-Jill, 22, 25, 188n4, 188n9, 192n10

MacDonald, Margaret Y., 187nn4–5, 197n3
Malina, Bruce, 48, 190n4
McGrath, James F., 190n31, 192n11, 193n1
McNeel, Jennifer Houston, 187n4, 188n5, 195n1, 196nn9–13, 196nn15–16, 196n19, 196nn22–25, 196nn27–28, 197n33, 197n36, 197n41
Meier, John, 62
Miller-McLemore, Bonnie, 39, 42, 190nn24–26, 190n32
Myers, Alicia D., 188n11, 189n5

Nelavala, Surekha, 65, 192n14
Newsom, Carol A., 196n27

O'Day, Gail, 53, 154, 191n12, 198n2
Osiek, Carolyn, 103, 131, 187nn4–5, 194n6, 197n37

Pfitzner, Victor C., 198n3
Pippin, Tina, 199n5
Polaski, Sandra Hack, 197n34

Rawson, Beryl, 187n4, 187n8
Reddish, Mitchell, 167, 174, 199n1, 199n3, 199n9, 199nn12–13, 200n20
Rehman, Luzia Sutter, 195n5
Reid, Barbara, 36, 87, 189nn17–18, 193n2, 194nn5–6
Roetzel, Calvin, 130, 131, 197n35, 197n38
Rohrbaugh, Richard, 48, 190n4
Rossing, Barbara, 199n4

Schneiders, Sandra M., 193n4
Schuller, Eileen, 196n27
Smith, Mitzi, 64–65, 171, 192nn13–14, 199n15
Spencer, F. Scott, 33, 81, 189nn8–9, 189n12, 192n4, 193n7, 194n1
Stegemann, Hartmut, 196n27

Tigchelaar, Eibert J. C., 196n27
Tulloch, Janet H., 187nn4–5

Westfall, Cynthia Long, 141, 198n9
Williams, Delores S., 194n2

INDEX OF SUBJECTS

adoption, 52–53, 54, 156–57
androcentrism, 1, 3, 43, 68, 87, 100, 110, 138, 182
angels, 25, 30–33, 34, 36, 38, 95, 101, 165, 170, 194n1
apocalypticism, 102, 114, 115–17, 119, 163, 168, 171, 178–79, 199n2
Aristotle, 13
authorship of New Testament letters, 99, 133–35

barrenness and fertility, 8, 12, 29, 30, 35, 100, 101, 178, 188n2
birth: birth imagery in John, 88–91, 182; end-times imagery, 113–15, 116–17, 178; God giving birth, 9, 88, 127–28, 148–50, 180; Jesus birthing church at cross, 53, 90–91, 178, 183; as joyful, 30, 90; Mary giving birth in Luke, 37; maternal mortality, 11, 178; midwives, 11, 38; Paul in labor, 118–20, 181; premature birth, 120–21; salvation through childbearing, 140–42; the Spirit giving birth, 88–89, 90; the Woman Clothed with the Sun giving birth, 165, 168
breastfeeding: ancient understanding of, 13; God breastfeeding, 128; human leaders as nursing mothers, 121–26, 128–29, 150–51, 180, 181, 183; Jesus as nursing mother, 151–52, 181, 183; and theology, 183; wet nursing, 12, 122, 123, 125; Zion breastfeeding, 9

conception, ancient understanding of, 13, 31, 88, 189n5

family, 7, 17–26, 40–41, 53, 56, 71–75, 109, 124, 143, 179–80
fertility. *See* barrenness and fertility

gendered language and metaphors for God, 9, 88, 91, 183. *See also* birth; breastfeeding
genealogies, 7, 15–23, 26, 177

Index of Subjects

Holy Spirit, 24, 25, 31–32, 34, 40, 43, 88–89, 90, 95

Ignatius of Antioch, 144
infant and child mortality, 11–12

Jerome, 163
Jesus: birth in Luke, 37–38; childhood, 41–43; comparison to Samuel, 36; conception by Holy Spirit, 31–32; countercultural views of family, 71–75; crucifixion, 51–53; and the Gethsemane prayer, 33; in healing stories, 55–67, 75–77; as the *logos*, 46–47, 51, 86; in Matthew's genealogy, 15, 16, 19, 22, 23; as mother hen, 84–86, 181, 183; relationship to his family, 40–41, 48–51, 71–72; relationship to Mary, 26, 27, 32, 48–51, 54, 72; and righteousness, 17; at the wedding at Cana, 47–51; as Wisdom or Wisdom's child, 86–88
Jews and Judaism, 11, 16, 40, 118

labor. *See* birth

magi, 16, 189n19
marriage, 10, 17, 18, 24, 25, 96, 109, 172, 191n1
Mary: in Acts, 94–95; and agency, 32–33; and the Beloved Disciple, 52–53; conception of Jesus in Luke, 31–32, 189n5; connection to Jesus, 26–27, 32, 48–51, 54, 72, 179; at the crucifixion, 51–53; as a disciple, 33; and the incarnation of Jesus in John, 46–47; as Jesus's teacher, 41–43, 177, 181, 190n31; in Luke's birth narrative, 29–43; in Matthew's birth narrative, 23–27; and mindfulness/intellectual engagement, 32–33, 38–39, 41, 179; as mother of the church, 53, 95; as prophet, 36; and righteousness, 17; scandal of pregnancy before marriage, 24–25; similarity to Tamar's story, 18–19; and suffering, 27, 35–36, 39–41, 42–43, 52, 179; virginity of, 30–31, 191n10; at the wedding at Cana, 47–51; as a widow, 52–53; and the Woman Clothed with the Sun in Revelation, 167, 173
maternal figures, symbolic: the church as mother, 152–54, 167; Deborah as mother, 159; Hagar as allegorical mother, 100–104, 180; Jerusalem as mother, 9, 85–86, 102–3, 153; Jesus as mother hen, 84–86, 181, 183; Jezebel (Revelation), 173–75, 181; Paul as mother, 112, 118–20, 121–26, 129–32; Qumran teacher as mother, 128–29; Rachel weeping, 27; Rufus's mother as Paul's mother, 106, 180; Sarah as allegorical/symbolic mother, 100–104, 159–60, 161, 180; the Spirit as mother, 88–89, 90; the Whore of Babylon, 168–72, 172, 175, 180, 181; Wisdom as mother, 87–88, 183; the Woman Clothed with the Sun, 165–68, 175, 179, 180; women as mothers in the family of faith, 72. *See also* birth; breastfeeding; motherhood
maternal mortality. *See under* birth
men in the Bible: Abraham, 3, 7, 15, 23, 30, 100, 101–2, 104–5, 155–56, 160; Adam, 8, 100, 140, 189n4; Beloved

Index of Subjects

Disciple, 52–53; Boaz, 19, 20–21; David, 3, 16, 19–20, 21–23, 24, 36, 188n8; Eli, 8, 35; Elijah, 66, 158, 173; Er, 18; Herod Antipas, 80–82; Herod the Great, 27, 80; Isaac, 101, 105, 156; Ishmael, 101, 104; Jacob, 7, 16, 27; Jairus, 59–60; James son of Zebedee, 56, 68, 77–78; John the Baptist, 30, 34, 80–82; John Mark, 95; John son of Zebedee, 37, 53, 56, 68, 77–78; Joseph (husband of Mary), 17, 19, 23–26, 27, 37, 38, 40, 43, 52, 191n10; Joseph (son of Jacob), 27, 158; Judah, 16, 18–19, 25; Moses, 16, 32, 127–28, 156–57, 181; Nicodemus, 88, 90; Onan, 18, 26; Paul, 3, 96, 98–111, 112–32, 133–35, 136–37, 140, 144, 145, 180; Peter, 37, 56, 68, 95, 120, 191n1; Rufus, 106, 108; Samuel, 8, 35–36; Shelah, 18, 19; Simeon, 40–41, 179; Solomon, 23; Timothy, 96, 145, 181; Uriah, 15, 22, 23, 25, 26, 188n8; Zechariah, 29–30, 32. *See also* Jesus

motherhood: and advocacy, protection, 19, 64, 77–79, 156–57, 158, 182, 183; and caregiving, comfort, 5, 9, 95, 123, 180–81, 182, 183; in the Greco-Roman world, 10–13; and identity, connection, 5, 8, 26–27, 32, 34, 123, 148–50, 152, 153–54, 160, 161, 179–80; and influence, authority, 9–10, 12, 45, 81, 96, 124, 125, 130, 131–32, 146, 157, 170, 175, 181; and love, 12–13; mothers as disciples, 33, 58, 75–76, 77, 78–79, 82–83; mothers as household managers, 9; mothers as teachers, 12, 41–43;

and new life, 5, 90, 117, 178; in Pauline communities, 105–10; pervasiveness in the Bible, 3, 8; and salvation (role in God's plan), 5, 8, 30, 37, 178; as social control, 145; and suffering, danger, 5, 11, 27, 42–43, 52, 67, 115, 116–17, 124–25, 158, 168, 178–79. *See also* birth; breastfeeding; maternal figures, symbolic; mothers

mothers: Asenath, 158; Bathsheba, 9, 15, 16, 21–23, 24, 25, 26, 27, 188n8; Bilhah, 8, 158; Elizabeth, 29–34, 43, 178, 189n3; Eunice, 96, 145–46, 181; Eve, 8, 100, 140–42; Hagar, 100–104, 156, 159, 180; Hannah, 8–9, 35–36, 159, 189n2; Herodias, 79–82, 177, 180; Jairus's wife, 59–60, 66; James and John's mother, 77–79, 177, 180; Jezebel (1–2 Kings), 173–74; Jochebed, 156–57; Leah, 8, 158; Lois, 145–46, 181; Mary mother of John Mark, 95, 180; the mother of the man born blind, 75–77, 180; Naomi, 20–21; Noah's wife, 158; Paul's mother, 107–8; Peninnah, 35; Pharaoh's daughter, 156–57; Rachel, 8, 15, 27, 158, 179, 189n2; Rahab, 15, 16, 19–20, 21, 22, 23, 24, 25, 26, 27, 157, 160–61; Rebecca, 15, 104–5, 108, 158, 188n2; Rufus's mother, 106, 180; Ruth, 3, 15, 16, 20–21, 22, 23, 24, 25, 26, 27, 159; Sarah, 15, 30, 100–105, 155–56, 159–60, 161, 180, 188n2, 189n3; the Shunammite woman, 158; Simon Peter's mother-in-law, 56–59, 180, 182; a stepmother, unnamed, 106–7; the Syrophoenician/Canaanite woman, 60–65, 177,

Index of Subjects

179, 180, 182; Tamar, 15, 16, 17–19, 20, 21, 22, 23–24, 25, 26, 27, 159; the widow of Nain, 65–67, 179; the widow of Zarephath, 158; Zilpah, 8, 158; Zipporah, 159. *See also* Mary; maternal figures, symbolic; motherhood

nursing. *See* breastfeeding

patriarchy: in the church, 154; effect of on ancient women, 9, 136, 173, 182; and expectations for/stereotypes of women, 19, 20, 21, 164–65, 171, 176; and feminine imagery, 154; and inheritance/widowhood, 52, 100; and marriage, birth, and motherhood, 10, 12, 17, 22, 23, 24–26, 31, 94, 188n8

Philo, 46

prostitution, 18, 19, 24, 157, 160, 168–69, 170, 174

pseudonymity. *See* authorship of New Testament letters

righteousness, 17, 19–20, 21, 22–23, 24–26, 27, 30, 47, 80, 188n6

Seneca, 13

virgins and virginity, 23, 24, 30–31, 144, 164–65, 172–73, 175, 191n10

virgin-whore dichotomy, 164–65, 169, 171, 172–73, 175

wet nurses. *See* breastfeeding

widows and widowhood, 10, 18, 20, 52–53, 56, 65–67, 95, 143–45, 158

Woman Wisdom, 46, 86–88, 181, 182, 183, 193n1

womanism, 34, 64–65, 79

womb: ancient understanding of, 13; and the birth process, 88, 114, 120, 168; Elizabeth's, 34; God's control of, 8, 29, 35; Jesus's, 90, 91, 178; *koilia*, translation of, 89–90, 194n8; Mary's, 32, 74, 190n34; Paul's mother's, 107–8; Rebecca's, 105; Sarah's, 100

women's bodies, ancient understanding of, 13, 31, 88

INDEX OF SCRIPTURE

OLD TESTAMENT

Genesis
1:28	7
2–3	140
2:2–4	156
2:7	189n4
2:23	140
3:6	140
3:20	8, 100
4:1	8
7:6–7	158
9:1	7
11:30	8
12:3	30
15:5	7
15:6	156
16:1–3	188n2
16:1–6	156
16:1–16	101, 159
17:17	30
17:17–18	156
18:9–15	156
18:12	189n3
19:27	20
20:18	8
21:6–7	30, 156
21:8–21	101, 159
22:1–19	160
25:21	8, 188n2
29–30	8, 158
29:31	8
30:1	189n2
30:2	8
30:22	8
35:22b–26	15
38	18
38:1–30	159
41:45	158
41:50	158

Exodus
1	156
2	156, 157
2:5–10	157
2:11–15	157
2:21–22	159
4:18–26	159
6:20	156
9:9	32
9:16	32
13:21	32
14:22	159
20:12	74, 138
22:22–24	66
23:26	8
40:24	32

Leviticus
12:1–8	40
20:11	107

Numbers
11:11–12	127–28
11:12	9, 128

Index of Scripture

Deuteronomy

5:16	138
7:14	8
14:28–29	66
20:16–18	61
22:23–24	24
22:30	107
23:3	20
24:17–22	66
25:5–10	18
27:20	107
28:11	8
32:11–12	85
32:13	9, 128
32:18	9, 127

Joshua

2:1–24	19, 157
2:11	157
6:15–27	19
6:22–25	157
6:25	161

Judges

4	159
5:7	159
11:1–40	81
13:1–3	8

Ruth

1:16	159
2:12	85
4:18–22	15, 19

1 Samuel

1:1–8	189n2
1:1–2:11	159
1:2	35
1:5–6	8
1:9–11	35
1:10–11	8
2:1–10	34
2:26	36
16:13	36

2 Samuel

11	23, 26
15–18	23

1 Kings

1	23
1:1–53	9
1:6	23
2:13–25	9
17:8–24	66, 158
17:13–16	158
17:19–22	158
17:24	158

2 Kings

4:8–37	158
4:9	158
4:22	158
4:30	158
4:32–35	158

Ezra

10:6–17	21

Nehemiah

9:21	9
13:23–27	21

Esther

5:3	81
5:6	81
7:2	81

Job

38:29	127

Psalms

2:8–9	165
17:8	85
34:8	152
57:1	85
61:4	85
68:5	66
91:3–4	85
113:9	8
118:25	85
146:9	66

Proverbs

1	86
8:22–31	46
9:4–6	86
31:10–31	9

Isaiah

1	85
1:17	66
10:1–2	66
11:6–9	117
13:6–8	113
25:6	51
42:14	9, 127
45:10–11	9, 127
46:3–4	9, 127

Index of Scripture

49:1	108	**Amos**		2:20	26, 179
49:15	9	1–2	85	2:21	26, 179
49:19–21	9, 85, 103	9:13	51	3:15	188n6
54:1	8, 9, 103			4:22	79
66:7–9	9	**Micah**		5:1–7:27	47
66:7–12	85, 103	4:9–10	9, 85, 103	5:6	188n6
66:9	8			5:10	188n6
66:10–12	9	**Zechariah**		5:20	188n6
66:13	9	7:8–10	66	5:45	188n6
				6:1	188n6
Jeremiah		**Malachi**		6:33	188n6
1:5	108	3:5	66	8:14–15	56–59
4:31	9, 85, 103			9:18–26	59–60
31:15	27	**Deuterocanonical Books**		10:34	73
				10:34–39	72–74
Lamentations				10:37–38	74
2:18–22	9, 85, 103	**Sirach**		10:41	188n6
		6:24–38	86	11:16–19	86–87
Ezekiel		51:23–26	86	11:19	86
16	169, 170, 175			11:28–30	86
16:35–43	170, 171	**New Testament**		12:46	52
23	169, 170, 175			12:46–50	72
23:9–10	170, 171	**Matthew**		12:48	190n27
23:22–35	170	1	15, 24	13:43	188n6
		1–2	27	13:55	52
Daniel		1:5	198n4	14:1–12	79–82
7:1–8	168	1:16	26	14:6	80
		1:18	24	14:13–21	192n11
Hosea		1:19	25, 188n6	15:21	61
1–3	169, 170	1:20	25	15:21–28	60–65
2	175	2	24, 26, 39	15:22	62, 64
2:3	170	2:11	26, 179	15:23	62
2:3–4	171	2:13	26, 179	15:24	62
2:9–10	170	2:14	26, 179	15:26	63
9:14	8	2:16–18	27, 80	15:27	63
11:1–4	9	2:18	179	15:28	63

Index of Scripture

15:31	192n11	7:24	60	1:49	34
20:19	79	7:24–30	60–65	1:50	34
20:20–28	77–79	7:27	61	1:51–53	34
20:25–28	79, 191n4	7:28	61	1:54	34
21:9	85	7:29	61	1:54–55	34
21:32	188n6	8:34	117	2	29, 43, 45
23:11	191n4	10:35–37	77–78	2:6	37
23:28	188n6	10:42–44	58	2:7	37–38
23:35	188n6	10:43–44	78	2:19	39
23:37–39	84–86	10:45	58	2:22–38	40
24:8	195n3	13	114	2:34–35	40
25:37	188n6	13:6–8	114	2:35	179
25:46	188n6	13:8	178	2:41–52	40
28:5–6	195n8	15:41	58	2:48	41, 179
28:8–10	195n8	16:6	195n8	2:51	41
28:19	64			2:52	36, 41
		Luke		4:16–30	47
Mark		1	29, 32, 43	4:18	42
1:13	58	1–2	74	4:38–39	56–59
1:21–28	47, 57	1:6–7	30	6:20–26	42
1:29–31	56–59	1:8	30	7:11	65
1:33–34	57	1:18	30, 32	7:11–17	179
3:20–21	71–72	1:20	32	7:13	66
3:21	72	1:25	30	7:15	66, 67
3:31	52, 182	1:29	32	7:16	66
3:31–35	71–72, 191n8	1:31	32	7:35	86, 87
3:33	190n27	1:32–33	36	8:1–3	95
3:35	72	1:35	31	8:19	52
5:21	192n5	1:38	32	8:19–21	43, 72
5:21–43	59–60, 68, 82, 179	1:42	34	8:21	190n27
5:40	59	1:43	34	8:40–56	59–60
5:42	59	1:46	34	8:51	59
6:14–29	79–82	1:46–55	34, 36, 42	8:53	59
6:20	80	1:46–57	34	8:56	59
6:22	80	1:47	34	9	32
6:28	80	1:48	34	9:35	31

Index of Scripture

9:58	38	7:38	91	9:36–43	93
11:27–28	43, 74, 191n8	8:10	49	12	95
12:51	73	8:20	49	16:1	198n10
13:34–35	84–86	9	75	16:1–5	96
14:26	74	9:2	75	16:11–15	93
19:38	85	9:3	75	16:13–15	95
22:11	36	9:8	76	16:16–18	94
22:24–27	192n4	9:20–23	76	16:40	93
22:42	33	10:10	50–51	18:1–4	94
24:5–7	195n8	12:23	49	18:18–21	94
		12:27	49	18:24–28	94
John		13	53	21:7–9	94
1	47, 86, 88	13:1	49		
1:12	53	13:34–35	154	**Romans**	
1:12–13	88	15:12	154	1:1	33
1:14	46	15:17	154	4	100
2	47	16:20–22	88, 90, 179	4:19	100, 198n4
2:1	47	17:1	49	5	100
2:1–12	45, 47–51	19:25	51	5:12	140
2:3	48	19:25–27	45	8	115, 117
2:4	48–50	19:26–27	52	8:14–17	116
2:5	50	19:27	49	8:18–23	116–17, 178, 179
2:11	50	19:29	50	8:22	112, 116
2:12	51, 52	19:30	91	9	104, 108
3	88, 90, 91	19:34	50, 91	9:6–8	105
3:3	88	20:11–17	195n8	9:9	198n4
3:4	90	20:15	49	9:10–13	105
3:5	90			11:26	105
3:5–8	89	**Acts**		11:29	105
3:16	90	1	95	16	106
4	91	1:12–14	94	16:1–2	105
4:10–14	90	2	95	16:3–5	95, 105, 136
4:21	49	4:29	33	16:6	105
7	90	5:1–11	93	16:7	105
7:30	49	8:1–3	121	16:12	105
7:37–39	89–90	9:1–19	121	16:13	106

Index of Scripture

1 Corinthians

1:11	105
1:27	130
3:1–3	125–26
3:2	112, 128, 129, 131, 136, 150, 151
5:1	106
5:5	107
7	109, 110
7:3–4	136
7:7–8	136
7:8	145
7:20	109
7:25–40	136
7:29–31	109
7:32–35	110, 144
8:1–13	200n19
9:5	191n1
11:5	137
15	100
15:3–7	120
15:8	112, 120–21
15:9	121
15:12–19	120
15:12–28	110

2 Corinthians

11:2	152
11:3	100
11:21b–29	117

Galatians

1:15	108
3	100
3:28	136
4	126

4:19	112, 117, 118, 130, 136
4:19–20	118–20
4:21–31	100–103, 198n4
4:26	153
4:30	103

Ephesians

5:21–6:9	138
5:22–23	152
6:1	138
6:2–3	138
6:4	138

Philippians

4:2–3	105, 136

Colossians

3:18	138
3:18–4:1	138
3:20	138
3:21	138
4:15	95

1 Thessalonians

2	121
2:5–8	121–24
2:7	112, 128, 129, 136, 150, 177
2:11–12	130
3:4	117
4:13–5:11	110
4:15	110
4:17	110
5	114, 115, 116
5:2–3	113–15, 178, 179
5:3	112, 115

5:4	115
5:5	115
5:9	115

1 Timothy

2:2	137, 139
2:4	139
2:8	139
2:8–15	139–42, 198n4
2:9–12	139–40
2:13–14	140
2:15	140–42
3	143
5:1–8	143–45
5:9–10	143
5:11–16	144
5:14	145

2 Timothy

1:5	96, 145–46

Titus

2:3–5	139

Hebrews

4:14–5:10	150
5:11–14	150–51, 197n29
5:12	150, 151
5:14	151
11	155, 156, 158, 159
11:1	155
11:4	155
11:7	158
11:8	155
11:9	158
11:11	155

Index of Scripture

11:11–12	155–56	**1 John**		12:9	165
11:16	194n3	3:11	154	12:11	166
11:21	158	3:23	154	12:12	165
11:23	156	4:7	150, 154	12:17	166, 167
11:23–28	156–57	4:8	150	13	168
11:24–25	157	4:11	150	13:1–4	168
11:29	159	4:12	154	13:2	168
11:31	157	4:21	150	13:7	168
11:32	159			13:8	168
11:35a	158	**2 John**		14	168
12:1	159	1	153	15	168
13:14	194n3	1–5	153	16	168
		5	154	17	168, 170, 175
James		6–13	153	17:1	169
1:1	149	13	153	17:1–6	169
1:15	149			17:2	169
1:18	149, 150	**Revelation**		17:5	169, 170
2:1	149	1	165, 173	17:9	169
2:17	160	2	174	17:15	169
2:25	159–61	2–3	165, 173	17:16	170, 171
		2:18–29	173	17:18	169
1 Peter		2:20	173–75	18:1–19:8	170
1:3	150, 160	2:22	174	18:6	171
1:3b–5	149	2:23	175	18:9–19	171
2:2	150, 151, 160, 197n29	4	165	19:3	171
2:2–3	151	5–11	165	19:7	172
2:4	152	12	166	19:8	172
2:9	150, 152	12:1	165	21:1–2	172
3:1–4	159–60	12:3	165	21:2	153, 172, 194n3
3:6	159–60	12:5	165, 179	21:9–22:7	172